NINE
DESPERATE
DAYS

ROBERT THOMPSON NINE DESPERATE DAYS

America's Rainbow Division in the Aisne-Marne Offensive

WESTHOLME
Yardley

Facing title page: Soldiers of the 165th Infantry Regiment, July 1918. (*National Archives*)

Westholme Publishing, LLC
904 Edgewood Road
Yardley, Pennsylvania 19067
Visit our Web site at www.westholmepublishing.com

ISBN: 978-1-59416-381-4
Also available as an eBook.

Printed in the United States of America.

In memory of all those who served in the Rainbow Division during the Great War. May your sacrifice and courage never be forgotten.

CONTENTS

MAPS

PREFACE

World War I, or the Great War as it was called in the 1920s and 1930s, has become something of a forgotten conflict in the collective American memory. That may be because it was followed twenty-one years later by another global war, World War II, and that second world war involved a more recent generation of Americans, a generation that included my own parents. As a result, many of us actually knew people who served in that war, people who have become rightfully anointed as America's "greatest generation." Also, even today, the entertainment industry continues to produce movies and television programs about World War II. As a result, it is a far more familiar conflict to most of us, which has pushed the Great War further back into our memories until it has almost completely faded from view.

This is truly tragic given that World War I was an instrumental force in shaping the world that followed and the one in which we all live today. Further, almost five million Americans served in World War I, and the nation suffered over four hundred thousand killed, wounded, and missing during barely a year of combat operations. Moreover, we must remember that the pain and disillusion caused by those losses led many Americans to embrace a renewed spirit of isolationism that drove American foreign and military policy between the two world wars and played an important role in allowing fascism to rise in Germany. For those reasons alone, perhaps it is important that we reexamine our participation in this first truly global conflict and how Americans rose to its many challenges.

In performing research for my book, *Suddenly Soldiers: The 166th Infantry Regiment in World War I*, I became very familiar with the service of the American 42nd Division, which was called the "Rainbow Division." Made up of National Guard units from twenty-six states, it was one of the first American divisions to arrive in France, debarking at Saint Nazaire on November 1, 1917, less than seven months after the United States declared war on Germany. Further, because the division was made up of men from so many different states and seemed to exemplify the nation's commitment to the Allied cause, the men of the Rainbow Division captured the hearts and imagination of the American people. By the end of the war on November 11, 1918, the division would spend a total of 164 days in combat, a number exceeded by only two other American divisions.

However, of those 164 days of fighting on the front lines, nine terrible days stand out—July 25–August 2, 1918. In his memoir, *Reminiscences*, General of the Army Douglas MacArthur said of the Rainbow Division's fighting during those pivotal days, "There was neither rest nor mercy." MacArthur, who was the division's chief of staff during the offensive, is known to have had a tendency toward dramatic hyperbole. However, in this case, his words present an accurate description of the fighting that occurred during what became known as the Aisne-Marne Offensive. During those nine days, the Rainbow Division would spearhead the Allied attack in what is considered to have been the final phase of the Second Battle of the Marne.

That battle was the turning point in the war because it stopped Germany's final offensive and began the process of eliminating the gains made by Germany during the first four years of the war. The Aisne-Marne Offensive phase, which sought to drive the Germans out of the Marne salient, was noteworthy because it was the first time American forces went on the offensive since arriving in France. They would no longer fight from fixed defensive positions in trenches. Rather, they would now advance, fighting a war of maneuver in the open, and would do so under command of an American corps-level organization for the first time, the US I Corps.

While a war of maneuver was the type of warfare long advocated by men like General John J. Pershing, commander of the American Expeditionary Force or AEF, events would show that the inexperienced American headquarters staffs at both the I Corps and the 42nd Division were unable to provide effective command and control of their forces in this type of combat. Commanding forces deployed in static defensive positions was one thing, but managing units engaged in a fluid and dynamic offensive was quite another. This was particularly evident in the I Corps and the 42nd Division staff's inability to coordinate and provide effective artillery support, which cost the men of the Rainbow Division dearly and contributed directly to the high number of casualties they would suffer.

All this was further compounded by the fact that, for the first seven days that the Rainbow Division was in combat in the Marne salient, their operations and the orders they received were predicated on a false premise that originated from the headquarters of French Sixth Army, which had overall control of the sector in which the US I Corps operated. This premise was based on the false notion that the Germans in the salient were in a panicked retreat to the safety of new lines behind the Vesle River. In point of fact, the enemy was actually performing a well-planned, well-executed strategic withdrawal from the Marne salient in which they would defend every inch of ground tenaciously. This premise would result in orders for the Rainbow Division to make ill-advised, headlong attacks against enemy forces of unknown strength in unknown positions with virtually no artillery support, resulting in horrific casualty rates.

There were many reasons I decided to tell the story of the Rainbow Division in the Aisne-Marne Offensive and, more specifically, in the fighting at La Croix Rouge Farm and along the Ourcq River. However, the most compelling reason was the desire to tell a story of what one historian referred to as the "naked valor" of the men who served in the division's four National Guard infantry regiments—New York's 165th Infantry, Ohio's 166th Infantry, Alabama's 167th Infantry, and Iowa's 168th Infantry—and their supporting machine gun battalions, Pennsylvania's 149th, Wisconsin's 150th, and Georgia's 151st. These regiments and battalions were filled mostly with citizen-soldiers, amateurs who had joined their local National Guard units before the war, never imagining that they would be called upon to fight in France in what was, up to that time, the most violent and costly war in human history.

Despite their lack of professional training and experience, they would advance in the face of furious machine gun and artillery fire and do so over and over, even when the orders from higher headquarters were almost criminally unsound. Even more remarkable was that they would achieve success despite the actions of those above them in the chain of command. It is true, however, that their success would often only be measured in yards when their orders called for miles of ground to be taken.

And every one of those yards would have an awful cost in terms of lives lost and terrible wounds suffered, both physical and emotional wounds that would disable some men for the rest of their lives.

Two things struck me as I worked on telling this story—the leadership displayed in the four infantry regiments and the deep love these soldiers had for one another. With the exception of one battalion commander, the leadership within these frontline combat units seems to have been extraordinary. This was even more remarkable because very few of the officers and noncommissioned officers had ever experienced combat before coming to France, and their professional training was limited to what their state militia organizations could provide. Also, most, if not all, of the junior officers came directly from the training program provided at Plattsburgh, New York, by the Citizen's Military Training Corps, a forerunner of today's Reserve Officer Training Corps program. Many of these young officers, whom the enlisted men initially referred to derisively as "Sears and Roebuck Officers," proved to be leaders who were both courageous and competent under fire. There were repeated instances where the captains who were company commanders fell and were replaced in the heat of battle by one of these young lieutenants, all of whom would take up the mantle of command and keep their men moving forward.

As for the deep affection the soldiers had for one another, many studies have shown that men often fight primarily for the men they serve beside. But here, that seems to have been even more the case. One must remember that the core members of these regiments consisted of men from the same hometowns. Therefore, the relationships and bonds between them had been formed over the course of their entire lives, not merely during a few months of military service, as was the case in other combat units. Their comrades were often men they had grown up with and who lived in the same neighborhoods back home. Sometimes, they were even members of the same family. As a result, the risks they would take on behalf of their comrades were often remarkable.

I was especially struck by the numerous stories of efforts to save a wounded friend despite the danger posed by heavy enemy machine gun fire. Again and again, I found stories about a wounded man being trapped in the open, unable to crawl back to safety. When one of his friends would realize what had happened, that friend would run forward to help his wounded comrade. Inevitably, enemy fire often killed the would-be rescuer. Then another soldier would make the attempt, despite seeing what had happened in the first attempted rescue. In many cases, man after man would unsuccessfully make the attempt to help their wounded buddy and would pay the ultimate price in the process until, finally, one soldier would be able to drag the wounded man to safety. These acts of love and devotion are, without doubt, the most remarkable things I found in my research.

In documenting the story of the Rainbow Division at the battle of La Croix Rouge Farm and along the Ourcq River I was aided by the excellent unit histories written about the division and its four infantry regiments as well as the personal memoirs, journals, letters, and diaries written by individual soldiers. At times, there were challenges dealing with accounts of incidents that conflicted slightly. But I was able to overcome these by carefully analyzing the facts presented by men who were sometimes at different places on the battlefield, saw events transpire differently from their perspective, and whose memories may have been affected by the passage of time. In the end, I strove to create what seemed to be the most credible version of the story.

Of all the sources I used, I must note the work of John H. Taber. Taber served as a first lieutenant in K Company of the 3rd Battalion of Iowa's 168th Infantry Regiment. He later wrote the regiment's official history, *The Story of the 168th Infantry*, which was published in 1925. Taber proved to be what I consider a superlative narrative historian. The story he tells is both factual and deeply compelling. And it is so compelling because Taber had the eye of a poet and the writing skills of a master storyteller. Whenever he recounts an event that he actually observed, Taber describes what his own memory held in terms so stark and vivid that the reader cannot help but close their eyes and clearly imagine the many terrible things Taber experienced firsthand. In doing so, Taber helps connect the modern historian to the personal and often painful aspects of historical events that help us to truly understand the experiences of those who were there. This also allows us to tell their story in a way that does them justice and provides the reader with far more than merely cold facts and analyses.

As with my previous book, I am very grateful for the photographic resources made available through the National Archives and Records Administration. Most of the photos used in this book came from their holdings, especially the special collection of World War I images they have catalogued for online access. I must also thank the staff at the National World War I Museum in Kansas City. Their excellent online archives provided numerous references and resources that would have been difficult to identify and obtain from any other source.

I also wish to express my deep appreciation to Major William Carraway, a historian with the Georgia Army National Guard. Major Carraway provided me with access to excellent photos taken during his trip to France for the 2018 centennial of the fighting at La Croix Rouge Farm and the Ourcq River and gave me permission to use them in the book. They help provide a marvelous visual context for the story, which is often so very important for the reader.

Also, I must thank my publisher, Bruce H. Franklin, and his very able and helpful staff at Westholme Publishing. Their professionalism and skills are greatly appreciated, and they always do a wonderful job of guiding me through the writing and publication process. But most of all, they have been an absolute joy to work with.

In this book, I have striven to use a truly narrative history style, one that provides the facts and documents their source while also telling a rich and colorful story. I hope my readers will be happy with the results.

1

THE RAINBOW APPEARS

April–October 1917

"The outfit . . . was training to go over where it was said that Hell was being manufactured faster than it could be used."
—Major Raymond Cheseldine, *Ohio in the Rainbow*

Newton Baker, the forty-five-year-old secretary of war, leaned back in his chair, listening intently to the two officers sitting opposite him in his office at the War Department. The senior of the two men was Major General William Mann, the head of the US Army's Militia Bureau. The second officer was Major Douglas MacArthur. He worked in the Mobile Army section of the General Staff, which had been charged with organizing the nation's efforts to mobilize its military forces following President Woodrow Wilson's declaration of war against Germany on April 6, 1917.[1]

General Mann was briefing Secretary Baker on the plans for mobilizing and organizing National Guard units to fight in France. At first, most of the General Staff opposed any thought of sending National Guard units to war in France. Even before war was declared, the small group of twenty-one officers who made up the General Staff had debated the issue, with the majority opposing the idea. But a vocal minority led by Major MacArthur insisted that the National Guard would be critical to America's ability to fight in Europe should that eventuality come to pass.[2] Once the nation was actually at war, it became clear to everyone on the General Staff that the MacArthur faction was correct.

The problem faced by the War Department was that the Regular Army was too small and was not adequately organized for the kind of war being fought in Europe. While the National Defense Act of 1916 had authorized the Regular Army to double its strength, by April 1917, the army still only had 5,800 officers and just over 120,000 men. However, even more revealing of its overall weakness was that the US Army did not have any units above the regimental level—not a single brigade, division, corps, or army organization existed.[3] Moreover, the army's doctrine and culture were essentially unchanged since the Spanish-American War.

US Army doctrine was still based on small units executing fluid tactics in the open without any significant supporting firepower. The infantryman with his rifle still reigned supreme and was the core element of American military doctrine. Therefore, the army had few machine guns, little heavy artillery, and no approach for the effective use of either weapon. Despite reports coming from the Western Front since 1914 on the use of artillery and machine guns, American doctrine did not change. Both weapons continued to be seen as tertiary supporting elements for the infantry rather than as crucial components of an integrated combat force.

But the French and British desperately needed manpower, and they needed it fast. So the army began to quickly organize existing Regular Army infantry, artillery, and support units into a new combat organization, the 1st Division, which they planned to deploy to France in June 1917. However, after that unit mobilized and headed across the Atlantic, the question became who would go next. Building up more Regular Army divisions would require gathering untrained men via enlistment and conscription, and that would take time—time the Allies did not have. The only answer was to mobilize and deploy National Guard units. Still, there was the question of how to best organize the various states' National Guard units, which was why Mann and MacArthur were in Secretary Baker's office.

The first thing Mann and MacArthur had examined was the critical issue of readiness. New York and Pennsylvania actually had an organized National Guard division within their respective states. Furthermore, both had sent men to the Mexican border to support Major General Pershing's punitive expedition against the Mexican partisan leader, "Pancho" Villa. Presumably, these two divisions would have the highest state of readiness. However, Baker, Mann, and MacArthur had concerns about the idea of these two divisions going to France next. If divisions from New York and

Pennsylvania went overseas, there might be negative public opinion in both states with the people there feeling that they were being asked to bear a greater burden than the rest of the country.[4] At the same time, citizens in other states might feel they were not being allowed to play their part in the nation's initial response to the call to arms.

Baker pondered the problem for a moment, and then he asked General Mann "whether there were not enough surplus units in the various States to make up a composite division which would have elements from many States, in all parts of the country, so that it would be in a true sense an All-American Division."[5] The secretary's idea clearly intrigued both Mann and MacArthur. They told Baker they would immediately go study the feasibility of this idea. Within forty-eight hours, it became apparent that forming such a division could be done, and they soon selected National Guard units from twenty-six different states to be a part of this new division. In early August 1917, when that task was complete, Mann and MacArthur decided to inform the press of this new division before giving a final briefing to Secretary Baker.

In addition to his duties in the Mobile Army section of the General Staff, MacArthur served as the press censor for the War Department. So he called reporters to his desk in the corner of the section's small office, which was just two doors down the corridor from the chief of staff's office. MacArthur began by telling them he had some interesting news. He went on to say, "We have organized on paper at least, the first National Guard division and the first division other than the First Division of the Regular Army, to be designated for service in France." He added that, while they had not numbered the new division, the idea behind it was to make the division "as representative as possible of the whole union." After explaining the process used to select the units, MacArthur uttered what would be some prophetic words. "In the makeup and promise of the future of this division," he said, "it resembles a rainbow."[6]

At that, one of the reporters knew he had just heard an excellent angle for this story. "Rainbow," he said, "there's the name for the division—I shall call it the Rainbow in my dispatch." The other reporters nodded in quick agreement. As the story was published in papers across the nation on August 14, the American people learned of the Rainbow Division for the first time.[7]

It would not be the last.

★

Not long after the news of the Rainbow Division hit the newspapers, the men and units who would fill its ranks began to arrive at Camp Mills, New York, which was located on a dusty plain on Long Island. When the story broke, the country's people were not the only ones to learn about this new division of citizen-soldiers. The men from those National Guard units, many of whom were just starting to mobilize, also learned about the Rainbow Division for the first time, which had now been officially designated by the War Department as the 42nd Division. Some units like the Ohio National Guard's 166th Infantry Regiment were on their way to their own initial mobilization and training camps. In their case, the Ohioans were heading to Camp Perry on the shores of Lake Erie. When they heard the news about the 42nd Division, they realized that they would be part of this new experiment for the National Guard.[8]

Since they had selected the units for the division, Secretary Baker made General Mann the division commander, and MacArthur, who was promoted to colonel, became the division's chief of staff. The organization they created would be required to meet the newly implemented table of organization and equipment for an American infantry division. The division would need a total of 991 officers and 27,114 enlisted men. Each of its four infantry regiments would have 3,600 men, and the regiments would be organized into two infantry brigades of two regiments each. The artillery brigade would consist of three regiments with twenty-four 155mm howitzers, forty-eight 75mm guns, and a trench mortar battery. Each infantry brigade had its own machine gun battalion, and there was another machine gun battalion assigned to the regiment's headquarters company, which would give the division 260 machine guns.[9]

The units Mann and MacArthur chose for the Rainbow Division included trench mortar support from Maryland's 117th Trench Mortar Battery. The division's light artillery guns were operated by men from the Illinois 149th Field Artillery and Minnesota 151st Field Artillery, while Indiana's 150th Field Artillery supplied the division's heavier six-inch artillery.[10]

Not surprisingly, there was also a large contingent of support organizations. The 117th Engineering Regiment was made with equal parts from South Carolina and California, while the 117th Engineering Train came from North Carolina. The 117th Field Signal Battalion hailed from Missouri, and there were military police companies from Virginia and a headquarters troop from the Louisiana 2nd Cavalry. There was also the 117th Ammunition Train from Kansas, 117th Supply Train from Texas, 165th Ambulance Company from New Jersey, 166th Ambulance Company from Tennessee, 167th Ambulance Company from Oklahoma, 168th Ambulance Company from Michigan, 165th Field Hospital from the District of Columbia, 166th Field Hospital from Nebraska, 167th Field Hospital from Oregon, and 168th Field Hospital from Colorado.[11]

The fighting heart of the division, of course, would be its four infantry regiments, which had been organized into two infantry brigades—the 83rd and 84th. The 83rd Infantry Brigade was to be commanded by Brigadier General Michael J. Lenihan, an 1887 graduate of West Point who had served on the American frontier, in the Philippines, on the General Staff in the War Department, and at the Army War College. Lenihan's brigade included the 165th Infantry Regiment from the New York National Guard and the 166th Infantry Regiment from the Ohio National Guard. The 84th Infantry Brigade, meanwhile, was placed under the command of General Robert A. Brown, who was also a West Point graduate, having been commissioned there in 1885. Like Lenihan, Brown had served at various posts along the frontier, in Cuba during the Spanish-American War, in the Philippines, and as a student at the Army War College.[12] His new brigade was composed of the Alabama National Guard's 167th Infantry Regiment and the Iowa National Guard's 168th Infantry Regiment.[13]

The 165th Infantry Regiment would eventually be arguably the division's most famous unit, due mainly to it being the subject of a major motion picture, the Warner Brothers 1940 production *The Fightin' 69th*, which starred James Cagney and Pat O'Brien. The 165th Infantry began as the 69th New York State Militia in the years before the Civil War. This unit, comprised of Irish immigrants from New York City, was redesignated as the 69th New York Volunteer Infantry Regiment during the Civil War and became part of the famed Irish Brigade of the II Corps in the Union's Army of the Potomac. The regiment fought in virtually every major battle of the war's eastern theater, and it ended the war with more combat casualties than any of New York's 115 regiments.[14]

During the Spanish-American War, the 69th New York was called to service and had made it as far as their embarkation port in Tampa, Florida, before the war ended. The regiment maintained its peacetime pattern of monthly drill sessions until 1916, when it was mobilized into federal service like other National Guard units under the authority of the

Militia Act of 1903 and the National Defense Act of 1916. The regiment
deployed to the Mexican border to support General Pershing's expedition,
and it did not return to New York City to muster out until March 1917,
where they paraded down Fifth Avenue. But when it returned to New
York City, the regiment was far below its authorized peacetime strength
with only 783 men, and 300 of those would leave the unit in the coming
weeks.[15]

As a result, when war was declared on Germany, the 69th New York
had to undertake a major recruiting campaign to reach the initial goal of
a Regular Army regiment's strength of two thousand men. Luckily, they
could rely on the tight-knit nature of the city's Irish-American commu-
nity for recruits. Rather than using garish advertising and holding bois-
terous town hall meetings, the regiment used the connections provided
by its remaining members and Catholic clergymen. These unofficial "re-
cruiters" were told that the regiment wanted special men, men who would
join for the right reasons and "who would be worthy successors of those
unforgotten patriots who at Bloody Ford and on Marye's Height earned
the title of 'The Fighting Irish.'"[16] So the veteran members sought out
friends they deemed reliable, and parish priests sent good men from the
parish athletic clubs.[17]

Father Francis P. Duffy, the regiment's venerable chaplain, related that
they did allow themselves one bit of advertising; however, it came with a
stern warning. "The one bit of publicity we indulged in," he later said,
"was to send round our machine gun trucks through the city streets with
the placard, 'Don't join the 69th unless you want to be among the first to
go to France.' That was the only kind of men we wanted—not impres-
sionable youth who would volunteer under the stimulus of a brass band
or a flood of patriotic oratory."[18]

One of the young men who answered the regiment's call for new enlistees was Martin Hogan. Hogan was only seventeen years old, and his
older brother was already a sergeant in one of the city's other National
Guard units. His parents had long since passed away, he was unmarried,
and young Martin had no responsibilities to prevent him from going to
France to fight. However, at seventeen years of age, Hogan was one year
short of the minimum age of eighteen. He decided that was not going to
stop him. "I felt that I looked old enough to pass a recruiting sergeant,"
Hogan later wrote, "and that the call for men was urgent enough to justify
me in camouflaging my age by one year. Anyhow, I thought, I can go to
France and grow up with the war."[19]

Father Francis Duffy (front row, second from right), chaplain of New York's 165th Infantry Regiment. (*National Archives*)

Hogan enlisted after hearing a speech in a theater one night that encouraged young men to join up. When the speaker asked for men to come up on stage to enlist, he was the first man to do so. When Hogan signed his enlistment papers, he chose the 69th Infantry because both it and he were Irish. The following day, he and the other men recruited at the theater reported to the 69th's armory and were given their physical examinations, after which they were assigned to K Company. All of the men with Hogan that day were about his age, which apparently did not make a particularly good impression. The first sergeant asked the captain who commanded the company to look the new recruits over. After walking up and down the line of new recruits and looking at some incredibly young, innocent faces, the captain said with obvious concern in his voice, "What are we getting now, Sergeant, a Boy Scout outfit?"[20]

Not long after the regiment's recruiting drive began, its commander, Colonel William Haskell, left the regiment for an assignment with the new National Army, which would consist of divisions formed from enlistees and draftees. Haskell had led the regiment during its days on the Mexican border and was considered by many to be the person most responsible for the regiment's noteworthy performance during Pershing's expedition.[21]

Haskell was replaced by Lieutenant Colonel Latham Reed, who had been Haskell's executive officer and second-in-command since November 1916. Reed, who had been in the New York National Guard since 1904, now had the job of orchestrating the recruitment effort.[22] When first joining the regiment, Reed had been somewhat aloof because he could sense the soldiers were suspicious of him. He was not Irish, and some of the men thought he might try to alter the character of the regiment. However, as Father Duffy later wrote, Reed proved to be "a good soldier keen, active, and aggressive" and thus won the loyalty of his men. Reed attacked the job of filling the regiment's ranks with "single-minded vigor," and he was primarily responsible for the recruiting campaign's success. [23]

As the new recruits joined the 69th, they had to receive at least some training as soldiers. So the regiment instituted a vigorous program of daily drilling on the vacant ground near the 23rd Street ferry. "The school of a soldier, school of a squad, platoon, company and battalion formation, regulations and the bayonet manual were thoroughly ground into us," wrote Martin Hogan. He added, "We worked too hard to be able to waste much time in thinking ahead about the war." Most of the new men lived at home and reported to the armory every morning for drill.[24]

On July 25, 1917, the 69th was mobilized into federal service just like all the other National Guard units around the country. Shortly after that, at the direction of the War Department, each regiment was told to increase its strength from about 2,000 men to 3,600.[25] While Lieutenant Colonel Reed likely wished to recruit more new men, the army had other ideas. They ordered that the additional soldiers needed would be transferred from other New York City National Guard units. As a result, every seventh man on the roster of the 7th New York was designated for transfer to the 69th, and the first increment of 335 new men arrived in early August.[26]

Any concerns about how these men might be treated by the current members of the 69th quickly evaporated. The entire 7th New York escorted the transferring men down Park Avenue to the 69th's armory at 26th Street and Lexington. On arrival, the men of the 7th formed a corridor up to the armory doors, which the transferees marched through. Once inside, they received an enthusiastic welcome, as one of the new men, Albert Ettinger, later remembered. "The ceremony was unforgettable," he wrote. "As we entered, the Irishers of the 69th gave us a rousing roar of welcome. Men were up in the balcony and hanging from the rafters, and they cheered and cheered because we were the first troops from other regiments in New York to make the transfer."[27]

On August 20, the regiment received one more new man. Still, this time it was in the form of another new commanding officer, the regiment's third in only three months. The new commander was Colonel Charles W. Hine, a West Point graduate, class of 1891. He had earned a law degree from the University of Cincinnati in 1893 and resigned from the Regular Army in 1895. Hine then worked in the railroad industry in various roles from freight brakeman to yardmaster and finally to company vice president. He returned to active duty during the Spanish-American War as a major in the Washington, DC National Guard and mustered out at the war's end. Hine was recalled to federal service in June as a colonel in the New York National Guard and subsequently given command of the 69th New York.[28] Father Duffy, for one, was impressed with Colonel Hine:

> He came into this conflict as organizer and commander of trains, a work for which his experience fitted him. He is a man of middle height with a strong body and an attractive face, healthily ruddy, strongly featured, with a halo of thick grey hair above. He is a man of ideas, of ideas formed by contact with life and business. He is a tireless worker, and demands the same unflinching service from every man under him. He has confidence in his men, especially the tried soldiers, and he has a strong liking for the Regiment and its traditions. The Regiment will do good work under the leadership of Colonel Charles Hine.[29]

On August 24, 1917, the 69th was redesignated as the 165th Infantry Regiment of the US Army and ordered to mobilize at its armory for immediate movement to Camp Mills on Long Island. They had increased their strength to 2,500 men and soon reached the required manpower of over 3,000 through additional transfers from the 12th, 14th, 23rd, and 71st New York. Martin Hogan later described the scene as the 69th marched toward Camp Mills:

> The regiment formed at the armory, turned toward Fifth Avenue, and once again the old 69th was outward bound on Uncle Sam's duty, its least unit filled with determination to represent the Old Gentleman effectively on whatever difficult mission might chance to fall to it. We turned north on Fifth Avenue. Great crowds lined the way and there was tremendous war enthusiasm. The strong impressions that we men got from this march, however, were not those of the large, triumphant

sort, of the cheering, of the affectionate calls of friends, of martial pride to know that we were on our way into a great, and probably glorious, adventure for home and country, but rather humbler impressions of a chastening sort, impressions of heartbroken mothers, wives, and sisters who tried to force their way by the police to kiss their "boy," a comrade in our ranks, good-by, of fathers who gulped out some choking word of love as their boys swung by with us. Seeing these heart-heavy dramas all along our line of march, I somehow missed the exultant spirit of the crowd and was mostly near to tears myself. We marched to Forty-eighth Street on Fifth Avenue, then took our way to the Thirty-fourth Street ferry, crossed to Long Island City, and entrained for Camp Mills.[30]

The other infantry regiment that joined the 165th Infantry as part of the division's 83rd Brigade was the 166th Infantry, formerly the 4th Ohio Infantry of the Ohio National Guard. The 4th Ohio Infantry Regiment had a long and proud lineage. Unlike most National Guard regiments, it could trace its ancestry back to the Mexican War of 1846–1848, where the regiment was part of General Winfield Scott's army that landed at Vera Cruz.[31] During the Civil War, the 4th Ohio, like the 69th New York, was part of the Army of the Potomac and took part in the fighting at Antietam, Fredericksburg, Chancellorsville, Gettysburg, Spotsylvania, Cold Harbor, and Petersburg.[32]

The regiment was reformed in April 1898 and called to federal service in May for duty during the Spanish-American War. Arriving in Cuba in late July, the 4th Ohio was part of the American forces attacking the town of Guayama in the days just before the end of the war. The regiment returned to Columbus, Ohio, and mustered out in January 1899. Shortly after that, the regiment was reorganized as part of the Ohio National Guard. During the seventeen years that followed, the companies that made up the regiment took part in the typical National Guard routine, conducting monthly drill sessions at their home armories with an annual summer encampment by the entire regiment at Camp Perry on the banks of Lake Erie.[33] Like its sister regiment from New York, the 4th Ohio also mobilized into federal service in 1916 and deployed to the Mexican border, returning home in March 1917.[34]

With the declaration of war, the 4th Ohio was ordered to begin recruiting new men in early April. The initial order from the state's adjutant general said, "You will at once recruit your company to War Strength of 152 enlisted men for each letter company, 37 enlisted men for Supply

The 165th Infantry Regiment leaves its armory in New York City for the march to Camp Mills on Long Island. (*National Archives*)

Company, and 74 enlisted men for Machine Gun Company."[35] However, like the other National Guard infantry regiments, these numbers soon increased, and each of the 4th Ohio's ten companies accelerated their efforts to bring new men into the fold. The 4th Ohio also mobilized all its companies at their home armories scattered across central Ohio on July 15, and they continued to recruit men until the regiment was formally mustered into federal service on August 5.[36] Then, on August 13, 1917, the regiment's companies each received a secret order to assemble at Camp Perry.[37] Once the regiment arrived there, it would no longer be the 4th Ohio Infantry. Instead, it would be designated as the 166th Infantry Regiment of the US Army.

The other similarity the 166th Infantry had with the regiment from New York was that it too was assigned a new commanding officer. In this case, however, it was someone the men of the regiment were familiar with—Colonel Benson W. Hough. Colonel Hough would prove to be a true leader in every sense of that word, and, as such, he was ideally suited to lead a regiment of citizen-soldiers. Born and raised in Delaware, Ohio, Hough was forty-two years old when he assumed command of the regiment and was a graduate of Ohio State University and a successful attorney.[38]

He enlisted as a private in the 4th Ohio in 1892 and served on and off in the Ohio National Guard, becoming an officer in 1902. He became the adjutant general of Ohio in 1915 but resigned in July 1916 so he could go to the Mexican border as a lieutenant colonel in the 4th Ohio. He mustered out of federal service with the rest of the regiment in March 1917 and then was commissioned a colonel on April 9, 1917, following the declaration of war.[39]

Hough proved to be a leader who was quiet, thoughtful, and, as one of his officers put it, "intensely human." He approached his job with great seriousness, and his judgment of men was "uncanny." Alison Reppy, a captain in the regiment, wrote that Hough was a "big man physically and intellectually, who hates formality and shuns publicity; a man who is reserved, yet friendly; a man who is ordinarily quiet and has but little to say, but who, when occasion demands, becomes a veritable volcano of action, sweeping aside all immaterial considerations and speaking directly and briefly on the real point at issue. It is this combination of qualities which binds men to him."[40]

From mid-August until early September, the 166th used their time at Camp Perry to organize the regiment and, most importantly, train the new enlistees and knock the rust off the veteran soldiers. Again, like the New Yorkers, the Ohio adjutant general increased the regiment's strength by transferring men from other Ohio National Guard units, ordering each company in every other Ohio National Guard infantry regiment to transfer sixteen men to the equivalent lettered company in the 166th.[41]

Naturally, the increase in numbers caused logistical challenges, with one of the first being a lack of tents to house all the men. One of the soldiers transferring in from another regiment was Enoch Williams, a twenty-two-year-old private from Dennison, Ohio, who arrived at Camp Perry in a train boxcar on the night of August 16. By then, trains carrying men had been arriving at Camp Perry for a couple of days. Enoch wrote home that day, saying they had arrived at 7:30 p.m. the previous evening after a tumultuous departure. "The whole Company escorted us to the station," he wrote his mother, "and we got some send-off." As the regiment got settled in and prepared for an unknown length of stay, the lack of tents meant Enoch and his comrades would have to sleep in the boxcars in which they arrived. Even after five days of sleeping in boxcars, there still were not enough tents to house the regiment. On August 22, Enoch wrote that, while they had finally managed to leave the boxcars, the regiment had told them to camp out on the porch of the supply building.[42]

Once all the companies had been re-organized and noncommissioned officers selected, training in extended order drill began. This involved the basics of combat maneuvering and small-unit tactics. Refresher training was conducted on the care and use of the rifle, along with training in the new manual of the bayonet. Also, since the machine gun was to serve in such a prominent role in France, officers from the machine gun school at Fort Sill, Oklahoma, arrived to provide additional instruction in the use of the weapon. More ominous, however, were the new classes in chemical warfare. Attacks using poisonous gas, mostly mustard and tear gas, were almost daily

Colonel Benson W. Hough, commander of Ohio's 166th Infantry regiment. (*National Archives*)

events on the Western Front in France, so any man who did not learn to effectively use his gas mask was risking death or horrible mutilation. With the commencement of all this new training, the men "began to realize that real war was but a step away."[43]

However, despite the seriousness of the training and the information provided about the Rainbow Division's purpose, some of the men doubted they would ever see combat. Not long before the regiment left Camp Perry, Enoch Williams wrote, "The talk is that we go tomorrow, but we are not certain. I never expect to go to France. The odds are four to one that we don't leave the U.S. Hardly anyone thinks we will leave the States."[44]

In early September, the 166th received orders to move to Camp Mills, where they would join the 165th Infantry, who had arrived there on September 1. The trains carrying the 166th left Camp Perry in the dark around 10:00 p.m. on the night of September 8, 1917, amid a steady, drenching rain. The men aboard the train were a miserable lot, "wet to the skin" as they "sat or sprawled three to two seats, trying to get a bit of rest before dawn."[45] The train made its way through Cleveland and then along the shores of Lake Erie to Buffalo, arriving there around 7:00 a.m. The train then paused briefly before moving east to Rochester, Syracuse, and Albany. Finally, it turned down the Mohawk and Hudson Valleys toward New York City and Camp Mills, where the regiment detrained around 3:30 p.m. on September 9.

The final two infantry regiments, the 167th and 168th, would be part of the division's 84th Brigade. The 167th was created from the 4th Alabama and, as such, was an oddity among the division's four infantry regiments, being the only one of the four that came from south of the Mason-Dixon Line. As such, it had the unique history of having been part of Robert E. Lee's Army of Northern Virginia during the Civil War and had actually fought against the 69th New York. In fact, the old 4th Alabama had fought from First Manassas until the surrender at Appomattox Court House in 1865, when there were only 202 survivors from a regiment that began the war numbering nearly 1,000.[46]

Like the other regiments, however, the 4th Alabama was mobilized for service on the border with Mexico in late June 1916. The regiment entered the mobilization camp at Vandiver Park in Montgomery, Alabama, and was soon mustered into federal service. The regiment left Montgomery by train on October 22, 1916, arriving in Nogales, Arizona, six days later where they pitched camp just outside of town on the road to Tucson. What followed was the same routine the other National Guard units endured, one of months of drill and hikes but no action.[47]

Another thing that made the 4th Alabama unique was their commanding officer, William P. Screws. Unlike some of the other infantry regiments in the 42nd Division, the men from Alabama would serve under one commanding officer from Mexico through the end of World War I. Another thing that made Screws unique was that, while a lieutenant colonel in the Alabama National Guard, he was also a captain in the Regular Army and had served in the dual role of regiment commander and federal mobilization officer when the regiment was called to service. Further, Screws was the only regiment commander to have been elected by the men to that post, as Alabama still maintained the old militia tradition of having the men choose their officers.[48]

Screws was a native of Alabama, having been born in Montgomery in 1875. He spent one year at the Marion Military Institute in Marion, Alabama, where he made the honor roll. He became a second lieutenant in the 3rd Alabama Volunteers in 1898, just in time for the Spanish-American War. After the war, he was promoted to first lieutenant of volunteers in 1899 and went to the Philippines. After returning to the United States in 1901, he was able to transfer to the Regular Army and was commissioned as a second lieutenant in 1902. The army sent him back to the Philippines where he saw combat during the Moro uprising. When he came back to the United States again, he was assigned to serve as a training officer, supervising National Guard units in Wisconsin, Illinois, Kansas, and Missouri before finally returning home to Alabama to oversee the training of its National Guard units.[49]

After almost five months in the Arizona desert, the 4th Alabama returned to Montgomery in late March 1917 and set up camp again in Vandiver Park, this time to start the demobilization process. However, before they could complete their exit from federal service, the regiment was told to stop their demobilization. War with Germany now seemed imminent, and the 4th Alabama was ordered to perform duties guarding critical war infrastructure such as rail yards and munition plants from sabotage by German sympathizers or agents.[50] As such, the 4th Alabama would be the only of the four infantry regiments in the Rainbow Division to remain in federal service continuously from the time they were called up to go to Arizona until the end of the war.

Colonel William P. Screws, commander of Alabama's 167th Infantry Regiment. (*National Archives*)

Orders came to return the regiment from guard duties to camp in Montgomery in May, where like all the other National Guard units in the country, they began their own recruiting campaign. The response across the state was overwhelming with groups of new enlistees forming in their hometowns. These various groups assembled and began "marching through Alabama." Everywhere they received tremendous ovations, the nation having been worked up to a high state of patriotism. By June 7, or thereabouts, all the contingents had reached Montgomery, and the men had begun their training.[51]

The 4th Alabama received orders in mid-August designating it as the 167th Infantry Regiment of the US Army. Along with those orders came the word to increase the regiment's strength, and the process to do so was the same as in other states, with men transferring from other Alabama National Guard units. In this case, the men came from the 1st Alabama Infantry, 2nd Alabama Infantry, 1st Alabama Cavalry, and 4th Alabama Infantry, which had a total of more than five thousand men. Screws, who was now a colonel, knew all the units intimately from his duties as the state's training supervisor. So he was able to get the authority to handpick the men he wanted from the other regiments.[52]

While these transfers might have been resented by the new men, the reality was the exact opposite. Captain Mortimer Jordan told his wife that almost all the transferees were excited about being part of the Rainbow Division. "The new men seem to be highly pleased with the transfer and have already begun to accuse their former comrades of being 'tin soldiers' while they belong to the 167th US Infantry," he wrote. "Some of our new men from the 1st [Alabama] Infantry had several fights on that account the day they transferred. They were 'rearing' to go with us."[53]

On August 27, the men began to break camp at Vandiver Park, now designated as Camp Sheridan.[54] In the early morning gloom of August 28, eight special trains awaited them in the Louisville and Nashville rail yards by the Alabama River. The army had kept the news of the regiment's departure quiet and barred the *Montgomery Advertiser* from announcing the movement in its pages. So the 167th began its journey to war without cheering, fanfare, or even goodbye kisses from parents, siblings, wives, or sweethearts. The trains all pulled out one after another for the three-day journey north to Camp Mills and their induction into the Rainbow Division.[55]

The legacy organization of Iowa's 168th Infantry, meanwhile, had originally formed in Council Bluffs, Iowa, in 1859 with the purpose of defending new settlements from raids by Sioux, Sac, and Fox warriors, as well as the lawless bands of bandits that roamed the plains. This initial organization was the foundation for the 3rd and 5th Iowa Infantry Regiments, which were merged as the 3rd Iowa in 1888.[56]

In April 1898, the regiment mobilized for duty in the Spanish-American War and entered federal service as the 51st Iowa Volunteers. In June, they took trains west to San Francisco in preparation for deployment in the Philippines, and they departed by ship for the journey there on November 2, 1898. They arrived on the island of Luzon in February 1899 just as the Philippine Insurrection began. The regiment fought in seventeen battles between then and their departure in September 1899.[57] This experience would later serve the regiment well for, when the regiment mobilized for duty in the war with Germany in June 1917, "its commanding officer; his lieutenant colonel, the three battalion commanders, the chief of the Medical Detachment, five company officers, and a number of enlisted men" had been in combat in the Philippines.[58]

Like its fellow National Guard regiments, the 3rd Iowa launched a massive recruiting campaign before being called to service and, by July

15, 1917, every company in the regiment had reached its full quota and "were besieged by eager applicants." On August 17, the outlying companies were ordered to report to the State Fair Grounds in Des Moines. The companies quickly began to arrive, and they made their camps on a hill just east of the exhibition grounds.[59]

This was also the date when the regiment received its designation as the 168th Infantry Regiment of the US Army and began using the transfer process to achieve the new required strength. In their case, the new men came from the 1st and 2nd Iowa Infantry, who transferred 813 and 840 men, respectively. All grades were included, with each company of the 1st and 2nd Iowa furnishing its proportionate share to the corresponding letter company of the 168th. By using this approach, every section of Iowa and almost every town in the state was represented in the 168th.[60]

The 168th began its journey to Camp Mills on September 9. The trains departed from the fairgrounds beginning at 5:00 p.m. as thousands of people gathered to cheer the men. Not surprisingly, the departure proved to be an emotional one. Major Winfred Robb, the regimental chaplain, later wrote, "With something gripping our throats, which we could not swallow, struggling to hold back the teardrops from our eyes, we stood upon the back of the train and watched the crowd of folks who came to see us off, become a blur and then indistinct in the distance. Our journey had begun."[61]

One young officer described the process of leaving for war as both heartbreaking and bitter:

> It was not until the first trains backed into the terminal at the Fair Grounds that the members of the 168th learned what leaving home was to mean to them. War, until then, had seemed such a remote and nebulous possibility that few had ever thought of themselves as actually in it. But now they realized, as did their friends and families, that every move was a step nearer to the uncertainty of the battle line. The fear that this might be the final parting, that this might be the last embrace, made more bitter the ordeal of farewell. It was amid smiles forced through tears, and stifled sobs from breaking hearts, that the crowded trains moved slowly out and disappeared in the distance.[62]

It took the 168th four days to reach Camp Mills. Along the way, large crowds greeted and cheered them in Chicago, Fort Wayne, Buffalo, Elmira, and Scranton. The men were gladdened by the "generosity and good will of the people that welcomed them en route." Finally, after waiting all night on a siding near Jamaica, New York, the first three train sections moved out to Garden City early in the morning hours of September 13, where they "disgorged themselves of their human freight."[63] The 168th had arrived.

Not surprisingly, the 165th Infantry was the first regiment to reach Camp Mills, given the short trip from New York City to the open plain near Hempstead, on Long Island. What had been farmland inhabited "only by Rabbits and skunks" quickly became a sea of tents housing over thirty thousand men. Army engineers had staked out the grounds indicating streets and locations for each regiment. The 165th's Pioneer Platoon arrived ahead of the regiment, quickly setting up their pup tents, a field kitchen, and then large model pyramidal tents that would house each squad at the head of each company's street. Once those were ready, the Pioneers erected the squad tents for their company and the regiment's headquarters company.[64]

As each regiment and support unit arrived, the camp became a beehive of activity, with soldiers setting up tents, kitchens, and even garbage dumps while organizing themselves for a stay of undetermined length. When the 166th arrived from Ohio, they were directed to set up camp in an area immediately to the right of the main entrance and across the road from the tents belonging to the 165th. While the regiment immediately had its supply of tents and cots, not everyone was pleased with their accommodations. Enoch Williams complained as soldiers have done throughout the centuries, saying, "This is a bum camp; they haven't got things fixed up at all."[65] Later, he would add that, while things were better, the constant clouds of dust raised by vehicles and men were a great bother. "The only thing that I find wrong with this camp is the dust," he wrote. "This place is the dirtyest camp I ever heard of. If you set anything down for two minutes, it's all dust."[66]

As the 168th arrived from Iowa, they found they were to be housed between their brigade partner, the 167th, and the 151st Machine Gun Battalion from Georgia with the 166th camped just to their west. Lieutenant John Taber later recalled that mess shacks had already been built when they arrived, and the regiment's tents were up and in place by noon. Once that chore was complete, the men had what would be an exceedingly rare afternoon off. Interestingly, they spent that precious downtime "chiefly in gazing in rapt awe at the airplanes circling and dipping gracefully in the sky above them. Many of them had never before seen an airplane, and to these it was a fascinating sight."[67] Little did they know at that moment that they would see many airplanes in the skies over France, but most of them would be German planes diving to strafe them.

When the 167th arrived on the trains from Montgomery, they were immediately ordered into quarantine by the Regimental Sanitary Department and the division surgeon. It seems that seven men had developed the measles during the trip north, so they had to go to their tents and remain there for two days only to be ordered back into quarantine again. "Naturally," wrote Captain Jordan to his wife, "the men are fretting over it and getting very restless. It looks to me as though some medical officers higher up have been afraid to take the responsibility of turning us loose."[68]

The quarantine worked, as there were only two more cases of measles at Camp Mills while the division was stationed there. But the health of all the troops was a major concern. The army's medical staff remembered what happened when thousands of men were thrown together at the outset of the Civil War. Diseases such as smallpox, measles, and chicken pox raged through the camps, and more men died from disease than from battle wounds. So the soldiers received virtually every vaccination that had been developed by that time.

Everyone was also examined for tuberculosis, and some did not pass muster. Lieutenant Leon Miesse of the 166th wrote home that "the Captain of A Co. (Capt. Peck) was declared unfit. I fear for the Capt. of Co. L for he hasn't been well since he has been here, and he looks bad."[69] The regiment's soldiers also received thorough physical examinations, as well as the vaccinations, including one for typhoid, which made many men ill. Enoch Williams reported that he had "a sore arm for we got a shot in the arm this morning. This is the sixth shot we have got."[70] Williams also wrote that he and his tent mates were under medical quarantine for several days, a common event in camp life during the war because many rural soldiers had not been exposed to the same diseases as their urban counterparts. "This life is not so bad," Williams told his mother. "The only thing that bothers me is that we are under quarantine. One of the fellows had spinal meningitis."[71]

However, of all the men, those from Alabama had the worst health issues. Major James W. Frew, one of the division surgeons, noted that, "From a medical standpoint the Alabama regiment caused us a great deal of worry and trouble. They were nearly all boys from the mountains and rural districts and as soon as they hit camp, they began to have their baby diseases. Measles, diphtheria, and scarlet fever were soon raging and the whole regiment was put under strict quarantine."[72]

Another major problem was the process of manning and organizing the upper echelon staffs from the division down to the regimental level. Each headquarters level required a dedicated staff not just to handle administrative and logistical issues but to be capable of developing and issuing complex orders for movements in combat. At the division and brigade levels, this was particularly challenging because there had been no brigades or divisions in the US Army since the Spanish-American War in 1898. Therefore, it was critical that these staffs receive the best officers the division had to offer. So a process of transferring qualified, talented officers up the chain of command began. Companies lost officers to a battalion staff or the regiment headquarters replacing the regiment's officers who had gone to the brigade or division headquarters.

Naturally, these officers had to be backfilled quickly, and the only sources available were typically young officers fresh from the training program provided at Plattsburgh, New York, by the Citizen's Military Training Corps, a modern forerunner of today's Reserve Officer Training Corps program. Integrating these new lieutenants into the companies was problematic because they were outsiders. The new men who had transferred into the various state regiments were one thing, but at least they all came from the same state. These new officers, however, were from states all around the country, and there were other issues because almost all of them were "college-bred men."[73]

When rumors began to circulate around the 166th about the impending arrival of these new, inexperienced officers, the grumbling from the enlisted men was very loud. One of the regiment's soldiers was heard to state, "As if it ain't bad enough to be hooked up with that crazy Irish crowd from New York, they're goin' to shove off a bunch of them green trainin' camp birds on us fer officers."[74] Further, these concerns were not merely confined to the enlisted men. When Lieutenant Miesse met the initial contingent of new officers, he was not duly impressed. Miesse, who had recently left Company L for a position at brigade headquarters, wrote his wife saying, "The new Officers came to-day that have been assigned to the Regiment, Co. L got three new ones. One of them is all O.K., but the other two I can't give very much."[75] Later, as the new officers tried to figure out their responsibilities, Miesse told his wife, "The boys in the Company call them the 'Sears and Roebuck Officers.' Most of them are not much good, but you can't say anything except to sit tight with your mouth closed."[76]

In the 167th, the enlisted men from Alabama resented the fact that almost all their new officers were "Yankees" from northern states. They also were either college graduates or came directly from a college campus, which was not the case with the regiment's own officers. The inexperience of these new lieutenants made the training more difficult because the officers were just as inexperienced as their men. Still, they were welcomed because the regiment, like all the others, was so desperately in need of them. One new officer, Second Lieutenant John Donaldson, later said that he was greeted warmly, writing, "A mighty fine bunch of fellows that treated us like Princes. . . . The officers mess is a dandy and if today's food is any criterion, Glory, Glory!"[77]

This massive intermingling of organizations from different regions of the country did not occur without some issues. The biggest of these involved the 165th and the 167th. Their two legacy organizations, the 69th New York and 4th Alabama, had fought one another during the Civil War, most notably at Fredericksburg in 1862, where the New Yorkers of the Irish Brigade were cut to pieces by the Alabamians as they tried to assault Marye's Heights. It seems the twentieth-century members of the two regiments decided to carry on the fight at Camp Mills. The brawls between the regiments were so bad that Raymond Cheseldine from the 166th would later say that the division's first combat communique ought to have read, "Elements of the Rainbow Division were engaged in hand-to-hand conflicts in the vicinity of Hempstead this evening."[78] As a result, the military police companies from Virginia were kept busy breaking up fights between the men from New York and those from Alabama. Eventually, however, the brawls ended and gave way to a relative sense of mutual respect between the two regiments.

Of course, two of the major reasons for forming the division at Camp Mills were to issue new equipment and perform training. Virtually all the units gathering at Camp Mills were poorly equipped. Those that had gone to Mexico wore out much of what they had, and what the states had on hand when their National Guard units were mobilized was insufficient both in quantity and quality. In the case of the 168th, their situation was made worse by the fact that they were the last regiment to arrive at Camp Mills. Therefore, much of the supplies of new equipment had already been issued, and the men from Iowa rushed to catch up. "While the line companies were sweating out on the drill fields," wrote John Taber, "the Supply Company was working at full speed to procure and distribute supplies and equipment." Eventually, every man in the 168th would get a woolen uniform and the short trench coat to replace the longer coat they had, but this process was not finished until the night before the regiment embarked for France.[79]

In all the regiments, old ordnance equipment, packs, haversacks, belts, canteens, and mess outfits were turned in and the latest army equipment issued. Each man got a complete set of new clothing, including a trench overcoat.[80] Enoch Williams from the 166th proudly wrote to his mother about all his new gear, saying, "I have two uniforms, three suits of underwear, five pairs of socks, two pairs of shoes, two hats, an overcoat, and a poncho. We have a bag to carry our extra clothes. On a hike, we have a pack to carry one blanket, poncho, half a shelter tent, underwear, and mess kit."[81]

However, despite all the army's efforts, there was a critical shortage of cold weather gear such as woolen sweaters, warm underwear, and heavy-duty shoes.[82] As a result, the division would deploy without winter clothing items that would prove to be critical in what was going to be one of the worst winters in French history.

But the equipment supply issue also would hold up the Rainbow Division's deployment to France. The army dictated that every division must be fully equipped before they could sail for Europe. The problems experienced by the division resulted in the 26th Division from New England, called the Yankee Division, leaving for France about a month before the 42nd Division.[83]

But the major activity at Camp Mills was training, and the daily training regimen was relentless. On the first day the division was assembled in camp, Mann and MacArthur issued their training program and schedule, which had three straightforward objectives. The first objective was to build discipline and unit cohesion, followed by a second objective to develop a high degree of physical fitness. Finally, the troops must learn from the school of the soldier. This meant drill, personal hygiene, and taking care of personal combat equipment. Mann and MacArthur also ordered that all company officers must know the required drill, be ready to lead both the drill and physical exercise, and ensure they instructed noncommissioned officers prior to each training day while the men ate and prepared for their daily activities.[84]

Reveille would sound at 4:50 a.m., and from then on until mess at 6:00 p.m. the men participated in close order dill and bayonet practice.[85] Every regiment set up its own drill field on the edge of the camp, and the men spent at least eight hours a day on the drill field under the severe and often profane tutelage of tough Regular Army drill sergeants who "hounded and harried" them without mercy. But the men of the division were determined to show their worth and took this punishment with no

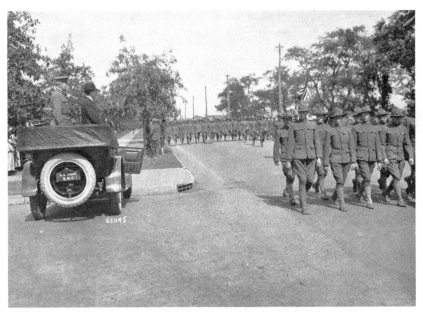

Secretary of War Baker and General Mann watch a review of the 42nd Division at Camp Mills. (*National Archives*)

more than the usual soldier's "beefing." The drill field was hot, rough, and overgrown with high weeds and became a "small world unto itself—a drilling, sweating, cursing little world, preparing to fight."[86]

Much time was spent on bayonet drill because the army had issued a new manual based on French and British experience on the Western Front. However, to make the men more interested in these drills, the officers told them that the Germans disliked "cold steel," and, therefore, the bayonet would be their most effective weapon. Furthermore, as John Taber recalled, the bayonet drill "did not arouse the pleasantest of expectations" and was intended to both make a soldier adept in the bayonet's use as well to fire him with blood lust:[87]

> To produce a good fighter, it is necessary first to awaken in him his primitive instincts. And the youngsters from the Middle West were far from blood-thirsty. Every jab punctured a mentally-pictured Kaiser; every thrust saw the finish of one of his subjects. If the knife became too deeply imbedded in the body, it could be withdrawn by planting the feet on his trunk and pulling, or by shooting him through point-blank; if he attempted to resist the withdrawal of a bayonet implanted

in his loins, there were means to force him to loose his hold. It was an ugly business, but necessary, and one that gave the men some sort of idea of what they had to face.[88]

Shortly after the training at Camp Mills began, Lieutenant General John Pershing, commander of the American Expeditionary Force (AEF), issued guidance to all officers in the army about pre-embarkation training. Pershing still clung to pre-war American military doctrine that stressed the primacy of the infantryman with a rifle. Despite all that he and other military leaders had observed of the war on the Western Front, they still had not embraced the importance of mass firepower support from artillery and the machine gun, and they never really would, which would cost the doughboys of the AEF dearly in the months to come. Pershing's guidance came in the form of a small booklet distributed to every officer, which also stressed the need for rifle practice and marksmanship training before embarkation for France.[89]

This final point is interesting because there was no rifle range at Camp Mills, and therefore, there was no shooting practice or training during the 42nd Division's time there. Instead, the emphasis was on speed and trying to develop a physically fit, cohesive organization before deploying overseas. The real training was yet to come in France, where the division's French Army instructors awaited them. It must be remembered that no one in either the Regular Army or National Guard was familiar with trench warfare or, more importantly, many of the weapons they would be required to use in combat. No one in the division had ever seen a hand grenade much less used one. There also were no trench mortars or automatic rifles in the army's equipment, so men would have to be trained in their use once they reached France.

As the weeks of training went by, most of the men began to wonder when they would leave Camp Mills and where they would really be going. "Everyone had a theory," wrote Raymond Cheseldine of the 166th, "and was only too glad to advance it. The camp was a hive of speculation."[90] Soon though, men like Enoch Williams, who had believed the regiment would never leave the country, came to realize that France was definitely their destination. In early September, Leon Miesse wrote his wife that "Hearing the talk runs and the way things look, we all expect to be on our way by the latter part of October."[91] Meanwhile, a few weeks later, Enoch Williams told his family that, "I don't think we will stay here all winter, but I think we will be here a month or so."[92] As it turned out, he made a surprisingly good guess.

On October 17, the division sent the word down to its units that they would leave Camp Mills after dark that night and that their tents were to be left standing so that no word about their departure would get out until they were on their way. After the evening mess was finished, the men of the Rainbow Division waited anxiously for the final order to come, many tired and sleeping on their backpacks. Finally, orders were whispered down the lanes that ran through each regiment's tents. Silently, the men marched through the darkness to the trains that would move them to the docks where their ships awaited them. "Those who were leaving first felt somewhat in luck," wrote Raymond Cheseldine. "Yet the solemnity of that first move in darkness overshadowed any thrill that was felt at the thought of actually 'going somewhere.'"[93]

Sadly, many of the men would not have a roundtrip ticket.

2

THE RAINBOW ARRIVES IN FRANCE

From Training to the Trenches,
November 1, 1917–June 18, 1918

"In the valleys in which we found ourselves, Joan of Arc was born,
had heard her mission and had received her command; and, as cru-
saders with the crusader's heart, the Rainbow was stirred with the
very martial spirit that she had, in her lifetime, inspired in others."
—Major Ronald Tompkins, *The Story of the Rainbow Division*

The training was never ending, and the intense cold of January and February 1918 made the learning process even more challenging. January
was particularly tough on the men of the Rainbow Division, as there was
continuous snow and sleet throughout the month.[1] The division found
itself in what was called the Seventh Training Area, which spread across
hundreds of square miles of French countryside dotted with small villages. The division would only be here for six weeks, during which the
pace of training was conducted "seriously and feverishly."[2] In the deep
snow and frozen hillsides, the division's French instructors drilled the
men incessantly in trench warfare and the use of the hand grenade, Stokes
mortar, one-pounder 37mm guns, and the Hotchkiss machine gun.

Leon Miesse of the 166th Infantry wrote to his wife that the men were
drilling seven hours per day with up to two hours of night classes or night
combat problems. The Guardsmen made quick progress, and Miesse told

his wife, "The men are fast developing into fighters and can handle the new implements of war with great alacrity." Demonstrating his growing confidence in the men of his company, he added, "I fear very much that the Kaiser has a surprise coming when this outfit is turned loose, for I never saw a more determined set of men."

Those determined men as well as all the men in the division would soon get their first test in combat. On February 16, the 42nd Division was ordered to move by rail north to that part of the Lorraine front known as the Lunéville, Saint Clement, and Baccarat sectors.

The process of moving the 42nd Division and the other divisions initially deploying to France was more than complex—it was an unprecedented undertaking. While they had moved a much smaller number of men to Cuba and the Philippines in 1898, no one in the War Department or Navy Department had ever contemplated moving this many men so far, much less across an ocean defended by enemy submarines. Within days of war being declared, the army formed a select committee of shipping executives to study the registries of American shipping and select vessels that might meet the army's needs. The committee initially selected thirteen American-flagged ships that were sufficiently fast and could carry enough fuel in their bunkers for transatlantic crossings.[3]

However, in some cases, these ships seemed barely capable of performing the job required of them. For instance, the SS *Mallory*, while it was a new ship built in 1916, had only operated in coastal waters between New York and New Orleans, which were nothing like the rough, deep, open waters of the North Atlantic. The SS *Pastores*, meanwhile, had been built in Belfast in 1913 and operated under the United Fruit Company, moving produce between the West Indies and Central America. As a result, the ship had simply not been designed to house thousands of passengers for a voyage across the Atlantic. Yet, these two ships would be assigned to carry thousands of American doughboys to France.

While it had been planned for the Rainbow Division to make the voyage in its entirety, the original deployment plan was altered to meet a change of conditions at the port of embarkation at Hoboken, New Jersey. This led to the division being distributed among ships at Hoboken, New York City, and Montreal. The six merchantmen in the Hoboken contingent began leaving on the night of October 18, and there was another departure on October 31. The first Hoboken group arrived at St. Nazaire on October 29, while the ships from New York City left on November 3 en route to Liverpool in Great Britain before finally arriving in Le Havre on December 1. Meanwhile, the ships from Montreal convoyed on October 27, also arriving in Liverpool on November 11. After a brief rest, they sailed down the Irish Sea and up the English Channel to Le Havre.[4]

The division's collective journey across the Atlantic was uneventful except for the miserable conditions aboard many of the ships and a breakdown on the SS *Grant* that required her to return to Hoboken for repairs, which delayed the arrival of part of the 168th Infantry.[5] Also, there was an outbreak of mumps that hit the 167th as they made their crossing. By the time their ships arrived in Liverpool, there were 600 cases reported, and the entire regiment had to be quarantined. Over 200 men were so ill they had to be hospitalized at the Belmont Military Hospital in the city. Once the quarantine was lifted, those Alabamians who were not sick received passes to visit Liverpool. Here, they once again demonstrated their penchant for rowdiness, picking fights with other Americans, British soldiers, and the military police.[6]

The bulk of the division arrived at St. Nazaire in early November, however, and within a few days, they began to move by train to their training areas. For most of the men, this meant riding in boxcars that one soldier referred to sarcastically as "the pride of the French National Railway system."[7] While these men had been transported in boxcars before, the American version was a luxurious palace compared to the French variety. These boxcars were tiny, perhaps only about eight feet wide and ten to sixteen feet long.[8] A painted label was on the side that said, "40 Hommes-8 Chevaux," which meant that the car's capacity was forty men or eight horses. Also, as one soldier pointed out, "the change from men to horses or vice versa, was often only a matter of a few moments."[9]

The soldiers were crammed thirty-two at a time into these cars. With all their equipment on their backs, it was so crowded that no one could sit down. Raymond Cheseldine of the 166th said that the crowding was so bad, it "would make a sardine box green with envy."[10]

By early December, most of the division was encamped at two training centers, the First Training Area near Morlaincourt and the Fifth Training Area near Vaucouleurs, both of which were a few miles south of the front lines near Tours and close enough to hear the dueling French and German artillery in the distance. Meanwhile, the entire artillery brigade, with the exception of the trench mortar battery, proceeded straight from St. Nazaire to Coëtquidan, where it was to receive its final training as a

Men from the 168th Infantry Regiment receiving trench warfare training in January 1918. (*National Archives*)

brigade before rejoining the division in February 1918. The trench mortar battery traveled to Fort de la Bonnelle, near Langres, for special training, returning to the division shortly before it made its first deployment in the trenches.[11]

As the division settled into a new training routine, political rumblings shook the chain of command. This activity began within days of the division's arrival in France when, on November 10, Colonel Fox Conner at AEF Headquarters issued a memorandum to the AEF Chief of Staff, Colonel James G. Harbord, recommending the entire 42nd Division be designated as the 1st Replacement Division of the American I Corps.[12] This meant that the division would function as nothing more than a pool of replacement soldiers for the units of other American divisions. On receiving this news, General Mann immediately went to see General Pershing at AEF Headquarters in Chaumont. He strenuously argued with Pershing, saying that the division "had been a uniting force as the nation mobilized for war."[13] But his pleas fell on deaf ears, and there could be no doubt that Pershing's position was fueled by the lingering disdain felt for the National Guard by the AEF commander and other Regular Army officers. However, General Mann and Colonel MacArthur were not about to roll over in the face of this challenge.

Whatever else Mann and MacArthur might have been, as career professional soldiers, they also had developed considerable political skills, especially Mann who had to work with numerous state officials while leading the Militia Bureau. The two men mounted a campaign to garner political support in the United States that resulted in a flood of letters and telegrams to both the War Department and AEF Headquarters protesting Pershing's plan for the Rainbow Division. At first, Pershing and his staff would not budge. They saw this issue as a test case for the AEF having direct control over all its forces. Colonel Conner wrote a second memorandum on November 22 stating, "If the drafted national guard is to be a reliable asset in this war it must be treated without special privileges." It went on to say, "The decision in this case is fundamentally important. It will probably establish the policy relating to employment of national guard divisions for replacements."[14]

But the army's chief of staff in Washington, DC, General Tasker Bliss, disagreed with Pershing and thought the idea of turning the 42nd Division into a replacement pool simply terrible. Moreover, his views were shared by President Wilson and Secretary of War Baker, both of whom believed that, given all the publicity surrounding the Rainbow Division, this would be a terrible mistake and one that would adversely impact the nation's support for the war effort.[15] It did not take long for this news to reach Chaumont. On November 25, only three days after Colonel Fox's memorandum defending Pershing's position, General Harbord reversed the AEF decision. In a new memorandum, he pointed out that the 42nd Division had "perhaps more esprit than any other division" and, more importantly, the War Department clearly would not agree to the change in the division's status. "I much fear that if you used it for replacement without notice to the War Department," he wrote, "that you would be reversed: on the other hand if you ask the War Department that you will not be permitted to do it."[16]

With that, the issue was settled. However, the political fallout was not. Pershing deeply resented Mann and MacArthur's actions. While the AEF commander refused to associate with MacArthur in the future, he took direct action against General Mann, whom he replaced as commander of the 42nd Division on December 15. While he cited Mann's age and overall health for his dismissal, the reasons for Mann's reassignment back to Washington were purely punitive. In this case, the War Department decided to let Pershing have his way.

Pershing replaced Mann with Major General Charles T. Menoher, an 1886 graduate of West Point and a colonel of field artillery in the Regular Army. He was also a graduate of the Artillery School and the Army War College and had served four years on the General Staff. More importantly, perhaps, Pershing knew Menoher well and trusted him.[17]

Major General Charles T. Menoher, who became commander of the 42nd Division in December 1918. (*National Archives*)

Upon their arrival in their respective training areas, the division's units began what was their real training—training for war on the Western Front. The course of instruction was based on all the Allies had learned during over three years of warfare on the Western Front. Officers and men assigned to use new weapons attended schools and daily drills under the watchful eyes of French instructors. For the four infantry regiments, the first weeks of training focused on weapons. Many of the more experienced members of the National Guard were very proficient in the use and care of their M1903 Springfield rifles, formally designated the United States Rifle, Caliber .30-06, Model 1903. However, as mentioned previously, none of the men had ever used some of the other vital weapons in the fighting in France.

For example, none of the division's soldiers had ever seen, much less used, a hand grenade. So daily training in the proper method for throwing a hand grenade was one of the first items on the training agenda. Most of the soldiers thought this would be easy since, after all, they had been throwing baseballs and footballs for most of their lives. However, they quickly learned that, if you threw a hand grenade like a baseball, it might certainly strike the ground at or near its target, but it then would bounce and roll far beyond it, exploding where it might do no harm to the enemy. So they had to learn to toss the grenade in an arc so it would land near the target and stay there.

As for the other weapons, these included the French-made Hotchkiss machine gun and Chauchat automatic rifle, as well as the British three-inch Stokes mortar.[18] When the 166th and the rest of the 42nd Division arrived in France, no unit in the US Army was equipped with an automatic rifle. An American-manufactured Browning Automatic Rifle was being developed, but it would take more than a year to get it ready and produced for field use. Therefore, the only weapon available was the Chauchat, which was developed by the French in 1915. It fired French 8mm model 1886 ammunition and was a relatively unsophisticated, crude weapon that could be mass produced very quickly. The Chauchat was light at only nineteen pounds and air-cooled with a magazine that held twenty rounds of ammunition. Its biggest problem was the scarcity of spare parts and poor-quality manufacturing, which often led to misaligned sights and shabby weapons assemblies.[19]

Like the Chauchat automatic rifle, the trench mortar was also something entirely new to American soldiers. The British three-inch Stokes mortar that the AEF received in France was a simple but ingenious invention. The Stokes mortar, like all mortars during the war, provided organic support fire for infantrymen by lobbing shells into enemy trenches and foxholes. The Stokes mortar was a simple muzzle-loading weapon. Essentially, the Stokes was a portable three-inch-diameter steel pipe that fired a high-explosive shell. The propellant charge was, in reality, a shotgun charge (without load) inserted in the base of the projectile. The mortar shell was dropped into the top of the barrel, slid rapidly down the tube, and the charge detonated upon hitting a fixed firing pin in the base of the tube. The resulting explosion forced the shell out of the tube and sent it on its way to the target.

The Stokes mortar was a crew-served weapon, and there were six mortars assigned to each unit within the Headquarters Company. That unit had thirty-nine men to handle the six mortars, one cart, one wagon, and nine mules. This team's job was to provide close support mortar fire in a variety of combinations. Squads, or groups of one or two men, could be organized and attached to parts of the regiment for specific fire missions, and they could fire their weapons in pairs or singly.[20]

Maybe the biggest training need would be on the use of the machine gun, which was a weapon that, along with heavy artillery, dominated the battlefields of the Western Front. While the American units had machine guns, the United States was unable to produce the guns in the quantity needed. Therefore, the Hotchkiss machine gun was issued to the 42nd Division and all the other AEF units in France. During late 1917, the newest version of the Hotchkiss was the Model 1914, which was a refinement of the older Model 1897 gun. When the war began, the French only issued the Hotchkiss to second-line territorial units, but soon, the French Army decided to make it the standard machine gun for all frontline units because of its reliability.[21]

The Hotchkiss machine gun was gas actuated and air-cooled, which gave it an advantage over water-cooled guns like the German Maxim. Another design advantage of the Hotchkiss was that it could be dismounted from its tripod and reassembled in less than a minute using one tool, and the French manufacturer made the weapon so that it was impossible to assemble improperly, a critical factor when inexperienced American gun crews were using the weapon.[22]

However, while reliable, the weapon did have its own unique problems. First, it was cumbersome as compared to similar guns, such as the Vickers and Browning, weighing over fifty-three pounds. That meant that the weapon and its ammunition needed to be transported by mule. Second, once the gun got hot, typically after firing around one thousand rounds, it took about four minutes plus sponging with cool water before firing again.[23]

Perhaps the most significant complication of using the Hotchkiss was that employing it in combat required a well-coordinated effort by a three-man team. That was because, while feeding the gun ammunition was relatively simple, each strip of ammunition held only twenty-four rounds of 8mm Lebel ammunition. That meant that the crew had to reload the gun several times per minute, requiring a well-choreographed process of reloading during periods when the gun was firing almost continuously.[24] This, in turn, meant that the soldiers in the division's machine gun battalions had to master this complex process in training if they were to be of any use in the trenches.

As the division's units in the First and Fifth Training Areas toiled to learn about their new weapons, no one was aware that the AEF and the French Army had never intended them to train there. Rather, the original plan called for them to train in the Seventh Training Area near Rolampont, which was about sixty-five miles to the south. However, the area was not ready for the regiment and the rest of the division when they arrived in France, and since the need to get the men trained was so great, they started their work in the First and Fifth Training Areas.[25]

Now, as December arrived, there were rumors of a German offensive coming near Toul. This meant that seasoned French troops were urgently needed in the area and that the untrained Americans would have to move to the Seventh Training Area near Rolampont. The reaction to this news frustrated some of the soldiers. One Ohio doughboy in the 166th was heard to say disgustedly that, "nobody knows nothin' over here. An' the officers is worse than anybody." Upon hearing that the Germans might be on the way, he added that "instead of gettin' ready to fight here, we get the dope that we've got to pull out an' let some Frogs come in to stop the Dutch. I didn't ask for this war, but now that we're here, what's all the training for if we're goin' to run before we've seen a German?"[26]

When orders were received to begin the move on December 11, 1917, the only way to get to Rolampont was on foot. The division's units had only enough trucks to carry rations and forage for their mules plus some carts and wagons that the mules pulled. Furthermore, the French did not have enough available trains to move the division. That meant they would have to march there. On December 12, 1917, the division formed up to begin what came to be known as the Valley Forge March.[27]

The march was brutal beyond description. The winter of 1917–1918 was one of the worst in French history, and the men of the Rainbow Division had to hike day after day through deep snow drifts amid subzero temperatures. Some of the men did not have overcoats and many did not have proper footwear. All of their shoes were the same summer weight gear they had been issued at Camp Mills, and much of that was worn out. As a result, as the division marched on the snow- and ice-covered roads south to Rolampont, you could trace their progress by the red trail left in the snow by thousands of badly bleeding feet. At times, the winds created classic white-out conditions, but the regiments kept moving on.

In many ways, the Valley Forge March demanded a level of courage and determination that some probably did not believe these National Guardsmen possessed. But they met the challenge head-on just as they would the horrors of combat that were yet to come. In later years, even General Pershing would be moved to commend them. Speaking at a reunion of the division in 1923, he said, "I recall your courage and your fortitude under all of these trying circumstances, with poor billets and bitter cold nights. But I also felt at the time, and can say now, that the experience prepared you as nothing else could have done perhaps for that trial of courage that came to you on many a battlefield. . . . I felt that nothing could have been more fortunate than that you had that experience."[28] After beginning the arduous march on December 12, the division paused from December 16 to December 26. Once they were on the road again, the weather became even worse than before. But the division completed its march to the Seventh Training Area on December 29. The entire journey and the men's attitude about it was summed up by one soldier. As he limped across the bridge at Rolampont with his feet wrapped in rags, slipping and sliding under the weight of his pack, covered in snow and bent against the gale-force winds that day, he said, "Valley Forge—Hell! There ain't no such animal."[29]

Once billeted in the new training area, the division's units renewed their training program with added urgency. With the travails of the Valley Forge March behind them, the men of the division knew that their first move to the front could not be too far off. While the severe winter weather did not provide any respite at first, the soldiers persisted in their efforts to learn these new ways of war from their diligent French instructors. Two battalions of the 32nd French Regiment now assisted the men of the division in learning the basics of trench warfare, conducting grenade and rifle range practice, and firing the Stokes mortars and the Hotchkiss machine gun.[30]

While the men toiled away in the cold, wet, and muddy practice trenches, they became acquainted with a vicious nemesis that plagued the soldiers of both sides: body lice. For the doughboys of the AEF, they came to be known as "cooties" or, on occasion, "crumbs." Before long, every man in the 42nd Division, officer or enlisted, would be infested with them. As one division commander would say, there were "too few baths and too many cooties." Cooties would be an unforgettable experience for the frontline doughboy.[31] At one point in the war, the chief medical officer of the 26th Division reported that the "command is 99% infested with lice; is filthy, bodily; needing bathing and delousing."[32] When the men searched for lice, they called the process "reading your shirt." One soldier wrote that, every morning, officers and men, whether "refined or roughneck," would meticulously strip to the waist for the process of reading his shirt. Leon Miesse of the 166th wrote his wife, "They call it the crumb number as crumb is another name for 'cooties' or body lice. . . . I certainly long for a good American bathtub."[33]

After six weeks in the Seventh Training Area, the division was pronounced ready for its first combat deployment. On February 16, 1918, the 42nd Division began to move by train from the Rolampont area north to a part of the Lorraine front known as the Lunéville and Baccarat sectors. With the exception of a brief period in August 1918, from now until the end of the war, the Rainbow Division would serve continually on the front lines. For these National Guardsmen, life would never be the same again.

At first, the men of the Rainbow Division were told that they were headed for a ten-day training session. All the units were ordered to pack up their excess baggage for storage, which they would retrieve after the training was complete. Further, the orders from division headquarters directed that the soldiers should retain only a thirty-day supply of field equipment. "Feverish preparation" began, but not surprisingly, no one was quite sure what ought to be included in thirty days' worth of field equipment. To make certain they did not take too much, everyone cut their gear and clothing down to the bone. While this seemed a very sensible approach at the time, no one could have possibly realized that they would not see their surplus baggage again until March 1919.[34]

The trains soon began rumbling out with the men once again packed tightly into the infamous 40 Hommes-8 Chevaux boxcars. The area they were headed for was what the French and the AEF called a "quiet sector." When the war began in 1914, the Germans drove deep into the region surrounding Lunéville and Baccarat, reaching Rambervillers and destroying villages along the way. Then they withdrew to a line that ran roughly from Reillon southeast to Domèvre-sur-Vezouze. After that, both sides dug trenches, strung barbed wire, and seemed to develop a tacit agreement not to intrude upon one another. Up to now, neither side had used gas along these lines, and "in the daytime, a shot was seldom heard."[35] Unfortunately, once the Americans arrived, that would all change.

From a military planning perspective, the move of the 42nd Division to Lunéville and Baccarat was relatively simple as compared to the operations that would come later in 1918. Despite that fact, the headquarters staff at AEF struggled to put together cogent, coordinated, and well-thought out orders. The problem was that there were simply not enough trained staff officers in the Regular Army. Following military reforms in the early 1900s, the War Department had created the command and staff courses at Fort Leavenworth and the Army War College in Washington, DC to provide what was essentially much-needed postgraduate education for Regular Army officers in effective planning. However, by April 1917, only 379 officers had completed the training at either institution.[36]

General Pershing later pointed out the sheer magnitude of this problem, saying that they "were confronted with the task of building up an army of millions that would require as many trained staff officers as we had officers in the whole Regular Army at the beginning of the war."[37] To successfully operate in the kind of modern war being fought on the Western Front, the AEF Headquarters' G1 (Personnel), G2 (Intelligence), G3

(Operations), and G4 (Logistics) divisions had to be able to function smoothly and develop plans that would effectively meet operational demands. However, this was not to be the case and, as a result, the plans developed by the AEF were often severely flawed. Orders to subordinate commands sometimes came too late or were incomprehensible. Worse perhaps, many times the plans and orders reflected an ill-informed or poorly conceived thought process. While there would be some improvement as the war continued, by the end of the war, AEF was still directing the achievement of impossible objectives, and operations were almost always plagued by a lack of needed fire support and logistics. Furthermore, this problem was even worse at the corps and division levels, where the staff struggled to effectively analyze and implement any orders received from a higher headquarters, be it American or French.

In the operations at Lunéville and Baccarat, one action of the AEF's G4 staff provides an example of planning that reflects a complete misunderstanding of operational support needs. G4 had worked out logistics plans with the French in terms of who would provide certain supplies. At this point in the war, the Americans were still critically short of some materiel. Therefore, it was decided that the French would provide the heavier artillery ammunition while the American Service of Supply, known as SOS, would supply all other forms of ammunition. The 42nd Division staff was to ensure an initial thirty-day supply of everything needed to support operations in the trenches went to Lunéville. But this thirty-day supply had been defined by the AEF's G4 staff, and many of their estimates for required supplies were far off the mark. For example, G4 had estimated that each trench mortar battery needed 600 rounds per Stokes mortar for thirty days of fire support. However, the Rainbow Division's 117th Trench Mortar Battery, armed with twenty-four mortars, would actually use four times that much in their first month of operations at Lunéville. In fact, in just twelve days from March 5 through March 12, 1918, the 117th fired 1,528 rounds, with over 800 rounds fired in a single night on March 9.[38]

The division arrived and was ready to move units to the front lines on February 21. Initially, the deployment was treated as a training event where French units would supervise the Americans, although this training event involved a very real enemy who would be firing live ammunition. The 165th Infantry plus two companies of the 150th Machine Gun Battalion were assigned on the far left of the Lunéville sector with the 164th French Division, with their front line in the Forêt de Parroy. To their immediate right was the 166th Infantry plus the other two companies of the 150th Machine Gun Battalion in the St. Clement sector with the 14th French Division. Meanwhile, the 167th Infantry, the 168th Infantry, and the 15lst Machine Gun Battalion were placed in the Baccarat sector under the 128th French Division, with the 168th on the far right of the sector near Badonviller.[39]

The division's other combat units were dispersed along the front. The 150th Field Artillery was placed to the far left with the 41st French Division in the Dombasle sector, while elements of the 149th Field Artillery supported the 164th French Division and the 165th Infantry. The rest of the 149th was assigned to the 14th French Division and the 166th Infantry, and the 151st Field Artillery and 117th Trench Mortar Battery supported the 128th French Division, 167th Infantry, and 168th Infantry.[40]

At first, only one-half platoon from each regiment deployed to the trenches, serving man for man with the French for a few days of instruction. Next, full companies moved forward, and, finally, full battalions took over each regiment's front.[41] As the men moved forward, many seemed to understand the importance of what was happening. John Taber of the 168th later wrote that the men felt that this was a "testing period." "Every one of them," he wrote, "now realized that in a few days, at least, he was to be put on trial—tested as a man and as a soldier, tested for personal courage, and tested for military efficiency before the eyes of his comrades, which to him were the eyes of the world."[42]

But there were also some concerns about the organization and staffing of critical support organizations such as the Sanitary Detachments that would provide first aid and move the wounded to the rear for treatment. In the 168th, Sanitary Detachment soldiers were issued Red Cross brassards to be worn on their left arm. Each brassard had a printed number that had been registered in both Washington, DC and Geneva, Switzerland, so that these men could be traced and identified if captured by the Germans. However, there were only forty-eight of these soldiers in the regiment, and only thirty of those were assigned to support the regiment's three battalions. So there were approximately thirty men available to act as first-aid workers in the front trenches—only ten to each battalion of more than 1,000 men.[43]

As the division's four regiments moved into the trenches on the night of February 21–22, most were careful to do so very quietly. When the 1st Division was the first American unit to take up positions at the front in a nearby sector, they had done so in broad daylight with a great show, which

The 2nd and 3rd Battalions of the 168th Infantry Regiment march through Rolampont in February 1918. (*National Archives*)

aroused German suspicions. In response, the Germans poured artillery fire down on their heads and conducted a raid on the first night in which they took several Americans prisoner. So, learning from the experience of their Regular Army counterparts, the National Guardsmen pushed their way through the mud to the trenches in the inky darkness and took their place in the line with as much stealth and quiet as humanly possible.[44]

Thus, the Rainbow Division went to war and began a process that would continue for the next four months. A battalion from each regiment would take its place in the trenches for ten days, a period the men called a "trick," while a second battalion was placed nearby as support and a third was farther to the rear as a strategic reserve. When the first battalion completed its trick, the second would move into the trenches, and the third would come forward as the supporting battalion, while the first battalion went to the rear in reserve. They all would soon discover that the British were correct when they said that trench warfare was "damned dull, damned damp, and damned dangerous."[45]

The trenches the men were to defend were, perhaps, not what they imagined during their time in the practice trenches in the Seventh Training Area. These trenches were not merely a single, long ditch in the earth. Rather, they were composed of a complex network of defensive positions that wound about the front. Each regiment was assigned responsibility for a specific subsector that had a line of four combat groups with each one referred to as a "Groupe de Combat" or GC. Two of the GCs, with their supporting "Poste d'Appui," or PA, just to their rear, formed a "strong point." Two or more strong points, with a reserve position to their rear, formed a single "Centre de Resistance," called a CR. That CR was given a name that would designate its specific area of responsibility.[46] For example, the 168th Infantry defended CR Chamois.

Each position was completely surrounded by tangles of barbed wire and, because each GC might be 400 to 500 yards apart, they were connected by small communication trenches built in a zigzag pattern called "boyaus." Each GC was defended by a platoon that maintained five or six posts. Each post was held by four men, with two always on duty during the night. Each post had a small shelter dug into the bank of the trench, which was covered with corrugated iron or strips of canvas and dirt. These "dugouts," as they were called, were used for sleeping quarters and equipment storage. During daytime hours, two or three men manned the entire GC.[47]

While the men's training in trench warfare might have been considered adequate, nothing could have prepared them for its reality. First, there was the discomfort caused by the cold and the mud, along with the presence of innumerable rats who scampered about up and down the trenches. The mud left a particularly strong impression on many of the men, Louis Collins of the 151st Field Artillery among them. After the war, Collins wrote:

> Never will the men of the 42nd Division forget the mud of Lorraine. Comrades may be forgotten, details of fighting go glimmering, marches and campaigns become hazy, but that awful February–March battle with the mud of Lorraine will stand out in their memories until final taps are sounded over the last surviving member of the division. For ten days the men of the 151st ate in mud, worked in mud, slept in mud, and dreamed of mud—when the mud would let them sleep. The picket lines in the echelons were in the mud; the men had to wallow through mud to get to the horses; and the horses had to wallow through mud to get to water. Every day it rained or snowed and the already villainous character of the mud became ever more villainous. . . . There is no mud like that of Lorraine.[48]

But the sights and sounds were far more disquieting. Flashes of gunfire would suddenly light the night, punctuated by the distant rattle of machine gun fire. Occasionally, a signal rocket or flare would erupt from the German trenches, portending what exactly the men did not know. All of this served as a reminder that this was no game, that thousands of men who wanted to kill you were only a few hundred yards away. Leon Miesse of the 166th described the trenches in a letter to his wife written immediately after his first trick:

> Imagine a ditch, such as they lay sewers in, 6 to 8 feet deep, water in the bottom, and then still more water and mud. Put a bunch of wire out in front of it and then on the darkest night imaginable, stand looking over the top, with an occasional zing of a sniper bullet and at frequent intervals light up the heavens with a star shell rocket which turns everything into day, and you have had near as I can tell you the experiences of the men of the Company. With us, we got very little sleep, never had my clothes off for the whole time, and sometimes not even my shoes. During that time, I washed my hands three times and shaved twice, scraped the dirt off my hair, and lived in a dugout with the Captain. . . . We have heard the scream of the shrapnel and H.E. [high explosive] shells and heard the spat of the M.G. [machine gun] bullet, and believe me, it is no pleasant sound.[49]

One of the first experiences the men had to learn to endure was enemy shelling. It took the Germans about twenty-four hours to realize that the Americans now manned the trenches opposite them. Once they knew this, they decided to turn the quiet sector into a very noisy one, regularly tossing artillery shells into the Rainbow Division's positions. The resulting roaring and crashing was enough to unnerve any man. Young Martin Hogan of the 165th wrote about being under enemy artillery fire, saying, "The earth around us boiled and churned and heaved and groaned and shivered. The air above us hissed and roared and snapped. The steady streaming rush of the messages of the guns withered our hearts as they smote and smote our trench."[50]

On the night of March 2, the Rainbow Division experienced its first combat death. That night, the men of the 1st Battalion from the 166th remained at their positions, anxiously awaiting the arrival of the 3rd Battalion, which was scheduled to relieve them. One of the men from D Company, Private Dyer Bird of Broadway, Ohio, stood vigil at a forward listening post. Private Bird had just turned eighteen on January 5. His mother had died when he was only three months old, and he had been raised by his grandparents in Broadway. He lived most of his life there but was working in Marion, Ohio, when war was declared. He enlisted in the Ohio National Guard a few weeks later.[51] His job on this night, like all those assigned to these posts, was to watch for any signs of German activity that might portend a raid or even a general attack. Staring out into the black night, he saw movement in no man's land. Probably concerned that his eyes might be playing tricks on him, he looked again and saw a German raiding party emerging from a nearby trench. He immediately hurled two grenades in their direction, and, as they exploded among the Germans, he turned to run back to the main line and warn his comrades. As he leaped from the trench, the Germans cut him down with gunfire. He fell forward into the mud, shouting out before he died, "The Germans are coming in the form of a wedge. Boys, I'm dying."[52] The 166th and Rainbow Division had lost their first man in combat. He would not be the last. Bird received an elaborate funeral, which was attended by French and American senior officers. But after Private Bird's death, there would be no more such extravagant funerals.

No more generals would come to honor the dead. In the months that followed, death would become a far too common event in the lives of the Rainbow Division's men. There would be so many men dying and, often, dying so fast that there was no time for elaborate burial ceremonies. Of course, a regimental band might come to play at a brief graveside ceremony, but there would be nothing like Dyer Bird's funeral again. Moreover, many of the dead would never be found. Their bodies were either left lying in no man's land, where no one could find them, or they were vaporized by an exploding German artillery shell. These men would end up categorized simply as "Missing in Action."

Private Bird's death was part of the elaborate but deadly game the two sides played in this "quiet" sector. Every night, both sides would send out patrols into no man's land. For the Americans' part, this usually meant detailing three to ten men and one officer to slip out of the trenches in the darkness and find their way through the tangles of barbed wire toward the German lines. For an hour or two, these patrols would roam about no man's land. Sometimes, they were assigned to capture German prisoners, while, at other times, the mission was to counter and block a German patrol believed to be headed for the American side of the barbed wire jungle that stretched between the trenches.[53] In any case, it could be a very treacherous and dangerous exercise that, in hindsight, seems to not have had sufficient potential for gain to offset what were very real losses in terms of life and limb.

Stokes Mortar crew from the 165th Infantry Regiment fires their weapon in the trenches at Lunéville in February 1918. (*National Archives*)

A few days after Bird's death, the division's first true test occurred. Now that the German High Command knew that Americans were in the front lines in Lorraine, they decided to strike what they hoped would be a devastating blow, one that would demoralize both the 42nd Division and the American people. But instead of a general attack across a broad front, they chose to conduct a large-scale raid that focused on one specific CR and unit, in this case, CR Chamois and the 168th Infantry. John Taber later explained the German's reasoning for a large-scale raid, saying, "A raid is ordinarily a very one-sided affair, and to the individual much more terrible than a general attack, for the concentration in men and guns is greater than could be possible on an extended front. The Boches were going to make this one particularly terrible."[54] The 15th Bavarian Sturm Battalion was chosen for the attack, and they apparently spent several days rehearsing for the raid on CR Chamois.

As dawn approached on March 5, 1918, the night had not been much different than other nights in the 168th's trenches. No man's land was covered in snow, and the moon's illumination made the terrain with its numerous skeleton-like tree trunks seem "strangely distorted." Suddenly, a single flare rose into the night sky from the German lines. This was not an altogether unusual event, and the Iowans of the regiment stamped their feet and crouched down, trying to gain some warmth in their badly chilled bodies. The men heard sounds typical for the hours just before dawn: a brief rattle of machine gun fire, the small thunderclap from a grenade exploding somewhere down the line, and the distant crowing of a rooster who knows dawn is coming soon. Then it suddenly grew quieter, and a slight breeze made it seem almost peaceful and serene as the clock struck 4:30 a.m.[55]

Suddenly and without warning, the entire northern horizon lit up with an intense brightness that only the sun itself usually provided. This was immediately followed by a thunderous, screaming roar as German artillery shells rained down on the men defending CR Chamois. The earth shook and trenches and dugouts collapsed as the high-explosive rounds fell. Men desperately tried to dig their comrades out from under these small avalanches that occurred everywhere up and down the sector's line. The exploding shells "tore our trenches literally to pieces on the left one-half of our sector," remembered Chaplain Winfred Robb. "For one hour and thirty-three minutes the roar of shells of both the enemy and our own literally shook the earth."[56] Another man, meanwhile, would characterize the artillery barrage as being "like an agile, hungry tiger leaping down upon its prey."[57]

As the first shells arrived, every post in the sector was abandoned as men ran to the nearest dugout. "Terrified bodies come rushing, slipping, stumbling, splashing to the dugouts," recalled John Taber, "dodging bits of flying debris, ducking showers of dirt, their path lighted by flashing explosions." Within the first few minutes of the barrage, all the telephone wires connecting the front lines with their reserves to the rear were cut. So the GC fired red rockets into the night sky to tell the American and French artillery to open fire on both the German batteries and no man's land. Men hovered near the dugout entrances listening to the deafening explosions, trying to detect any shift in the barrage that might indicate enemy infantry was now coming across no man's land. The intensity of the artillery barrage was turning "the whole Chamois system into a hecatomb of horror and confusion."[58]

As shells burst all around the first-aid dugout, the Sanitary Detachment's Lawrence Stewart heard a man calling for help, "their voice thick with fear." Someone shouted out over the thunderous roar that a dugout had been hit, caving it in and burying several men in the process. Stewart ran out into the inferno of exploding shells, forcing his way through dozens of fallen sandbags and a collapsed trench wall to the remnants of the dugout. He knelt down and tried to pry up some of the boards but discovered they were nailed down tightly. Stewart began to run back to the first aid dugout for help but soon met a lieutenant and another soldier coming to his assistance. The soldier was sent back to get stretchers while Stewart and the lieutenant tried to pull away the wreckage. About that time, another group of men arrived on the scene and, as the German shells continued to rain down, they dug down and uncovered the bodies of three men, two of whom were dead and the other severely injured. They got the wounded man on a stretcher and started for the aid station at Badonviller. Stewart recalled that the trenches "were narrow and so twisted that four men carrying a stretcher could scarcely pass through. The mud was up to our knees, the communication trench destroyed and under heavy shellfire." Somehow, they survived the journey to the aid station. [59]

Later, upon reflection about the events of that night, Stewart would write:

> ... it's one thing to charge out into No Man's-Land in the heat of battle, ready to jab the first German you see; it's quite different to endure the same shellfire, the same pandemonium, and at the same time see your friends fall wounded and dying about you, while you keep yourself cool and steady enough to relieve them as much as possible of pain, carrying them back through the rain of shells at a tortuous, snail's pace. And that day we knew War.[60]

As the artillery fire gradually shifted to the rear, the German infantry attacked, hoping to make easy work of the American survivors. They were to be severely disappointed. As the Germans came within range of the American trenches, they met a withering blast of fire from the Iowans' rifles, Chauchats, Stokes mortars, and machine guns. As their infantry were cut down, only a few Germans actually made it into the trenches, and these were cut down within seconds. The remaining Germans limped back to their own trenches, leaving dozens of dead men hideously sprawled across the Americans' wire. Major Walter Wolf later reported that "for a month thereafter, we were picking his dead from our wire and our portion of No Man's Land."[61]

The Rainbow Division had met its first test under fire. While some at AEF Headquarters did not see the attack of March 5 as anything but a minor affair, others knew better, General Pershing among them. The AEF commander arrived at the 168th's sector shortly after the fighting ended,

Secretary of War Baker, General Menoher, and General Lenihan inspect the 166th Infantry Regiment in March 1918. (*National Archives*)

and the battalion that had absorbed the attack was relieved. Standing by the road, Pershing watched intently as the men trudged wearily by on their way to the rear. There was no pomp or ceremony, just a procession of exhausted men whose uniforms were filthy, covered in mud, and torn by barbed wire. Marching slowly in single file, most never even looked up to see the ramrod erect figure of their commanding general nor the staff that surrounded him. Rather, it seemed to take everything they had to just focus on the back of the man ahead of them in line. To his credit, Pershing did not ask for a formal report from the regiment or division staff. Instead, he would call out now and then to a passing officer from the battalion and ask him a question about the attack and his men's performance.[62] From those informal reports, shouted out across the road, Pershing learned all he needed to know—the Rainbow Division was not merely an annoying political experiment but was, in fact, on its way to being one of the best fighting divisions in the AEF. As Martin Hogan from the 165th later observed, the division's time in the trenches of Lorraine "was our baptism."[63]

On March 27, the division was relieved of duty in the trenches and began to march back to the training area at Rolampont. However, they

A contemporary view of the village of Ancerviller, which was in the Baccarat sector. (*Major William Carraway, Historian, Georgia Army National Guard*)

had only gone a few miles when orders came for them to stop, turn around, and march to the Baccarat sector. On March 21, the Germans had launched what would be the first in a series of major offensives, this one near Amiens. They were pushing the British and French back, and the 128th French Division had been ordered to pull out of Baccarat and head immediately to Amiens to help stem the German tide. Therefore, someone had to take over their positions in Baccarat, and the 42nd Division had been ordered to move there immediately.

For the first time in the war, an American division would be entrusted with an entire divisional, two brigade-in-the line, sector. On April 1, the Rainbow Division relieved the French in the Baccarat sector. The 84th Brigade assumed defense of the four CRs along the right portion of the sector while the 83rd Brigade took responsibility for CR Ancerviller on the left. From this point forward, that is how the two brigades would always align for battle, with the 83rd on the left and the 84th to their immediate right.[64]

Day-to-day operations in Baccarat continued just as they had in the three previous months with two notable exceptions. The first occurred in early April just after the division had relieved the French when the division started to receive its first replacements, all of them new draftees. This would not have been quite so bad a situation except that company commanders quickly learned these new men had received almost no training. In a rush to get replacements to the front, the army not only did not provide these young soldiers with the special training the 42nd Division's soldiers had received from the French, but they also did not provide even the basic sort of training the division's veterans had received at home in their local National Guard armories. In one case, most of the draftees sent to the 166th Infantry had been in the army less than thirty days, in France less than nine days, and three of them had never fired their Springfield rifles. This situation would only grow worse as the war progressed, and, as a result, the casualties among these draftees were extremely high. Raymond Cheseldine would write that their deaths in combat were "little short of murder."[65]

The second exception occurred on May 27, when the Germans made their first major gas attack on the men of the Rainbow Division. Up to now, there had been isolated gas attacks along the line, but now the Germans unleashed a barrage of mustard gas along the entire Baccarat sector. In the 168th alone, over 400 men were gassed and forty-seven died.[66] Martin Hogan of the 165th remembered the attack vividly, saying "The first that I noticed in my excitement was that. . . water was streaming from my eyes almost as though they were hydrants. I could not see my hand before my face." Soon he noticed a thick gray mist closing around him, and he fell to his knees. "Crawling I knew not in what direction," he later wrote, "I was starting to feel my hands and knees stinging as though they had been burned."[67]

On May 9, while still in the Baccarat sector, the 165th Infantry had a change in command. Colonel Barker was ordered to return to the War Department where he would serve on the General Staff. His replacement was a Regular Army officer and 1897 graduate of West Point, Colonel Frank R. McCoy. McCoy had been serving as General Pershing's aide at AEF Headquarters and had a solid reputation as a tough, competent soldier. Father Duffy was most impressed upon meeting him, describing him as "a man of good height, of spare athletic figure, with a lean strongly formed face, nose Roman and dominating, brows capacious, eyes and mouth that can be humorous, quizzical or stern, as I learned by watching him, in the first five minutes. He has dignity of bearing, charm of manner and an alert and wide-ranging intelligence that embraces men, books, art, nature."[68]

The division remained in Baccarat until June 18, when they were relieved by French infantry. The men were supposed to receive a rest after 120 days at the front. However, in what would become a pattern for the entire war, that rest period was not to be. Less than forty-eight hours after pulling out of the Baccarat sector, the division received orders to march to nearby rail stations, where they would board trains for an unknown location.[69] They had proven themselves by enduring the trench warfare routine of the "quiet" sectors in Lorraine where they conducted nighttime patrols, dodged artillery shells, and fought the rats and mud.

Colonel Frank R. McCoy, commander of the 165th Infantry Regiment. (*National Archives*)

Now, the Rainbow Division was moving 130 miles to the west where they would become part of what the men called the "Big Show."

3

THE RAINBOW MEETS THE GERMANS IN CHAMPAGNE

June 18–July 20, 1918

"None shall glance to the rear, none shall yield a step. Each shall have but one thought, to kill, to kill, until they have had their fill."
—General Henri Joseph Eugene Gouraud, 4th French Army, General Order for the Champagne Defensive, July 7, 1918

The shelling had been like nothing ever seen in war. Even the hardened French veterans were stunned by the intensity of the German artillery barrage that came crashing down on the Allied lines in Champagne. An Iowa soldier later wrote, "One never conceived of such a thunder of sound. It was paralyzing, crushing."[1] The high-explosive rounds fell for nearly four hours before finally shifting their fury south of the intermediate line, which was the first main line of defense for the French divisions and Americans of the Rainbow Division. As the shelling moved south, those in the intermediate line scrambled out of the dugouts where they had sought safety from the German shelling and went to their assigned positions in the trenches. They checked their rifles, fixed bayonets, and made small stacks of hand grenades within reach as the Hotchkiss machine gun and Stokes mortar crews made sure their weapons were ready.

Ahead of them in the dim light before dawn were a small detachment of French soldiers located a few miles away in the original main trenches. The defensive plan from General Gouraud had called for these trenches to be abandoned so much of the German artillery fire would fall on empty fortifications. The mission of the few brave Frenchmen who remained there was to ride out the artillery barrage, watch for the advance of divisions of German infantry, and, when they saw the flood of gray-clad Germans coming, send red rockets into the night sky as a warning to those in the intermediate line.

For the former National Guardsmen of the Rainbow Division in the intermediate line, the anticipation was beyond intense. They knew they were about to make a desperate stand against an enemy with far superior numbers, a stand that could not fail. While there was another line of defense to their rear, where most of the division was deployed, they did not want the enemy to get past this line. The course of the war might very well turn on their ability to hold their ground. Around 4:00 a.m., as their eyes looked anxiously to the north, they saw several red rockets arc into the early morning gloom.

The Germans were coming.

The division began moving to the area around Châlons-en-Champagne in the Marne region on June 21. There had been no time to even clean the mud of the trenches off their uniforms as they boarded trains for the journey. Colonel MacArthur was personally directing the loading of the 84th Brigade when General Pershing and his staff arrived on the scene. It seems the general had a penchant for appearing without notice and berating his field officers as a means of keeping them on their toes. This time, it was Douglas MacArthur's turn to feel Pershing's wrath once again. Seeing the men's condition, Pershing decided to dress MacArthur down in full view of the brigade's men and return to his usual criticism of the 42nd Division. "This division is a disgrace, the men are poorly disciplined, and they are not properly trained," Pershing roared. "The whole outfit is just about the worst I have ever seen. They're a filthy rabble." MacArthur leapt to his men's defense by reminding the AEF commander that the men were just leaving three months in the trenches. But Pershing was having none of it and visibly became even more irritated. "Young man," he shouted, "I do not like your attitude. MacArthur, I'm going to hold you personally responsible for getting discipline and order into this division— or God help the whole pack of you."[2]

The trains carrying the division's men and equipment moved through Lunéville, Nancy, Toul, Bar Le Duc, and Neaufchateau before the division began arriving at Vitry-le-Francois in the Marne River valley on June 22. From there, they would move steadily forward until reaching the area around Châlons-en-Champagne. The weather was warm and sunny, so pleasant one would not have thought there was a war raging just a few miles away. Leon Miesse of the 166th even found time for a swim in the Marne Canal.[3] Despite years of war, the Marne River valley remained relatively unscarred. It was here that Marshal Joffre turned back the first great German offensive of the war in September 1914. However, since then, it had been relatively quiet. One British soldier wrote that the area presented "a pleasant well cultivated scene, unmarred by the shell holes, trenches, and barbed wire to which we had become so accustomed on the static front."[4]

The region was characterized by five rivers: the Aisne, Vesle, Ardre, Ourcq, and Marne. All these rivers flowed generally east to west except for the Ardre, which ran northwest into the Vesle. However, most Americans would not have considered many of these to actually be rivers but, rather, just large streams. Still, the rivers presented advantages to any defender in that their banks often rose as high as 200 feet, with those along the Aisne even higher. Further, these rivers produced marshy flats that would slow the movement of vehicles and artillery.[5] The Marne also was home to dense forests, as well as large grain fields, filled mostly with tall corn and wheat. The latter provided what General John Pershing later called "excellent cover" for infantry and machine gunners.[6]

The reason for the division's transfer to this part of the front was another German offensive, this one specifically designed to end the war on Germany's terms. Starting on March 21, 1918, the Germans had conducted a series of four major offensives. The first had been named Operation Michael. It lasted fifteen days and was the most successful of the four. In it, the Germans attacked a thinly held area in the Somme using seventy-two divisions, driving the British back more than twenty-five miles across a fifty-mile-wide front. The British and the Germans each suffered more than 200,000 casualties.[7]

Next came Operation Georgette on April 9. This attack sought to weaken the British before a third attack was launched against the channel ports. In this offensive, the Germans advanced only five miles in the area around Armentières, while both sides each lost approximately 110,000 men. The third offensive, Operation Blücher-Yorck, came in late May and was mounted against both the British and French lines on the Chemin des Dames. It penetrated deep into the Marne Valley, causing panic in

Paris and creating a large salient that penetrated twenty-five miles into the Allied lines. This time, each side lost about 130,000 men.[8] The fourth offensive, dubbed Operation Gneisenau, came in early June. The Germans attempted to enlarge the Marne salient but had minimal success due to a lack of German reserves and a stubborn defense mounted by the French.[9]

That lack of progress in June's offensive led to General Ludendorff planning a fifth offensive, which he called Operation Friedensturm or the "Peace Offensive." Ludendorff gave it that name because the objective was to envelop and capture the ancient French city of Reims, threaten Paris, and inflict such severe losses on Allied forces that the French would be forced to propose peace negotiations. The target would be French forces in Champagne, and this time, German planning and preparation would be meticulous. Three German armies totaling fifty-two divisions spent more than five weeks getting ready for what would be an attack across a thirty-five-mile front.[10]

Ludendorff's plan was to assemble 500,000 men backed by thousands of artillery pieces. He expected to sweep away the forces of the French 4th Army under General Henri Gouraud, which numbered less that 100,000 men. This was probably sound thinking by Ludendorff since, along the front lines east of Reims, Gouraud had only forty thousand men to face Ludendorff's 300,000.[11] This area east of Reims was where the Rainbow Division would be deployed.

Luckily for the Allies, Henri Gouraud was both an experienced and wise general. He knew very well what a desperate challenge his forces would face on the plains of Champagne. He also knew that there was only so much he could do given the German's advantage in both men and artillery firepower. So he devised a plan for defense in depth that was both innovative and daring.

The main French defenses were in a line of trenches just south of the Py River. Clearly, any German offensive would focus on these trenches, likely subjecting them to a massive artillery barrage using both high-explosive and gas shells, followed by an assault employing thousands of German infantrymen. Therefore, Gouraud proposed to let this massive German blow fall on empty trenches. He planned to order his men to quietly withdraw at the last moment to a second line, called the intermediate line, and a third defensive line, which included the positions that the 42nd Division would occupy. Once the Germans found the first line of trenches empty, they would have to make their attack against the intermediate line across one to three miles of open ground. When they did so, Gouraud would strike them with a massive barrage from both French and American artillery. When the enemy overran the intermediate line, the bulk of the 4th Army's forces would meet their advance from a second line of resistance about a mile behind the intermediate line.[12]

The final element of the French general's defense in depth would be the establishment of signal posts about a half-mile forward of the intermediate line. The men stationed at these positions would signal when the Germans began to move forward and then hold their positions until killed or captured, inflicting whatever damage they could on the advancing hordes of German infantry. Therefore, these positions were named "sacrifice posts,"[13] which proved to be a terrible but appropriate name.

On July 2, the 42nd Division was assigned to the 21st French Army Corps of Gouraud's 4th Army and ordered to move immediately to the vicinity of Suippes. The 21st Corps sector ran from a left flank just south of the town of Aubérive eastward to a point near the Route Marchand, a distance of almost eight miles. The entire area was a maze of trenches and dugouts. In accordance with Gouraud's plan, most of the infantry moved into the intermediate line with supporting French and American artillery placed nearby. At first, the Rainbow Division's infantry remained in the second line of resistance, but as the French became better acquainted with the Americans, the division's infantry began to move into the intermediate line.[14]

As the Americans moved forward, they looked out across the open plain in front of them and were not impressed. The terrain was stark and white with chalk that filled the air with dust. Most of the men referred to the area as the "Lousy Champagne." It was mercilessly hot as the July sun bore down on the trenches, and Raymond Cheseldine described the scene this way: "The chalk plains glared white in the blazing sun, their baldness relieved here and there by the red of the poppy and the blue of the corn flowers."[15] Father Duffy from the 165th commented that one man felt it looked "just like Texas."[16] Lawrence Stewart was the kindest in his comments about Champagne, later writing, "Our new home was in one of the most active sectors of the Western Front, but it nevertheless possessed a strange picturesqueness. The ditches in which we lived were dug in hard, chalky-white ground and shone dazzlingly in the sunlight. The country was dotted with dwarfed, twisted pines similar to those found in the mountains of our own United States."[17]

As the battalions assigned to the intermediate line deployed, the division's men were not placed in a continuous line. Rather, they were inter-

Terrain that the 42nd Division would defend at Champagne in July 1918. (*National Archives*)

spersed along the line with French infantry units. While the 42nd Division and its regiments maintained control of these battalions, Gouraud had a method to this particular madness. In a conversation after the war, MacArthur told division historian Henry Reilly, "The reason for alternating our units with French units was to allow as many French troops as possible to see American troops in the front position and thus to know positively that the German propaganda that the American reinforcement was a myth or greatly exaggerated at best because there were not enough of them in France to effect the situation, was the utter falsity which it was."[18]

As a result of Gouraud's plan, the 84th Brigade was assigned to reinforce the 13th French Infantry on the right in Sector Souain, which was in the middle of the intermediate line and on the main highway from Châlons-en-Champagne through Suippes north to Sommepy-Tahure on the Py River. The 83rd Brigade, meanwhile, moved to support the French 170th Infantry Division on the left in Sector Esperance. The town of Saint Hilaire-le-Grand was just south of the center of the intermediate line in this sector and on the old Roman Road running from Suippes to Reims.[19]

In Sector Esperance, F and G Companies of the 2nd Battalion, 165th Infantry, supported by H Company, were on the extreme left of the 21st

French Army Corps area. To their immediate right was the 116th French Infantry and the 10th Chasseur á Pied. Next in line to the right was E Company from the 165th's 2nd Battalion, followed by K Company from the 166th Infantry's 3rd Battalion. To their right were units of the 117th French Infantry, and Sector Esperance's extreme right was held by I and L Company from the 166th with their own M Company in support. All three infantry battalions were supported by Wisconsin's 150th Machine Gun Battalion.[20] To the right of the 166th were other units from the French 170th Division.

In Sector Souain, F Company of the 167th Infantry was posted just north of the town of Souain on the left side of the road running north to Sommepy-Tahure with E Company aligned on the right side of the road. To their right was the 109th French Infantry who had G and H Companies of the 167th immediately behind them. To their right rear were E and F Company of the 168th Infantry along with the 21st French Infantry. Here, machine gun support came from Georgia's 151st Machine Gun Battalion.[21]

Each sector had its own dedicated artillery support. The 83rd Brigade on the left was supported by the guns from the 149th Field Artillery, while the 84th Brigade had fire support from the 151st Field Artillery. In both cases, the American guns were positioned amongst the supporting French artillery. Their mission was to fire deadly barrages into the attacking German infantry as they moved from their own lines to the old French trenches and then back to 200 meters in front of the intermediate line's trenches. Finally, the heavy artillery of the 150th Field Artillery was assigned a position from which its howitzers and those of the French could provide fire support to the entire 21st French Army Corps area.[22]

The remaining battalions from the Rainbow Division's four infantry regiments were echeloned to the rear of the intermediate line along the second line of resistance, which was entirely under command of the Rainbow Division.[23]

In the center of the no man's land between the old French trenches and the intermediate line were the four sacrifice posts of the 21st French Army Corps area. Three of these were manned by French infantry ranging in size from a platoon to a small French battalion of three companies.[24] The remaining sacrifice post was assigned to the 166th Infantry's 3rd Battalion. The battalion commander, Captain Roger Haubrich, chose I Company to man the post. Because the men who go forward to the sacrifice post were being asked to fight until annihilated, wounded, or captured,

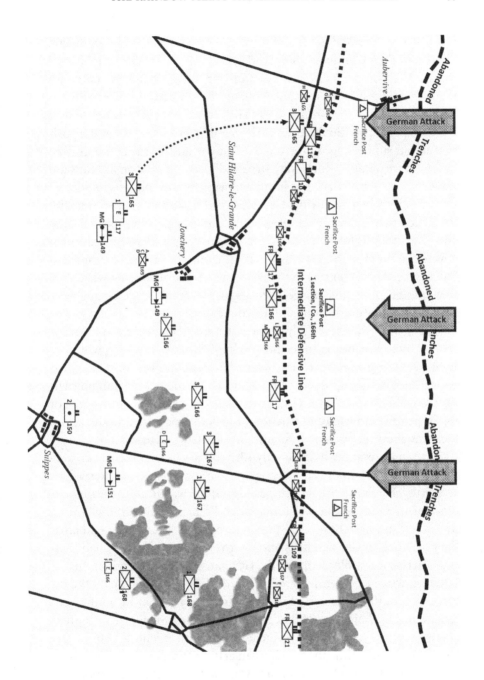

Map 1. Positions manned by the 42nd Division at Champagne.

Haubrich felt he could not morally order men to take such an assignment. So he told the I Company commander, Captain Henry Grave, to ask for twenty-five volunteers as well as an officer to command. When Grave made the request to his men, Lieutenant Clyde Vaughn, a twenty-three-year-old schoolteacher from Liberty Hill, Texas, stepped forward to lead the detachment, as did the twenty-five soldiers needed to cover the position and its supporting anti-tank gun.[25] Vaughn and his men were to await orders to move out, which were expected to come as soon as Gouraud was sure the enemy attack was imminent. Vaughn was told he should send up red flares when he saw the Germans coming and then open fire with his detachment's rifles, machine guns, automatic rifles, and the anti-tank gun. The idea was for him and his men to break up and slow the German advance, even though they would almost certainly be overwhelmed and "submerged by it—just as the rocks break up the advancing wave."[26] If they could do enough damage, perhaps the Germans would be unable to strike a fatal blow against the intermediate line.

The men worked feverishly in the hot sun and chalk dust to repair or rebuild their trenches, each seeming to know what was coming would be unlike anything any American soldiers had seen in the war. As the days passed and the date approached mid-July, all the men of the Rainbow Division could do was wait as Gouraud watched for some definitive sign of the impending attack. But sometimes a general's best friend is luck, and luck was about to pay two different visits to Henri Gouraud.

First, in the evening hours of July 13, a solitary German officer crossed the Py River to scout the French positions he and his men would soon be assaulting. He found the French positions quickly, but unfortunately for this German officer, the skeleton crew of French soldiers still guarding the lines also found him. They took him prisoner before he could cross the river back to German lines and discovered that the officer had foolishly carried a complete copy of the German attack orders with him.

Then, while the French were interpreting and breaking down the information in the orders, five French soldiers led by a daring young lieutenant staged their own raid across the Py. They managed to capture twenty-seven German soldiers, including an officer who told his interrogators the exact time for the German artillery barrage and subsequent infantry attack down to the minute. As a result, the Allies now knew that the enemy artillery would open fire at 12:10 a.m. on July 15 and that their infantry would cross the Py at 4:00 a.m.[27] They also learned that General Ludendorff was supremely confident of his plan because he expected his men to be in Châlons-en-Champagne only forty-eight hours after commencing the offensive.[28]

When General Gouraud learned of this intelligence, he not only alerted his command but also ordered American and French artillery to open a massive barrage on the German positions starting at 11:45 p.m., twenty-five minutes before the planned German bombardment.[29] Gouraud hoped this barrage would not only do damage to the assembling German infantry but also sow confusion among both the German soldiers and their commanders.

As the clock ticked toward midnight, the men of the Rainbow Division waited in anticipation for the Allied artillery barrage to begin. At precisely 11:45 p.m., the guns opened fire. The Americans had heard their own artillery fire many times since they entered the trenches in February, but nothing prepared them for this barrage. The crash of the massed guns "fairly lifted men from their feet."[30] Thousands of guns that had been silent and hidden now roared to life, belching flame. The dark night was suddenly illuminated as the guns "fired with an intensity that caused the atmosphere to shake with a constant rolling, unbroken sound."[31]

The roaring symphony the artillery produced was a mix of the deep blasts from the heavy guns, sharper detonations from the middle calibers, and a constant bark from the 75mm cannon. The symphony was endless, shaking the air with the swishing sound of the departing shells. Major Wolf remembered it as "a hellish music."[32] The light from the gun flashes caused the stars to disappear from sight as the deadly projectiles arced through the night sky toward the men and artillery of the Kaiser's army.

This sudden artillery assault caught the Germans completely by surprise. They were busy moving men forward to their jumping off points for the attack, and their own artillery batteries were making sure all was in place for their own barrage. As the French and American shells came crashing down, soldiers dashed for whatever cover they could find, trenches and dugouts collapsed under the impact of high-explosive rounds, and supply wagons burst into flames.

If nothing else, the unexpected Allied attack caused confusion. When the artillery fire began, a German infantry regiment commander named Kurt Hesse was napping in a shell hole behind the German lines after completing his unit's final preparations for the coming advance. Suddenly, he awakened to the sound of heavy artillery fire. He quickly glanced at his watch and saw that it was not yet time for the German barrage to begin. He thought, perhaps, they had made a mistake. But when he jumped out of the shell hole and looked around, he saw that shells were falling everywhere around him—the French and the Americans had opened fire first. He ran to his dugout to contact his battalion commanders but discovered the Allied artillery fire had cut his telephone lines. He darted out to check on his men and found that the incoming artillery was focusing on railroad crossings and crucial road junctures, anywhere the Germans might assemble their infantry. The intense and accurate concentration of the Allied shells caused mass confusion on the roads where German infantry were trying to move forward to their jumping-off points. When Hesse got to his battalions along the first line, he found his positions littered with hundreds of dead and wounded and discovered that two of his battalions had been severely mauled by the shelling.[33] The initial phase of General Gouraud's defensive plan was working to perfection.

As the men in the Allied trenches to the south watched the shells arc overheard on their way to the German lines, they kept glancing at their watches as the clock ticked toward 12:10 a.m., the time when the intelligence report said the Germans would open fire. Despite the damage being done by the Allied artillery, the German guns were ready. Precisely at the appointed time, the American and French soldiers "suddenly saw the sky behind the German lines opposite light with a tremendous flare, stretching farther to the right and left than any individual could see."[34] A fraction of a second later, the roar of the firing guns came sweeping across the Champagne Plain to the ears of those in the Rainbow Division.

Ludendorff had assembled more than two thousand pieces of artillery to support the offensive. That made for an average of one gun for every twenty yards of the forty-mile front, making it the largest concentration of artillery ever assembled in history up to that moment. The German plan was to begin by shelling the first line trenches, which they did not realize had been abandoned. Then, once they had secured those trenches, they would begin a rolling barrage to support the infantry advance. As the name implies, rolling barrages preceded the attacking infantry in a carefully choreographed process that provided supporting fire while on the move. Each barrage might be different, but they all moved forward in measured steps, focusing artillery fire on one line before moving forward to the next set of targets at a designated time. If successful, this allowed the infantry to move forward through areas cleared of enemy defenses. The exact speed and timing of rolling barrages varied based on the nature of the terrain and the strength of the enemy's position, but a

Wrecked field kitchens and dead horses left by the German bombardment on the night of July 14-15, 1918. (*National Archives*)

typical rate for advancing infantry was about 800 feet in ten minutes.[35]

At the same time, the heavier long-range German guns would send shells toward what was the second line of resistance and the rear areas where Allied supplies were gathered. By the time the barrage would end, German shells had landed as far as twenty miles away in Châlons-en-Champagne. The German artillery was so terrifying that it would become the basis for comparison with every subsequent German artillery barrage. As time would tell, nothing would compare with it. One soldier from the 167th Infantry said that, for him, the German artillery barrage that night was when "real war began."[36] In a letter written a few days later, Raymond Cheseldine of the 166th wrote, "A perfect night, and then the sky lighted by countless flares, the air full of shrieking shells and bursting shrapnel, the atmosphere choked with powder smoke and gas, the earth torn into bits by great explosives – the calls of men, the rattle of wagons, the shrieks and cries of horses and mules, the whirr and thrum of airplanes—never can I forget it if I live forever."[37]

The shelling continued nonstop for four hours. Major Wolf recalled the "transformation that these minutes worked is beyond the conception of the single mind. Along the roads, ammunition boxes were tumbled in irregular piles, men lay dismembered. Animals lay across the trails, and most important roads passed over and plowed through by the hard-ribbon caisson and ammunition columns."[38] When the guns finally paused, on came the first waves of gray-clad German infantry.

Despite the Allied shelling, the German infantry had eventually made it to their jumping-off points. The first wave included six first-class divisions, a Guard Cavalry Division along with the 2nd, 88th, 1st, 5th, and the 7th Bavarian Divisions. They had only recently returned to the front after two weeks of rest in the rear. Three divisions made the attack on the French in the center, and two assaulted the positions on the Allied right manned by Alabama's 167th and Iowa's 168th, while one full division made its way against the left where Ohio's 166th and New York's 165th awaited them.[39]

As Gouraud had planned, the first resistance the Germans encountered were the French and American sacrifice posts. In the dark, they could not be sure they had not found the major line of Allied resistance. So they deployed accordingly and began to attack these isolated forward posts. In the sacrifice post manned by men from I Company of the 166th Infantry, Lieutenant Vaughn had sent his men into the dugouts when the German artillery fire began. He later recounted that he had "paid close attention to the bombardment so as to ascertain the moment when it began to lift." As the enemy barrage began to move south toward the intermediate line, he sent his men out into the trenches. "My men were scattered in groups of four to six up and down the trench for some thirty or forty yards," he remembered. "I took my stand with the men in the front section. I placed my sergeant in the rear section."[40]

Around 4:00 a.m., as Vaughn peered into the darkness to the north, he saw groups of men emerging and coming toward him. Knowing they had to be Germans, he ordered his small detachment to open fire. They fought furiously, sweeping the enemy infantry with automatic rifle and machine gun fire while blasting the advancing lines with their anti-tank gun. The firing from these twenty-six men was so intense that it staggered the first wave of German shock troops, forcing them to stop, reorganize, and lay down covering fire for their own men who now advanced only a few yards at a time. Eventually, numbers and superior firepower would prove too much for Vaughn and his men. Every man in the sacrifice post was either killed or wounded before the survivors ran out of ammunition. Vaughn himself was hit in the face by a German bullet that tore away part of his jaw and chin. The Germans took the survivors prisoner, but Vaughn and his detachment had managed to hold up the German assault on the intermediate line until almost 8:00 a.m. while killing hundreds of the enemy whose bodies were stacked in piles in front of the sacrifice post.[41] More importantly, the time these men and the others at the French sacrifice posts bought the Allies meant that the enemy would have to continue their attack against the intermediate line in broad daylight.

Another benefit from the fierce defense by the sacrifice posts was that, now, the German infantry was not supported by its artillery's rolling barrage. As they fought to subdue the sacrifice posts, the barrage had continued south until it passed the intermediate line. That meant there was nothing to prevent the American and French soldiers in that line from making a strong defense of their trenches.

On the Allied left, the men of the 165th crawled out from their dugouts as the German artillery fire moved past them and moved into their assigned positions. As some of them readied to open fire, a few veteran French infantrymen who were there restrained them, for, in the dim light and dust, a Poilu's light blue coat might look a lot like a German's gray uniform. But, after about an hour, one of the Frenchmen pointed out into no man's land and cried out, "Boche, Boche!"[42] Martin Hogan remembered these moments, saying, "Bayonets were tested and then rifles laid on the enemy, while the men leaned against the trenches staring at Fritz— thousands of him—with keen interest."[43] At that point, the Germans began their assault, sweeping the tops of the 165th's trenches with machine gun fire and dropping in shells from their Minenwerfer mortars. Then, they rose up and charged toward the New Yorkers, preceded by a wave of rifle grenades and hand grenades.

French and American 75mm artillery continued to fire into the advancing Germans, and the New York infantry opened fire with rifles while having their bayonets fixed and ready. Dozens of Germans were cut down, but many were able to jump into the 165th's trenches. The fighting was now hand-to-hand with rifle butts and bayonets being the primary weapons. "Clubbed rifles were splintered against skulls and shoulder bone," wrote Martin Hogan. "Bayonets were plunged home" over and over again and withdrawn covered in blood, as the New Yorker's trench became "a gruesome mess" that would forever be seared in young Martin's memory.[44] The Germans soon fell back in disarray, and their attack on the Allied left subsided.

Farther down the line to the east, the weight of the German assault hit the 166th's positions about the same time as the attack on the 165th. The

117th Sanitary Train ambulances bring 42nd Division wounded to a field hospital near Suippes, July 15, 1918. (*National Archives*)

fighting here was bitter and violent, as the four companies of the 166th's 3rd Battalion tried desperately to hold their ground against the overwhelming waves of German infantry. All along the Ohioans' front, the German infantry advanced carefully toward the tangles of barbed wire in front of the 3rd Battalion's trenches. Still, the Ohio doughboys proceeded to shoot slowly and calmly, picking off one German after another. As the enemy came closer, the pace of the American firing increased, decimating the enemy ranks as they neared the wire. Not a single German managed to cross the wire, and the waves of enemy infantry "again and again broke and retreated in disorder, and the ground before the wire changed from the white of chalk dust to the gray of dead German soldiers."[45]

On the far right, the bulk of the German infantry advanced through the Allied shellfire toward some cover provided by the shattered remnants of a small woods directly in front of the French 109th Infantry, G and H Companies of the 167th's 2nd Battalion, and E and F Companies of the 168th's 2nd Battalion. When the remainder of what had been two German divisions moved forward from the trees, the Alabamians and Iowans opened a withering fire. Lawrence Stewart later wrote, "They worked their machine guns for all they were worth, astonishing both the

Men from the 165th Infantry Regiment coming off the line at Champagne, July 19, 1918. (*National Archives*)

French and the Germans by the coolness and the directness with which they aimed."[46]

Here, as on the left of the Allied line, some Germans made it into the 167th and 168th's trenches using the communication trenches as a route into the main lines. But these penetrations were quickly pushed back through fierce counterattacks that saw waves of American hand grenades being thrown into the midst of the advancing Germans. The Germans fell back in confusion and, after ten hours of artillery fire and infantry combat, the fighting subsided. Leon Miesse of the 166th wrote his wife later, saying, "From prisoners afterward, it was learned that they lost from 50 to 60 percent of their men and that one Division of the Boche, which was to make the attack was so cut up by our artillery that they had to be taken back and replaced by another Division before the attack started. . . . One of our men counted 150 [dead] in just a small place."[47] The enemy continued to fire artillery shells into the Allied positions, but what would be the Germans' last great offensive of the war had ended in disaster.

As events would later prove, the fight on the plains of Champagne marked a turning point in the war. The Germans had suffered tremendous losses while utterly failing to achieve their objectives. Reims remained in Allied hands, and Paris was safe from any German attack. The Rainbow Division had lost 1,567 killed and wounded in a single day, about 79 percent of their total losses during the preceding five months in the trenches of Lunéville and Baccarat.[48]

As the only American division involved in the battle, the 42nd Division received a great deal of attention and praise for its performance on July 15. Some of that praise came from the Germans. Kurt Hesse, an officer in the 5th Grenadier Regiment, 36th German Infantry Division, later wrote, "The Americans kill everything! That was the cry of horror of July 15th, which long took hold of our men. At home meanwhile they were sarcastic about the imperfect training of this enemy, about the American 'bluff' and the like. The fact that on July 15th more than sixty per cent of our troops led to battle were left dead or wounded upon the battlefield may substantially be charged to his credit."[49]

The next step in the war would bring an end to fighting in the trenches and initiate something new in the war: offensive operations fought in the open. Furthermore, for the first time, the AEF and the Rainbow Division would go on the offensive. On July 21, the smoke had barely cleared from the fighting at Champagne when the first units from the division entrained at St. Hilaire-au-Temple and headed for a new position north of Château-Thierry, where they would join the forces gathering for a great Allied offensive.

4

THE RAINBOW ADVANCES

July 21–25, 1918

"Death beckoned the bravest and the strongest in the deceptive
fields of that bright green countryside."
—General Douglas MacArthur, *Reminiscences*

As the men of the Rainbow Division approached the Marne salient, they
found the area deceptively peaceful and pastoral. Lovely villages and pic-
turesque farms lined roads as they marched east from the train stations.
The fields were filled with yellow, ripening wheat, and the skies were
bright blue. After the smoke and death in Champagne, it was a welcome
relief to see such countryside.

However, they soon heard the familiar rumble of artillery in the distance, which became louder and deeper with every step they took. Within
just a few hours, many of them would reach the town of Château-Thierry,
where the boundary of the combat area really began. Up to now, the division had seen war's destructive effect on French villages and towns, but
nothing had prepared them for what they saw here. One New York soldier
recalled that there "was nothing but stone, dust heaps and dead Germans,
with scattered equipment, bits of broken trucks, dead horses, and general
misery and desolation."[1] Put more simply, a doughboy from the 151st
Field Artillery would later say of Château-Thierry, "Nothing was left but
latitude, longitude, and broken brick."[2]

Once the men moved northeast beyond Château-Thierry, they encountered open fields once again, but these were very different from what

they had seen to the west of the battle area. Here, the fields were dotted with hundreds of gaping shell holes, broken wagons, dead animals, and soldiers' bodies from both sides. The dead soldiers were a mix of French poilus in their faded blue uniforms, German infantry in their gray coats, and American doughboys in khaki. Most of the latter came from the Rainbow's sister National Guard division, the 26th from New England. There had not been time to bury them during the bitter fighting here, and then the German shelling made it impossible to do so safely. As a result of the hot temperatures, "the air was clammy with death."[3] Many soldiers had to don their gas masks to deal with the horrific odor, which at times made it almost impossible to breathe.

Martin Hogan of the 165th later wrote, "All around was a chaotically pitted country, wounded to the death with great rents and shell holes, deep gouged sores as far as the eye could reach. It was a pathetic country. Its trees were splintered and mangled with shell hits; its fields were plowed and scarred deep below the fertile soils, and the road upon which we were traveling was torn up and battered."[4]

Eventually, the soldiers' pace would slow as the guns' roar and the shelling came much closer. Ahead lay the Germans, who were retreating, or so the men of the Rainbow Division had been told. No one in the division, even the G2 intelligence staff at 42nd Division Headquarters, seemed to really know what was happening. But, as they would soon find out, the enemy was withdrawing but doing so methodically while defending every inch of ground.

The cost in pursuing the Germans, who were going to leave the Marne Salient no matter what the men of the Rainbow Division might do, would be higher than anyone could have imagined.

For several months, Marshal Ferdinand Foch, the Supreme Commander of the Allied Armies, had wanted to launch a counteroffensive against the Germans. However, until mid-July 1918, he had neither seen the opportunity nor had sufficient reserve forces to do so. Since the German offensive in March 1918, the initiative and the advantage in manpower belonged to the enemy. However, with the victory at Champagne and the increasing American strength in France, all that had changed.

German morale had taken a severe blow at Champagne. Their severe losses meant that, for the first time since the Russian withdrawal from the war in early March 1918, which allowed the Germans to shift millions of men to the Western Front, superiority in manpower had swung in the Allies' favor. Pershing noted this, saying, "Thanks to this unprecedented movement, Allied inferiority in March had been within three months transformed into Allied superiority of over 200,000 men."[5] Now, Foch could launch his counteroffensive. From this moment until the end of the war, the Allies would never fight on the defensive again.

For this initiative, Foch chose what was called the Marne salient as his target. This salient had been formed by German gains during their offensives that began in March 1918. Its base was thirty-five miles long, running from a point about seven miles northwest of Soissons east to the Vesle River at a point about three miles west of Reims. Its apex was approximately twenty-five miles deep, centered on the Marne River near Château-Thierry. The German forces in the salient had been fighting for four months and were "disorganized, depleted, and exhausted."[6] Further, most of the forty divisions stationed there were concentrated in the eastern part of the salient, leaving only a small portion under the command of General Johannes von Eben's Ninth Army to defend the western side of the salient. Therefore, Foch decided to launch his offensive against the west boundary of the Marne salient.

The opening blow, which was slated for July 18, would be made by General Mangin's Tenth French Army, which would employ nine French infantry and cavalry divisions and the AEF's two best divisions, the 1st and 2nd. These units would strike east, aiming to capture Soissons and cut the vital German lines of supply and communication along the road that ran between that city and Château-Thierry. Meanwhile, the French Sixth Army, led by General Jean Marie Joseph Degoutte, would attack northeast toward Château-Thierry using four French divisions and the American 4th and 26th Divisions.

By July 20, Mangin and Degoutte's armies had cut the road between Soissons and Château-Thierry, compelling the German forces remaining in the salient to withdraw north to the Vesle River. However, it is critical to note that this would be a disciplined, well-planned withdrawal and not a panicked general retreat—the Germans were too well led and trained to allow a disorderly rout. Their plan called for them to escape to the Vesle with the bulk of both their men, artillery, and supplies. To do this effectively, they would fight a delaying action designed to slow the Allied advance. They turned the area from Château-Thierry to the high ground north of the Ourcq River into a series of strong points, using the many French farms with their stone houses and buildings into small fortresses covered by well-placed machine gun units that made every building and every clearing into a killing ground.[7]

They would also use their army's "long arm," massing hundreds of artillery pieces above the Ourcq River to cover the entire area where the Allies would advance north from the Marne River. In this case, again being the consummate professionals that they were, the Germans made sure to carefully register every key road, road intersection, farm, water spring, river crossing, and woods that the Allies might use. This would allow them to rain shells down on both the French and American infantry and their own supporting artillery.

The area was essentially rectangular in shape with a mixture of woods, open fields of wheat and clover, heavily defended farms, small towns, and the Ourcq River. The river itself was not a significant obstacle, being only a few feet wide and waist deep. The biggest problem the river posed was the open ground one would have to cross south of the river and the high ground on the far side. North of the river, that high ground ran from Hill 184 on the west to Hill 220 in the east, giving the Germans the advantage in both observation and concealment. Using these advantages, they could effectively cover the approaches to the Ourcq with both artillery and machine gun fire.[8]

There were also several towns near the Ourcq that the Germans could use for cover, and each would have to be taken if the Allies were to push the Germans back toward the Vesle. There was Seringes-et Nesles, a village of almost 300 people with ninety houses on the western edge. Below the river was Villers-sur-Fère, with a population of nearly 500 in 139 homes plus an umbrella factory and a brickyard. Next, to the east and north of the river, was Sergy. It had a population of just over 250 people and 78 houses. Finally, there was Nesles, which had an old chateau and a cluster of buildings in two small farms.[9] In total, it was the perfect area from which to mount a spirited defense and a holding action.

Even before the Allied offensive was launched, Foch seemed to know that the area around the Ourcq River was crucial and that the Germans would use the high ground above the river as their last line of defense to protect their forces as they withdrew to the Vesle. On July 16, two days before the Allied attack began, he said, "a powerful offensive in the direction of Fère-en Tardenois," which was north of the Ourcq and just west of Seringes-et-Nesles, was of "the greatest importance." To gain control of this area, he stated that the "plan to devote the Tenth Army and the left of the [French] Sixth Army to it is to be adhered to at all costs and to be carried out on the date contemplated."[10]

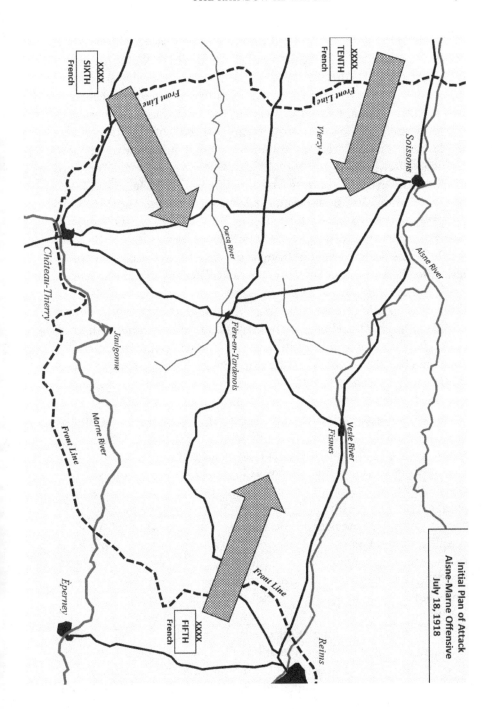

Map 2. The initial plan for the Aisne-Marne Offensive.

As the 26th Division advanced forward from Château-Thierry, they met fierce resistance and began to suffer severe casualties almost immediately. As a result, on July 21, the 42nd Division was ordered to start moving east toward the Marne salient, where they would join the French Sixth Army under General Degoutte as part of the newly formed American I Corps. Initially, all Degoutte ordered was that the 42nd be stationed in the I Corps zone and "remain in the army reserve until new orders employing it elsewhere."[11]

The 26th Division's ability to overcome the German defensive concept had been complicated by two factors related to command. The first factor posed a particular problem for the American I Corps and the National Guard units like the 26th and 42nd Divisions. Up to now, these units had fought purely defensive actions from fixed positions. Now they were being tasked to fight an offensive action characterized by fluid and dynamic maneuver. An attack made using maneuver is far more challenging to execute than a static defense because troops and their commanders must be able to react to the changing configuration of the terrain they find as well as how the enemy sets up its defenses. Unit commanders, especially above the battalion level, had little experience with the attack. Furthermore, few, if any, had any actual working knowledge of how to conduct a successful maneuver-based operation. As a result, many mistakes would be made because commanders were novices at this type of war fighting.[12]

The second factor was a seriously flawed analysis made by General Degoutte and his staff. From the beginning of the offensive, it appears that Degoutte was convinced the Allies were fighting a broken enemy who was desperately trying to escape and could easily be pushed into a mad, panicked retreat. As a result, he repeatedly ordered a headlong pursuit of the enemy. On July 21, he issued orders saying, "All units will push straight ahead," and told French cavalry to move forward so they could pursue a fleeing enemy as soon as they broke for the rear. He also saw little need for artillery support in these same orders, saying that "only a relatively small, but well-equipped, force of artillery" would be needed.[13] Throughout the offensive, the French Sixth Army issued similar orders for frontal assaults with little planning or knowledge of the actual tactical situation and seemingly little to no consideration of the reports being sent to them of a stiff, disciplined, and determined German resistance. This pattern of issuing orders for poorly planned attacks by the infantry with almost no artillery support continued throughout the offensive and would cost the Rainbow Division dearly.

What made this crucial error in judgment by Degoutte and other commanders in the French Sixth Army even worse is that the same scenario had played out before. When the Germans were stopped in the First Battle of the Marne in 1914, the Allies made the same mistake. At that time, the French and British assumed that the Germans, who were withdrawing in long columns along every available road, were a beaten enemy that could be pushed into a mad dash to the rear. When the Allied forces undertook a vigorous pursuit, instead of a fleeing enemy army, they encountered one that had carefully selected and manned positions along the Aisne River, where they conducted a highly disciplined defense-in-depth to cover their army as it withdrew to a new line. As the 42nd Division historian Henry Reilly would later write, "In other words, it was not a case for pell-mell determined pursuit of a defeated retreating enemy, but was one for careful reconnaissance and patrolling followed by a first-class plan of attack and a carefully arranged coordinated assault in accordance with that plan."[14] Tragically, however, that was not what would happen.

When the orders arrived for the Rainbow Division to move out on July 21, several units were already heading south away from the Champagne battlefront. Late on the evening of July 18, as the men in the 168th Infantry were preparing to turn in for the night, their company commanders rousted them from their tents, telling them to roll packs and prepare to move out.[15] By 2:00 a.m., the Iowans were heading down the road to Châlons-en-Champagne with the 167th following the same route.

The same was true for the other units, except that those regiments on the left flank marched to Vadenay. Father Duffy of the 165th said that all they were told was that they "would be relieved by morning. Why? No one knew. Where were we going? No one knew."[16]

Lawrence Stewart of the 168th later recalled his regiment's night march to Châlons-en-Champagne:

> Along the front the darkness was streaked with the flashes of the guns, which cleft the night and lighted up the way. The roar of the cannon beat upon our ears like the roll of a thousand kettle-drums. The lightning like flares showed merciless havoc along the road. Bodies of dead horses, mixed in with the charred and blackened ruins of buildings, littered up the ground. And so the column pushed ahead, like a long brown serpent twisting evenly down the road. Once an enemy airplane detected these movements and came to say farewell, dropping "eggs" on the road over which we were passing. Without

much formality we scattered to the wheatfields on the other side, taking refuge in the long ripening grain, and suffered no casualties.[17]

Stewart's story also highlights a growing concern among the men of the division: the impunity with which German aircraft attacked them. In 1918, the concept of air superiority was in its infancy and, at this point in the war, the Germans seemed to enjoy a decided advantage. Throughout their time in Champagne, German fighters would strafe the American troops by day and bombers would attack them by night. This continued throughout the coming offensive in the Marne salient and, while German air attacks might not contribute much materially to the German defense, it created a sense of frustration and futility among the men of the Rainbow Division.

On July 21, the first infantry regiments began to board trains for what to them was an unknown destination. Of course, many men hoped that they were at last heading for a long-promised period of rest, perhaps one that even included passes to visit Paris. The 167th Infantry was the first to entrain, marching the ten miles from their camp outside Châlons-en-Champagne at Courtisols through L'Épine to the rail station at Coolus. It was late when the Machine Gun Company, Headquarters Company, Supply Company, Regimental Headquarters, and 1st Battalion boarded the first of the five trains needed to move the regiment. As a result, the 2nd and 3rd Battalions would entrain in the early morning hours of July 22.[18]

Meanwhile, eight miles to the north, the 165th was marching from their camp at Vadenay to the train depot at Saint-Hilaire-au-Temple. Father Duffy said of the lack of information regarding their destination, "'We don't know where we're going but we're on our way' might be taken as the traveling song of soldiers." As the New Yorkers boarded the trains throughout the day of July 21, they too suffered from German air attacks. Father Duffy recorded the following in his diary:

> Our 2nd Battalion and the Wisconsins, which formed one of the sections, had the mean end of a one-sided battle while waiting at the station. The German bombing planes came over and started dropping their "Devil's eggs." C-r-r-unch! C-r-r-unch! C-r-r-unch! the face of the earth was punctured with deep holes that sent up rocks and smoke like a volcano in eruption; the freight shed was sent in flying flinders, but the train was untouched. Animals were killed, but no men.[19]

The 168th Infantry's trains also departed from Coolus but not until the morning of July 23. They left the camp at Courtisols around 3:00 a.m., marching in a downpour through L'Épine and Châlons-en-Champagne.[20] They would be the last of the regiments to entrain, as the 166th had boarded their trains at Saint-Hilaire-au-Temple the day before, July 22.[21]

Normally, the train ride from the Champagne area to Château-Thierry would have taken only four hours. However, the track connecting the two areas had been damaged by German shelling, so the Rainbow Division's trains had to follow a circuitous route that took over forty-eight hours to traverse before arriving near Château-Thierry. From Châlons-en-Champagne, the trains traveled southeast to Saint Dizier, where they turned to the west toward Troyes before moving northwest to Noisy-le-Sec in the suburbs of Paris. As the trains approached Paris, some of the men thought that they were, indeed, heading for a parade in Paris followed by a much-needed leave and rest. But while they could see the Eiffel Tower through field glasses, the station at Noisy-le-Sec was the closest they would get to the City of Light.[22]

For most, this was a bitter disappointment. Lawrence Stewart of the 168th recorded that it was about 2:00 p.m. when his train entered the station at Noisy-le-Sec. "It was hard to realize," he wrote, "that the heart of the sublime French metropolis was lying not more than four miles from us ... our glimpses of the capital were of the most tantalizing sort—a distant view of the Eiffel tower through the golden mist of sunshine, a graceful bit of avenue, the suburban trains as they roared in and out of the stations."[23]

An Alabamian in the 167th said that their arrival in the Parisian suburbs set off what he called "Dame Rumor." "Dame Rumor," he wrote, "immediately set to work, starting the conclusion that the counteroffensive had been successfully completed, and that the regiment, no longer required at the front, was being sent to Paris to parade in a celebration after the great victory." However, as soon as the train changed tracks and turned to the northeast toward Château-Thierry, the men's hopes were crushed and "once more the men realized that 'Dame Rumor' is none too reliable."[24]

However, there was one more memory of the time in the Noisy-le-Sec depot that many men seemed to recall vividly—the reception they received from the French people. John Taber of the 168th wrote in his diary, "Demonstrative crowds along the way and on the bridges cheered and waved flags as we went by. The Americans seem to be very popular right now, and, maybe we need cheering."[25] Lawrence Stewart had similar memories, saying that their train's journey through the Paris suburbs was "accompanied by the shouts and flag demonstrations of the French, who thronged the streets alongside the railroad track or hung from their upper story windows flourishing American banners."[26]

Even the venerable Father Duffy of the 165th took note of the enthusiastic greeting they received. "We were impressed with the new enthusiasm for American soldiers among the French people," he wrote. "Every station, every village, every farm window was hung with colors, some attempt at the Stars and Stripes being common. And stout burghers, lovely maidens, saucy gamins, and old roadmenders had a cheer and a wave of the hand for '*les braves Américaines, si jeunes, si forts, si gentils,*' [the brave Americans, so young, so strong, so kind] as the troop train passed by."[27] Unfortunately, a far less welcoming reception awaited them in the Marne salient.

As the Rainbow Division's trains made their way slowly westward, the National Guardsmen of the Yankee Division, the 26th, were fighting their way into the salient. At 4:00 a.m. on July 21, the New Englanders began their advance by driving approximately four miles to reach the vital Soissons–Château-Thierry highway in less than eight hours. Up to this point, German resistance had been minimal, as they withdrew toward better defensive positions. The 26th's men rested briefly before resuming their advance in the afternoon. This time, however, their attack began to bog down as they encountered the first of the German's fortified positions in and around Épieds and Trugny.[28]

Here for the first time, General Degoutte's misplaced belief in a general German retreat ran into reality, but no one in the upper echelon of command seemed to notice. The American I Corps Headquarters, believing these German positions were merely lightly defended rear guard outposts, ordered the 26th Division to attack that evening with no artillery support. After several unsuccessful attempts, the 26th was able to briefly gain entry to both towns before furious German resistance pushed them out. The next morning, July 22, the Yankee Division tried again, but withering German machine gun fire and a counterattack by the German 201st Division drove them back.[29]

The 26th's efforts provide a snapshot of the poor decisions being made up the chain of command, poor decisions that would continue for days. During the early morning of July 22, the officer commanding the battalion trying to gain entry to Trugny sent the following by runner to his brigade commander: "Am held up on my right flank by hostile machine-gun fire in woods to northeast of Trugny. Need one-pounders or machine guns to knock them out. My right flank is apparently exposed. Hostile infantry has evidently pulled out leaving machine guns in possession of woods." This was followed shortly by an even more desperate plea for help: "Hostile heavy artillery is bombarding us heavily. Hostile machine-gun fire on both flanks; nearest are firing from our right rear. Send something over there, or we will have to stop or pull out altogether." A few minutes later, the same battalion commander sent a final desperate request for help, saying, "For Christ's sake, knock out the machine guns on our right. Heavy casualties. What troops should be on my right and left, and where are they?" [30]

That same afternoon, the Americans were able to get some artillery support, but yet another assault failed. The attacking forces found that they had no friendly forces on either flank despite desperate pleas for such support. Instead, they were subjected to more murderous machine gun fire, and now heavy German artillery fire added to the deadly enemy resistance. As tactical commanders begged for help, those at the brigade, division, and corps levels should have realized things were not as they had been told, that this was not merely a small rear-guard action. But it seems no one was convinced, and the poor New England Guardsmen paid a terrible price for such blind stupidity.

In fact, after the division had established a line outside Épieds and Trugny that night, the French Sixth Army and I Corps were still insisting on a "continuation of the push straight forward."[31] Luckily, the division commander, General Edwards, decided to risk insubordination by issuing orders for a flanking maneuver rather than another frontal assault. This achieved some success, but the German opposition, consisting mostly of scattered but well-positioned squad-sized groups of infantry and machine gunners, still held on, ably performing their mission of delaying the American advance while the rest of the German forces withdrew toward either their next defensive line above the Ourcq River or their new front line of resistance on the Vesle River. Finally, the 26th Division took Épieds and Trugny on July 23 only to discover that the Germans had withdrawn to the north and northeast.

The Yankee Division would advance a short distance forward to the edge of the Forêt-de-Fère, where they dug in. The division's men were exhausted, and they had suffered terrible casualties. In the ten days since the beginning of the German Marne offensive on July 15, the 26th Division suffered more than 4,000 casualties, with over 3,000 of those being in the five days from July 18 to 23.[32] It was not surprising, therefore, that

the French Sixth Army ordered the Rainbow Division to relieve the beleaguered Yankee Division on July 23.[33]

From the train depot at Noisy-le-Sec, the division's trains switched
tracks and headed northeast, first to Meaux and then to stations at Trilport and La Ferté-sous-Jouarre. The first unit to arrive was the 167th Infantry. Part of the regiment detrained at Trilport, about twenty-one miles
southwest of Château-Thierry, on July 22, while the rest of the regiment
arrived at La Ferté-sous-Jouarre the next day. The 2nd Battalion marched
six miles to Ussy-sur-Marne, and the remainder of the 167th went to Sammeron, a small village just across the Marne from Ussy-sur-Marne. Since
orders to move forward had not yet been received, the men spent July 23
resting and swimming in the Marne, which provided the first opportunity
for the men to bathe in many weeks.[34]

However, the bathing in the Marne by the soldiers camping in Sammeron caused some issues with the locals that, once again, highlighted
the Alabamians' ability to engage in various hijinks. When the men swam
out into the river, they decided to take possession of a small house that
was floating midstream and served as the municipal washhouse, where
the women of Sammeron went to wash clothes. But the Alabamians
thought its roof served as an excellent place from which to dive into the
river. Soon, however, too many enthusiastic men were on the roof, and
the house began to sink into the Marne. The Alabamians tried to stop the
house from sinking completely, but their efforts were to no avail and the
town's washhouse soon disappeared below the river's waves.

Worse yet, when this was happening, an elderly woman was at the house
washing her family's clothes. When she realized the washhouse was sinking, she became hysterical, yelling and jumping up and down as the water
steadily rose to her waist. Luckily, two soldiers went to her rescue and got
her safely to shore as her clothes went to the bottom of the river with the
washhouse. The regiment subsequently was forced to apologize and pay
the town "a large number of francs" to cover the cost of a new washhouse.[35]

The remaining infantry regiments arrived on July 24. The Iowans of
the 168th left their trains at Trilport around 3:00 a.m. John Taber, a young
lieutenant in the regiment, remarked in his diary that, as they detrained,
they unloaded weapons, baggage, and kitchens before forming the regiment and making "a hard march up hill and down dale," covering the
seven miles to Jaignes in about three hours. Taber described Jaignes as "a
delightful village, set way up on a hill above the Marne." The lieutenant
drew what he called "the prize billet of all," a nicely furnished room over-

looking a lovely garden. Taber added that, while he was very tired, he figured the regiment would be in Jaignes at least twenty-four hours and decided to wait for nightfall before getting the first sleep he would have in a real bed in some time. He enjoyed a bath and a "sumptuous" meal that included roast duck, fresh vegetables, and champagne. But before he could climb into his bed, the regiment received orders to pack up and be ready to move out that night.[36]

The New Yorkers of the 165th also arrived in Trilport on July 24 and made the shortest march of all the regiments, only four miles to Changis-sur-Marne. Martin Hogan took note of the lovely French countryside between the train station and the village. "It was a pleasant country through which we marched," he later wrote, "and seemed little touched by war."[37] Father Duffy described Changis-sur-Marne as follows: "The broad, silvery Marne forms a loop around the little village and the commodious modern chateau (owned, by the way, by an American), in which we live. We revel in our new found luxury."[38]

The Ohioans of the 166th detrained at La Ferté-sous-Jouarre mid-morning on July 24 and began a seven-mile hike through Méry-sur-Marne and Nauteuil-sur-Marne to Crouttes-sur-Marne. This line of march took them along the Marne River, which they crossed twice on the way to Crouttes-sur-Marne. The summer weather was lovely, as was the scenery. The soldiers noticed the pastoral beauty of the area, so very different from what they had seen in Champagne. This part of the Marne Valley was filled with lush green meadows and wheat fields, and one would not have known there was a war raging a short distance away. When the regiment arrived at their destination and was billeted, the men unslung their packs, stripped down, and, like other members of the division, dived into the waters of the Marne for a swim and a bath.[39]

The first element of the Rainbow Division to move up to the line in the Marne salient was the 84th Brigade, which began preparations to advance in the late afternoon of July 24. This was somewhat unusual because the division's leadership had always wanted the division to be committed to battle as a single entity. But realizing the urgency of getting help forward to the 26th Division, Degoutte's orders of July 23 specified that the division "go into line by entire brigades at least, rather than bit by bit as its elements arrive."[40]

I Corps, under the command of General Hunter Liggett, set up its headquarters in Épieds. Initially, the new American corps had command of not just the 26th Division and 42nd Division but also the French 167th

Division, which was aligned to the left of the 26th Division. This organization would now shift with the 84th Brigade moving to relief of the 26th Division. In addition, orders from the French Sixth Army directed that the division relieve the French 167th Division on July 27.[41] As a result, the 83rd Brigade would begin to advance late in the afternoon of July 25.

In the late afternoon of July 24, just as the 167th and 168th were settling into their new camps, they received warning orders directing them to pack up and prepare to move. When he read the orders to the 168th, Colonel Ernest Bennett, the regiment commander, immediately prepared to send the orders down to his three battalion commanders. About that time, a major from division headquarters arrived to have a hurried meet with Bennett about the amount of transportation needed to move the regiment. It seemed that, for the first time, the men were to have the luxury of being moved by truck. As he was preparing to leave, the major told him, "You probably will take up the fight in the morning. The 26th Division is exhausted. They have fought magnificently." Then he added, wryly, "Tell one of your men to get me a pair of Boche field glasses."[42]

Bennett's staff and the supply company swung into immediate action. They issued extra bandoliers of ammunition to the men and gathered up reserve supplies of rations, mostly hardtack and the infamous canned corned beef known to the men as "corned Willy." Company first sergeants inspected the men's rifles and bayonets and made sure everyone filled their canteens. As the men hurried about camp preparing, some even looked forward to the prospect of traveling by truck. However, all too soon they would learn that more often than not, the use of trucks to move forward meant one thing—the desperate need for a "pinch hitter."[43]

Soon, the 168th was ready to go, but it was long after dark before the French trucks arrived in Jaignes. Each battalion had gathered its men in a separate group to load onto the trucks. To their surprise, the Iowans discovered that the trucks were driven by French colonial troops from the central highlands of Vietnam, which was then referred to as French Indochina.[44] As the long line of trucks pulled up, the Vietnamese drivers hopped down from their cabs to show the Iowans how to load both the men and their equipment and supplies. The typical truckload was sixteen men, but some were crammed with as many as thirty. In all, it would take seventy-five trucks to move each battalion from the division's regiments.[45] By midnight, the 168th was on its way.

The 167th Infantry, meanwhile, was gathered and ready to go by 4:00 p.m. on July 24. However, the men from Alabama got to experience the

Artillery wagons from the 42nd Division pass through Château-Thierry during the Aisne-Marne Offensive. (*National Archives*)

classic army phenomenon of "hurry up and wait." Everything and everyone was in position to load up in Ussy-sur-Marne, but the departure was delayed until 7:45 p.m. As the hours passed, the trucks still did not show up. Finally, the men heard the rumble produced by the solid-rubber-tired French trucks. The trucks roared into Ussy-sur-Marne and, just as in Jaignes, the men met their Vietnamese drivers, who dismounted from their trucks and lined up in the same order as the trucks they drove. Then a Vietnamese-speaking French officer assigned sixteen men to each driver, who immediately led his group off to his truck and showed them how to get aboard. The 167th was on its way to the fight by 11:30 p.m.[46]

The trucks carrying both the 167th and 168th rolled through the shattered remnant of Château-Thierry during the night, but as the men peered out from their trucks, it was too dark to see anything. One doughboy later said that, ever since the Marines made their legendary stand at Château-Thierry in late May, the town's name "had an American ring in the ears of the AEF." But he noted that the name also signified tough, desperate fighting that filled the men of the Rainbow Division "with a certainty that, as the Champagne was the frying pan, so this would be the fire."[47]

The convoy of trucks carrying the 168th arrived a few miles beyond Épieds around 6:00 a.m. on July 25. The city had only been seized a few hours before by the 26th Division, who had moved forward toward the Forêt-de-Fère. As a result, the smoke still rose from its grim ruins as a steady rain now fell. The Iowans lined up and began to march forward as German shells landed in a field a few hundred yards ahead of them. Above them, German and French aircraft dipped and dived in dogfights, and the sky was spotted with bursts of anti-aircraft fire. The column soon passed by a large overturned German artillery piece and a group of dead German soldiers. John Taber wrote in his diary that the entire scene was like that of "an exaggerated chromo of a civil war battle." A few minutes later, as they entered a wheat field, they found the ripe, yellow wheat filled with the bodies of men from the Yankee Division's 101st Infantry Regiment. They had been cut down by German machine guns hidden in the nearby woods, but there had not been time to bury them yet. It was a most dispiriting sight.[48]

The 167th arrived about an hour after the 168th, unloading their trucks at Courpoil, approximately a mile and a half northeast of Épieds. The men paused briefly for a hot meal and a little rest, as few had slept during their jarring overnight ride. Soon, however, they headed northeast through the wheat fields toward the Bois de Fary and the positions of the 26th Division in the Forêt-de-Fère. John Hayes of I Company later said that German reconnaissance planes swooped down through the rain every few minutes using breaks in the clouds to watch the Alabamians move forward.[49] Colonel Screws, the regiment commander, later said, "the Boche practically saw my troops going forward, as there was no chance to get to the front line without crossing a long open space."[50]

Because the regiment's mules had to march cross-country, everything had to be carried by the men. The Sanitary Detachments carried their stretchers and boxes of medical supplies, while the infantrymen were bogged down with rations, full canteens, and 250 rounds of ammunition. Meanwhile, the Machine Gun Companies had to use hand carts to roll their heavy Hotchkiss guns and ammunition through the muddy wheat fields during the five-mile march.[51]

The 168th had paused just a few short kilometers from the edge of the woods, briefly taking cover in shell holes in the wheat fields. As they had approached the area, they passed a battery of French 75mm guns that were preparing to open fire. One of the poilus who spoke English called out to an Iowan, "Are you going forward this morning?" The American

Soldiers of the 42nd Division marching through the Forêt-de-Fère. (*National Archives*)

replied, "Yes, and if you'll just pick up your little 'ol *soixante-quinze* [75] and hitch on, we'll try to get you to Berlin before night." The Poilu frowned seriously and said, "But surely you don 't expect to get that far?" The doughboy reluctantly conceded, "Well, there is some talk of stopping at the Rhine, but I dunno, I dunno about that. These fellers are Hell when they get started."[52]

Finally, the time came for the 168th to advance into the woods and relieve the battered remnant of the Yankee Division. The Iowa men climbed somewhat reluctantly out of their shell holes and made their way through the deep slimy mud, which Lawrence Stewart said was "worse here than in any previous campaign," as the French 75s swung into action, sending shells toward the Germans on the far side of the Forêt-de-Fère. Unknown to the Iowans, this would be the last artillery support they would receive for almost five days.

As they moved closer to the woods, the sights that greeted them were even worse than they had seen up to now, providing a grim preview of the fight that lay ahead of them. John Taber wrote of the scene:

> But if there were any illusions as to the nature of the task that was in store for the regiment, all that was necessary to dispel them was a glance at the fields round about. Shell holes, twisted rifles, crusted bay-

onets, machine guns with half-emptied cartridge belts, and Germans—dead Germans—beside them, littered the trampled wheat. And every few yards, in the open stretch or before the hedges that had screened an enemy nest, were crumpled khaki forms pitched on their faces their hands gripping rifle stocks in the vise of death. This was the sight that greeted the men of the 168th as they moved forward to battle. In making a relief there is nothing so destructive to morale as to come upon the bodies of dead comrades: it makes one think; and thinking is bad, even for soldiers who have schooled themselves to look upon death as the common fate of all.[53]

By noon, the Iowans had stopped short of the Forêt-de-Fère and dug in under the cover of the trees in the Bois de Fary, as the French artillery barrage was likely to spur return fire from the German guns. It did not take long for that to happen just as predicted, and within minutes German shells were landing nearby.[54] Meanwhile, the 167th had come forward and began moving into the forest somewhere to the 168th's left, exactly where no one knew, as the situation in the dense woods quickly became terribly confused.

Soon after the 168th was in place, Colonel Bennett and three of his staff met with Colonel John Parker, the commander of what was left of the 102nd Infantry, in the woods just south of a lake, the Étang de la Logette. They discussed the process for relieving the 102nd that night, and Parker told Bennett and the others that his entire regiment now numbered less than one of the battalions in the 168th. As a result, Parker added, he could not hold his line as he would have liked to, and he had no clear idea about where the German lines were or what their strength might be.[55] The usual procedure would have been for the 102nd to provide guides who could lead the Iowans and the Alabamians to the correct positions in the line, but Parker had so few men that he only had one guide for the 168th and none for the 167th.

Colonel Bennett ordered his 1st Battalion under Major Emory Worthington to take over the front line from the 102nd and scattered elements of the 101st Infantry as well as one battalion from the 112th Infantry. The regiment's 2nd Battalion under Major Claude Stanley moved up to the support position while the 3rd Battalion under Major Guy Brewer positioned themselves as a reserve in front of the ruins of the Maison Boutache where the 168th's Post of Command (PC) had been established.

At the same time, the 167th was stumbling forward to the 168th's left on their own without any guide to help place them in the proper position.

An officer from the Illinois National Guard who saw the 167th moving into the woods toward the incoming German artillery fire asked some Alabama officer where they were going. They told him to ask Colonel Screws, who the Illinois officer could easily pick out because, as usual, Screws had a large burning cigar in his mouth. The officer called out to Screws, "Hello, Bill. Where are you going?" The Alabama colonel replied, "Damn if I know, but I am on my way."[56]

Meanwhile, the 168th's 1st Battalion was led into position by a guide who supposedly knew the terrain. However, shortly after relieving the 102nd's men, Major Worthington sensed that something was wrong. After surveying the situation, Worthington realized that the defensive line was so indefinite that he could not locate the friendly units from the 167th that were supposed to be on his left flank.

About this time, General Brown informed Colonel Bennett that the troops relieved by the 1st Battalion had wandered out of the area and were not the group that needed to be relieved. Those in the actual sector assigned to the 168th were straggling back without waiting for relief. Obviously, the 102nd's guide had no clue where the correct units were. This had created a serious gap between the 167th and 168th, which was why Major Worthington had not been able to establish contact with the 167th. Moving Worthington's battalion would be impossible, as German shelling had now become quite heavy. So Bennett ordered E and F Companies from the 2nd Battalion to go fill the gap on the left and make contact with the 167th. They were in position around 9:30 p.m., but this shift by those two companies proved a daunting challenge. Not only were enemy heavy artillery shells now crashing into the woods, but it was also "so dark that one could scarcely see his hand before his face—even in the daytime it was hard enough to maintain liaison in the dense and tangled brush."[57]

On the Iowans' left, the Alabama regiment managed to establish skirmish lines using men from their 1st and 2nd Battalions. These men would act as individual scouts on a line rather than acting as part of patrols or assault forces. Each soldier was responsible for his personal part of the front. It was certainly not an ideal situation, but under the circumstances it was the best they could do.[58]

The long night that followed made for one of the worst of the war and one long remembered by those who were there in the Forêt-de-Fère. Lawrence Stewart recalled the night as being "black as ink, drenched with ghostly mists and pierced with the eerie whine of falling explosives."[59] All night long, the Germans raked the woods where the 167th and 168th lay with both antipersonnel and high-explosive rounds. The shelling caused numerous casualties, and those rendering aid to the wounded could not see what they were doing in the dark. So their only solution was to use flashlights, but these had to be shielded and used carefully lest the Germans see them and bring down even more murderous fire on their positions. John Taber would write, "The roaring guns, the flashing bursts, the frequent gas alarms, intermittent showers, a chilling wind, and lack of shelter combined to make it a night of pure misery," adding, "Never was daybreak more anxiously awaited."[60]

When daybreak did finally come and the sun broke through, those in the forward skirmish lines could barely make out a group of stone farm buildings surrounding a huge walled-in central building that was "medieval in style and fortress like in effect." Worse, these building and the surrounding area seemed to be teeming with German machine guns.[61] The Americans were getting their first look at the La Croix Rouge Farm.

It would have to be taken, no matter the cost.

5

THE BATTLE FOR
LA CROIX ROUGE FARM

July 26, 1918

"The 167th Alabama assisted by the left of the 168th Iowa had
stormed and captured the Croix Rouge Farm in a manner which for
its gallantry I do not believe has been surpassed in military history."
—General Douglas MacArthur, quoted in
Henry Reilly's *Americans All*

It was raining steadily as it had all day on July 26 when Private John Hayes
and the rest of the 167th Infantry's I Company began their advance
through the woods and undergrowth of the Forêt-de Fère a little after
5:00 p.m. Ahead of them across several hundred yards of open ground
was La Croix Rouge Farm, a complex of stone farm buildings and a large
walled-in farmhouse that the American officers at I Corps had said was
merely a "machine gun nest."[1] Like every other farm in the area around
Épieds, this one was occupied by the Germans. But here, the Germans
had created a veritable fortress armed with dozens of heavy 7.92mm machine guns. It was certainly not just a "machine gun nest." Furthermore,
each weapon was served by a five-man crew, and those men were determined not to give any ground to the Americans.

1st Lieutenant John Powell was leading the company forward when
German lookouts saw the Alabamians coming through the woods. All at
once, red flame leaped out toward them from more guns than Hayes and

his comrades could count. The German machine guns swept back and forth across the entire area as "twigs and leaves cut from trees by the fusillade began falling" and "whistling machine gun slugs knocked bark from trees." Hayes dropped to the ground as his platoon sergeant, William Boyd, hurried past him, saying, "This is the real thing."[2]

The steady advance continued despite the heavy enemy fire and, after about thirty minutes, I Company reached the part of the woods where the Germans had meticulously cleared the undergrowth to give them a clearer field of fire. Up to now, the company had only suffered two or three men wounded, but that would soon change. Hayes could now clearly see the fortified farmhouse across all that terrible open ground, and the German gunners could clearly see him and the rest of I Company. There were guns in front of them and on each side, but no one in I Company could see them distinctly enough to return their fire. Lieutenant Powell grabbed his field glasses and began to move down the slight slope ahead of them in an attempt to locate some of the machine guns that were now cutting down dozens of his men. Powell only got about thirty yards before machine gun bullets ripped into his body. Another young officer took command and sent two men forward to help Powell. They were able to reach him and bring the lieutenant back, but he would die before they reached the aid station in the rear.[3]

As the company advanced into the open field, the murderous enemy fire became even more violent. Hayes and the others in the company took whatever cover they could find, including trees, rocks, and even some scattered cords of firewood. From these positions, they began to locate German positions and open fire on them with their rifles. One by one, some of the enemy guns were silenced. But there were many more guns to overcome, and the advance across the fields toward La Croix Rouge Farm would be long and bloody.[4]

Other than the German shelling of the Forêt-de-Fère, the night of July 25–26 had been uneventful for men of the 167th and 168th. However, that did not mean it had not been a miserable night. It had rained most of the night, and that rain continued in the morning. The men were also famished. Since moving forward during the evening of July 24, the men had nothing to eat but their reserve rations of hardtack and "corn Willy." The wagons of the two regiments' Supply Companies had started out just after the trucks carrying the men left the banks of the Marne, but they

La Croix Rouge Farm, whose stone buildings were turned into a fortress by the Germans. (*National Archives*)

had been struggling to reach the front ever since. The roads from Château-Thierry were crammed with advancing troops and vehicles, and the rains had turned the roads into muddy bogs. When the field kitchen carts finally reached Épieds, they quickly began preparing hot meals, which were sent forward by ration carts. However, it would be late in the day before they reached the Forêt-de-Fère.[5]

Colonel Bennett had set up his PC at the Maison Boutache. At the same time, Colonel Screws made his PC in his tent, which he erected in a gully alongside a muddy trail about a half a mile to the rear of his regiment's skirmish line. As it became light, he ordered small patrols forward to determine the enemy's exact position and strength. This proved to be a daunting challenge. As the patrols made their way forward through the woods toward La Croix Rouge Farm, they encountered German snipers who opened fire on them from the trees and farmhouse up ahead. As soon as a German lookout could see them, the Germans would open fire with their machine guns, forcing the patrols to quickly retreat. As a result, the Americans remained essentially ignorant of both the location and extent of the enemy's defenses.[6]

This lack of information was not confined to these two frontline regiments. However, as one moved up the chain of command from the 84th Brigade to 42nd Division, I Corps, and French Sixth Army Headquarters, the ignorance was clearly more willful in nature. Although the weather prevented any aerial reconnaissance that would provide substantial intelligence of German strength and positions across the front and even though the initial advancing French and American units had encountered stiff resistance and taken heavy casualties, the official position of the French Sixth Army was unchanged—the enemy was in full retreat, and there were only small rear-guard units with which to contend. This was reflected in the I Corps situation report for the period ending at 8:00 p.m. on July 25, which noted the La Croix Rouge Farm as part of the enemy line and merely said "La Croix Rouge Farm (machine-gun nest here)."[7] The orders for July 25 from General Degoutte's headquarters showed the optimism of a staff convinced that the enemy was fleeing the salient. They directed that the American I Corps seize the Ourcq River crossings and the town of Sergy by the morning of July 26. This, they said, would allow French cavalry to chase the retreating German forces.[8]

But Sergy and the river crossings were still more than four miles away to the northeast from La Croix Rouge Farm, where the 167th and 168th were positioned on the morning of July 26. That anyone believed they should have advanced as far as the Ourcq River by this time clearly demonstrates that those at higher headquarters were either delusional or were ignoring all evidence that conflicted with their wishful thinking.

The German positions at La Croix Rouge Farm were far stronger than the Americans opposite them realized. But the men from Alabama and Iowa suspected that the intelligence from higher headquarters was more than a little faulty. As they lay in their skirmish lines, the doughboys could hear the Germans talking to their immediate front, and every time they moved a few feet forward, the Germans opened fire on them. So, obviously, any idea that all the Germans had retired across the Ourcq River was sheer fantasy.[9]

For their part, the Germans seemed well aware that a substantial force of American and French infantry was occupying the woods to the west, southwest, and south of their position, and they were ready to defend the farm. These same men had fought the American 26th and French 167th and 29th Divisions to a standstill, and they applied all they had learned in four years of war to fortify the farm. They had turned the ancient farmhouse into a massive machine gun position, capable of sweeping the fields in front of it in every direction. The farm was manned by veteran soldiers of the 23rd German Infantry Division and the 10th Landwehr Division, who set up interlocking bands of fire over measured distances with their heavy 7.92mm machine guns.[10]

These guns were well camouflaged and placed in trenches that formed a V shape with the farmhouse at its apex. The trenches in the V's arms went for about 200 yards to the southwest and northwest toward the woods where the Americans were positioned. Meanwhile, other machine guns were dug into the north and south along the road just east of the farm that led toward Le Charmel.[11]

The German infantry also had rifles and automatic rifles capable of accurately hitting targets out to a thousand yards. Some of the riflemen were positioned in trees to serve as snipers. Furthermore, there also was no shortage of ammunition, as the Germans had built an ammo dump in the forest about a mile east of the farm.[12]

The Germans had also carefully prepared the battlefield. Across the open fields to the west and southwest were the woods that separated the two opposing forces. On the American side of the woods, there was a dense maze of bushes and undergrowth that obstructed their view of the farm and made moving forward difficult. However, on the other side, the Germans had carefully cleared the underbrush to give them an unobstructed view of the Americans when they advanced.[13]

But the Germans also added one deadly finishing touch to their preparations. After they had cleared the underbrush, they painted bands on the trees at the edge of the woods. These bands, painted in red or white, were about waist high from the ground and served as aiming points for their machine gunners.[14] Lieutenant Colonel Walter Bare, executive officer of the 167th, later noted how exact these markers were. The way they were placed on the trees "gave the machine gunners the exact military crest of the terrain and were so arranged that if the enemy was advancing standing up, they would be shot in the lower limbs."[15]Private John Hayes of the 167th's I Company saw these bands as something more sinister: "From long experience, the Germans had prepared a cunning death trap in which they sat like a great spider, ready to spring on its prey."[16]

Back in the Forêt-de-Fère, both regiments waited. On the far left in the 167th, the 1st Battalion's skirmish lines faced an area of the forest that was mostly clear of undergrowth, giving them little protection from enemy riflemen and machine gunners. The 3rd Battalion to their right occupied thicker woods that were good for cover but hard to run through. Both battalions were still in skirmish lines about a thousand yards east of the farm but, since they were only 200 to 300 yards from the nearest German riflemen, the battalions' men were constantly in range.[17]

The 168th remained to the 167th's right, occupying the southwest edge of the woods on the farm's clearing, most of the southern side of that clearing, and then along a line facing northeast and parallel to the Fère-en-Tardenois-La Croix Rouge Farm-Le Charmel-Road.[18] However, confusion resulting from their initial mistaken alignment the night before remained at daybreak on July 26. Neither the 1st nor 2nd Battalions knew precisely where the other was positioned, no one could find Major Worthington, the 1st Battalion commander, and his men were unsure of their orders.[19] To make things even worse, there was a gap between the 167th and 168th that caused further confusion amid incoming artillery shells. Both regiments worked to establish flank contact that morning, but they did not finally connect until afternoon.[20]

During that morning, as patrols tried to scout the German positions, Major Dallas Smith, commander of the 167th's 3rd Battalion, met with Major John Carroll, commander of the 1st Battalion and a longtime friend. Smith told Carroll that he believed they would see heavy losses if they made an assault on the farm. Carroll said that he was awaiting a report from his Intelligence Section, which ought to tell them more. A few minutes later, the patrol from that section arrived back at the skirmish line. The officer leading the patrol had been wounded but managed to return. They had gained little new information because they were constantly under observation by the Germans who fired at them at will.[21]

To make matters even more dismal, both Colonel Screws and Bennett were operating without any decent maps of the area around La Croix Rouge Farm. Screws had a low-scale map, which did not tell him much, and Bennett had nothing except a rough sketch of the area given to him by the departing commander of the 102nd Infantry. Still, being the professional soldier he was, Screws decided to make contingency plans for an attack should the brigade choose to order an assault. Screws sketched out a plan calling for the regiment executive officer, Lieutenant Colonel Bare, to take a position behind the 1st Battalion on the left. He would be responsible for organizing both men separated from their units once the fighting started as well as any units that became disorganized. Lieutenant Powell from I Company of the 3rd Battalion would play a similar role on their right. After reviewing the plan with his two battalion commanders, Majors Carroll and Smith, they returned to their respective battalion PCs to brief their company commanders.[22]

Around 1:00 p.m., Major Claude Stanley, commander of the 168th's 2nd Battalion, received his first direction regarding an assault on La Croix Rouge Farm. A message came from Colonel Bennett saying, "Get in contact with the enemy, if you have not already done so. The line will advance at 2 p.m. If you receive no further orders, advance at that hour." It then stated that Stanley's first objective was the road just behind the farm, followed by the village of Fresnes, about two miles to the northeast, if it could be taken without serious resistance. Bennett also sent a rough drawing showing the outlines of the battalion's sector.[23] The source of Colonel Bennett's orders is uncertain because, oddly, the 167th did not receive similar direction.

While there seems to be no information on what, if any, direction Bennett had received from the brigade at this point, he had sent Major Stanley all the information available, which was not much. Stanley noted that there was not a word about the enemy's positions, weapons, or strength. Apparently, the idea behind getting in contact with the enemy was for Stanley's infantrymen to find out the information firsthand.[24]

At this time, Stanley's officers were desperately trying to establish a solid line across the sector connected with the 167th on their left and the French 168th Infantry on their right. Also, Stanley's supporting companies were just coming up, and the Machine Gun Company still had not arrived. There was no way for him to attack at 2:00 p.m. So, at 1:20 p.m., Stanley sent a reply to Colonel Bennett that said, "Impossible to advance at 2:00 p.m. Cannot be in position. Troops [French] on right do not advance until 7."[25] When he received Stanley's message, Bennett wisely canceled the attack.

The other issue Stanley reported to Colonel Bennett was a critical need for Chauchat automatic rifle and Hotchkiss machine gun ammunition. As the 167th and 168th awaited orders to attack, this was a problem that plagued both regiments. They had advanced with only the ammunition they could carry on their backs, which meant they did not have enough for a sustained attack, much less to battle any German counterattacks that might come. The cause of this problem seemed to lie in the performance of the 117th Ammunition Train from the Kansas National Guard. Apparently, they and their commander, Lieutenant Colonel Frank Travis, felt no sense of urgency and were moving slowly and casually toward the front. For Travis's part, he exercised little influence on the speed of the unit and, in fact, would soon be relieved of command with a comment from 42nd Division Headquarters that "he was unfit to command the Ammunition Train [due to] a lack of interest and appearance of timidity for his personal safety."[26] In other words, the division believed Travis was a coward.

Around midafternoon, Screws, Bennett, the commanders of the 101st and 102nd Field Artillery of the 26th Division, and their respective staff officers were called to the 84th Brigade PC to meet with General Brown. About 3:00 p.m., the meeting began with Brown reading an order for the 167th and 168th Infantry to attack La Croix Rouge Farm at 4:50 p.m. This meant they were being told to attack in broad daylight against an enemy of unknown strength deployed in unknown positions. Screws and Bennett were both dumbfounded, and Screws later said he listened to the orders being read in "utter amazement." "I protested as far as a Colonel could and still save his head," he recalled. Screws reminded Brown of what he believed was in his front and told the general that a better plan would be to "fall back out of the woods and bring as much artillery down on the enemy line as possible." Screws pleaded for at least some artillery preparation and was told there would be nothing more than a rolling barrage during the attack. However, as events would show, the Alabamians and Iowans did not even get that much artillery support.[27]

Why Brown refused to wait until the battlefield was better prepared is a question that defies any answer based on good military thinking. However, there is little doubt that the attack was ordered in such a hurried, cavalier manner because of the pressure coming from higher headquarters to move faster, and the orders came from officers who still believed all they faced were the small rear-guard forces of a fleeing enemy.

Screws then asked Brown if the 167th French Division on his left, which was also under the control of I Corps, would jump off for the attack at the same time. To the shock of both Screws and Bennett, Brown said the French had no orders to attack but that he was sure they would probably advance when they saw the Americans do so. The lack of planning and coordination by Brown and his staff was absolutely stupefying.

By the time General Brown was finished discussing this "plan," it was almost 4:30 p.m., only twenty minutes before the prescribed time of the attack. Screws issued verbal instructions to his regiment's staff and wrote out a set of instructions, one for each of his two assault battalions, the 1st and the 3rd. The colonel handed the written instructions to Lieutenant Colonel Bare and instructed him to deliver them with all possible speed. By now, it was only ten or fifteen minutes before the jumping-off time, and Bare was almost three miles away from the 3rd Battalion PC. He found a motorcycle waiting for him and hopped into the sidecar. The driver sped away as fast as he could safely go across the fields and narrow forest pathways. When he reached Major Smith's PC, Bare leaped from the car to deliver the instructions. Major Smith read the orders and was horrified. He told Bare that this attack would result in terrible losses if

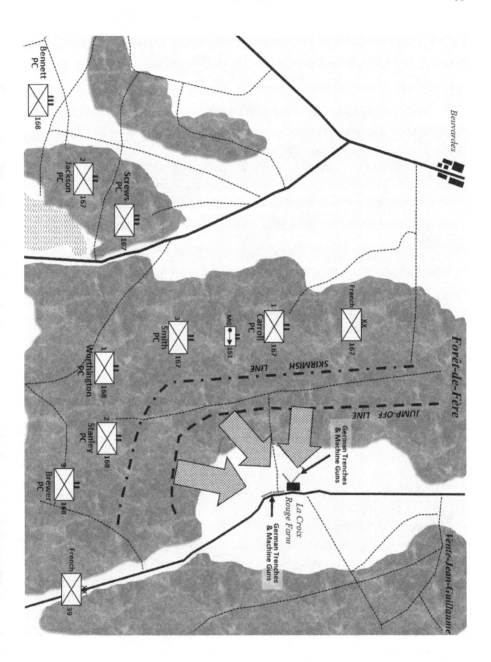

Map 3. The attack by the 167th and 168th Infantry Regiments on July 26, 1918, at La Croix Rouge Farm.

they did not have artillery preparation and support. A short while later, just before the attack began, Smith told his fellow battalion commander, John Carroll, "John, there will be many of these officers and men we will never see again."[28]

Bare then drove away toward the 1st Battalion PC to the north. As the driver started away, heavy German shelling began. As he and Bare got within about one thousand yards of Major Carroll's PC, they discovered a large tree had fallen across the forest trail. The forest was too dense on either side to go around the tree, and Bare and his driver could not lift the heavy motorcycle over it. There was nothing to do but make a run for it, which Bare did. By the time he got to Major Carroll, it was already past 5:00 p.m.[29]

The orders called for Carroll's 1st Battalion to attack supported by the 167th Machine Gun Company, whose men would have to carry their heavy Hotchkiss machine guns with the riflemen as they all attacked across the open fields between the skirmish line and the farmhouse. Once they reached La Croix Rouge Farm, Carroll's men were supposed to turn to the northeast, moving across yet more open ground beyond the farm until they reached the Vente-Jean-Guillaume woods about a mile away. Meanwhile, Smith's 3rd Battalion was told to attack through the woods and across the open ground, move past the farmhouse, and establish a line in the woods about a thousand yards to the east. The orders prescribed that the infantry "move at a single bound—speed 100 meters in three minutes to the final objective," which was impossible given the defenses that lay in front of the Americans.[30] Needless to say, with the late start and the lack of a coordinated attack by the 1st and 3rd Battalions, the 167th's assault was not off to a good start.

However, if possible, things were even more confused in the 168th Infantry on the right. Major Stanley had spent the afternoon getting his 2nd Battalion in place for the attack he anticipated was coming. E and F Companies would be his assault companies, with E on the right and F on the left nearest the 167th's 3rd Battalion. Each company would advance with two platoons attacking while the two other platoons followed in support. At the same time, G and H Companies would support the attack, positioned on the far right about 600 yards away. His Machine Gun Company would provide supporting fire, but, unlike the 167th, they would not advance with the assault forces. Stanley could see that the terrain between the jumping-off line and the open ground was heavily wooded with thick underbrush. As a result, there were no trails over which the heavy machine guns could be moved forward. Therefore, he ordered the Machine Gun Company to place their weapons in the woods to provide supporting fire as the battalion attacked.[31]

Around 3:40 p.m., E and F Companies were in place. Their commanders, Captains Casey and Yates, reported to Major Stanley at the 2nd Battalion PC to receive final instructions. Yates, who had just returned from a discussion with the French on their right, told Stanley that the French were ordered to advance to the road running southeast from the farm and then make a turning movement to the left. Captain Yates said that his orders were to move straight past the farm and into the woods beyond. This, the French replied, was impossible, and they had been told that the Americans were not going to advance until much later.[32]

Hearing this, Major Stanley immediately went to the French PC, where they confirmed what Yates had told him. As one historian noted, "Here was a situation brimming with all the potentialities of a glorious jumble."[33] Suppose the French proceeded with their plan, and the Iowans followed their orders. In that case, the Germans could sit back and watch the French and Americans destroy one another in their own crossfire. Stanley sent a message to Colonel Bennett explaining the situation. Still, he knew that, since the French and Americans were under the command of two different corps, there was no way this would get sorted out in time. So he took the initiative and made an agreement with the French battalion commander that, if the French turning maneuver was successful, the Americans would halt at their first objective, the road from the farm to Le Charmel. But all this had the effect of delaying the attack by the 168th once again.[34]

So, instead of advancing, the 168th remained in place as German artillery fire fell down on them amid a continuing rainstorm. The "dripping green woods were heavy with the smoke of bursting shells and the mist of toxic gases," mostly phosgene and tear gas. Shrapnel was flying everywhere, and the trees were being shattered by the high-explosive rounds, sending deadly splinters flying through the woods where the men hugged the ground, trying to avoid being killed or wounded. With every explosion, the 168th's casualties were increasing, and they were gaining nothing. They had been ordered to be ready to attack twice, and both times they were told to hold.[35]

When the meeting at the 84th Brigade PC was concluded, Colonel Bennett did the same thing as Colonel Screws—he wrote an urgent message for his assaulting battalion's commander and sent it on its way. In this case, he gave the message to Captain Lloyd Ross, his operations officer. Just as Lieutenant Colonel Bare had done, Roberts made "superhuman efforts" to get the message to attack to Major Stanley before the time designated for the jump-off. However, even if the conditions had been better, the captain probably could not have gotten there in time. And conditions were far from good. Roberts struggled down forest paths made slippery by the constant rain and fought desperately not to get stuck in the thick mud as German artillery shells burst all around him. By the time he found Major Stanley at the 2nd Battalion PC, it was 5:12 p.m., twenty-two minutes past the time for the attack.[36]

Stanley's four company commanders were at the PC when the message from Colonel Bennett arrived. The major read the message out loud, and the company commanders dashed out to get back to their respective companies and carry out the brigade's orders. Major Stanley would later note that "This was the first information that we had received as to what we were to attack and that there was a turning movement contemplated." Then, he, his staff, and runners went forward to the edge of the woods to watch E and F Companies advance to the attack on La Croix Rouge Farm.[37] As Stanley made his way forward, German artillery seemed to focus on the 300 to 500 yards from the clearing into the woods. Before he and his staff could get to the jumping-off line, Stanley's adjutant, Lieutenant Peckham, and most of his runners were killed in the enemy barrage. Finally, Stanley reached the woods' edge only a minute before the assaulting troops made their attack.[38]

The terrain where the attack was to be made created a battlefield where the advantages were all with the defenders. The stone buildings of the farm sat in the center of a rectangular clearing that was one-half-mile wide and a mile long, with a narrow passage leading northward through the woods. The farm rose above "fields of bronzed wheat on the up slope of a gently undulating prairie." As such, it commanded the open ground to both the west and south to the edge of the woods, forming a "natural stronghold."[39] The road that ran past the farm to the southeast, which was hedged in by bushes and small trees and lined with machine guns, was the Iowans' objective. At the same time, the Alabamians would make a frontal assault on the farmhouse and its V-shaped trenches filled with machine guns.

The advance by the battalions of the two regiments was supposed to happen simultaneously. Yet, the timing of the orders, the lateness of their arrival, and the fact that battalion commanders all received the orders at

View of La Croix Farm from the southwest, where the Iowans of the 168th Infantry Regiment began their attack on July 26, 1918. This photo shows the deadly open ground that both the 167th and 168th Infantry Regiments had to cross in their attack. (*National Archives*)

different times made that impossible. On the left, the 1st Battalion of the 167th advanced fifteen minutes before the 3rd Battalion stepped off. The battalions' lines were irregular, and the 1st Battalion moved forward at a much faster pace.[40]

C and D Companies led the 1st Battalion attack from the far-left flank, passing through A and B Companies, who remained lying down in the dense woods providing supporting rifle and machine gun fire. As the two companies ran into the woods where the Germans had cleared the underbrush, the Germans opened a traversing fire with their machine guns from the trenches in front of the farmhouse. Lieutenant Colonel Bare, who advanced with the 1st Battalion, recalled that, in just the woods' edge to the battalion's front, the Germans had massed twenty-seven machine guns. Dozens of men fell almost immediately, and the rest of the men took whatever cover they could find about 100 yards into the clearing where they were trapped for over an hour. The 167th Machine Gun Company, which was attacking with the 1st Battalion, struggled to get their guns across the open field and was hit hard as well. Their commander,

Captain Julien Strassburger, was killed along with three of his men before he made it a hundred yards. The initial attack by the 1st Battalion had lasted only fifteen minutes.[41]

The 3rd Battalion assault did not go much better. Major Smith's men started taking heavy losses as soon as they emerged into the open, and they took cover behind trees, rocks, and even small piles of firewood that had been left in the fields. From there, Smith's riflemen started to determine precisely where some of the enemy machine guns were located and opened fire on them, taking down several German gun crews. But, while they were taking cover, a group of Germans managed to infiltrate the woods to their left and rear from where they opened a deadly fire on the 3rd Battalion. Private Hayes wrote that, in those critical moments, a thought ran through his mind that they "were trapped between two German forces and would in a matter of minutes all be killed or captured."[42]

Luckily, salvation from two different sources appeared at that moment. The first came in the form of Lieutenant Edward "Shorty" Wren, a former Auburn football star. Wren came forward with a small detail armed with a 37mm one-pounder[43] gun and opened fire on the machine guns to the battalion's front, quickly silencing them. At the same time, a small detachment of infantry led by 1st Lieutenant Robert Espy of B Company attacked and drove back the infiltrating Germans on the left.[44]

Meanwhile, to the right, the 168th began to move to the attack. Officers blew shrill blasts from their whistles as the men of E and F Companies stood up to move forward with their bayonets fixed. As they stepped out from the woods in "faultless formation," German artillery poured a deadly barrage into the woods behind them, hitting the supporting companies hard. As E and F Companies advanced, they were protected from machine gun fire for a short distance by some slightly rising terrain. However, as soon as their helmets were seen above the slope by the Germans, the enemy opened fire from what some said were as many as fifty machine gun positions. The opening fusillade tore "great gaps" in the Iowans' ranks, and the men immediately hit the ground. They formed a skirmish line and began to return fire, although, like the Alabamians to their left, they had difficulty precisely locating the German's positions. Describing the scene, John Taber wrote, "The air was a tumult of shell crashes, shouted commands, snapping bullets, crackle of machine guns, and calls for stretcher-bearers." As more men were hit, Major Stanley's men slowly crawled forward, continuing the advance toward their objective, the road to Le Charmel.[45]

La Croix Rouge Farm and the road that led to Fère en Tardenois and Le Charmel. This road was the objective of the 168th Infantry Regiment. The shallow trenches used by the German machine gun crews can clearly be seen along the road to the left. (*Major William Carraway, Historian, Georgia Army National Guard*)

On the far right, E Company was in trouble. The French, who were supposed to cover their right flank, only advanced 100 yards before stopping their attack. This meant that the German machine guns on the eastern edge of the clearing could sweep E Company's right flank with enfilading fire. F Company also found itself in difficult straits but soon received some unexpected assistance. Two platoons from D Company, which were in support of the lead companies, got lost amid the smoke and underbrush, veered to the left, and, as they emerged into the open, suddenly found themselves in the middle of the fight. Their leaders, Lieutenant Harrison Peyton and Sergeant Lance Morrow, used their common sense and steadily fed their men into the line to help F Company.[46]

Lieutenant Peyton continued forward until a sudden ferocious burst of enemy fire temporarily stopped him. As he took cover, two of his men dove into a shell hole just behind him. No sooner had they jumped into the hole when another German shell exploded between the two men. Peyton was uninjured and was shaking off the daze caused by the explosion when he heard a low groan coming from one of the two men in the shell hole, Private James Gallagher. Peyton went to his side, saw the gaping wound in Gallagher's body, and heard him saying, "Holy Father, guide well the soul I know you will soon release." The words clearly were coming amid terrible pain, and the young private spoke haltingly. Gallagher looked up at his lieutenant and said, "Lieutenant, Lieutenant, I am . . . dying, please, won't you . . ." The soldier gasped in pain, unable to finish his sentence. Peyton said, "Yes, Gallagher, what is it you want me to do?" With great difficulty, Gallagher replied, "Write my Mother that I did my duty."[47]

Just then, the lieutenant heard another voice at his side. This one came from Private Basil Cowell and was calm and steady. "Lieutenant," Cowell asked, "will you write for me, too? I'm done for." For a moment, Peyton thought this must all be part of a horrific nightmare, but he leaned over Cowell to see a waxen, bloody face. Cowell seemed calm and at peace as he died next to his buddy, Jim Gallagher.[48]

Around 7:00 p.m., as the battle raged, the 167th's 1st Battalion began a second assault using men from C and D Companies, who had not been part of the first attack, combined with surviving soldiers from A and B Companies. The second attack began when Lieutenant Ernest Bell led two platoons from D Company forward while Lieutenant Espy attacked with two B Company platoons. From the start, this attack achieved success, despite heavy casualties. Within minutes, about 100 of Bell and Espy's men were leaping into the German trenches, savagely fighting the German gunners hand-to-hand using every weapon at their disposal, killing them "with rifle, pistol, and bayonet."[49]

To their right, 3rd Battalion needed more men in the attack. So Major Smith ordered the soldiers from his mortar platoon to join the riflemen in M Company. As the company advanced, their first sergeant, Norman Summers, saw the carnage around him. "Some of our men were blown to pieces," he wrote, adding, "Some had their arms and legs blown into tatters. . . . It began to get dark. Shells were bursting on all sides. . . . Long red flashes came from German machine guns. Heavy undergrowth made progress difficult. As I was advancing a boy at my side was shot down by a German machine gun. . . . I will never forget the look on his face as he went down."[50]

Seeing the forward trenches falling into American hands, German units began to fall back, which sealed the fate of the remaining Germans on the farm's north and west sides. Those Germans quickly began to run for the woods to the east, leaving "their guns, rifles and hundreds of boxes of ammunition." The 1st Battalion continued forward to seize the farmhouse and most of the compound.[51] The Germans soon organized a counterattack against the 1st Battalion, and, as the enemy advanced, Major Carroll shouted, "Save your fire men! We'll give 'em hell with the bayonet!" His men ceased firing and waited for the Germans before again fighting them hand-to-hand. The 3rd Battalion soon joined Carroll's men as the Germans withdrew and the farm complex fell into American hands.[52]

On the right, Major Stanley had spent a "terrible hour" watching as his men fell everywhere. He could clearly see every detail of the fighting, and what he saw filled him with dread. When the attack began, F Company was late stepping off because the runner who had the orders to advance had been knocked down twice by exploding shells. The platoon led by Lieutenant Harold Fisher lost ten men while they waited for the signal to go. As Fisher was waiting for the signal to advance, he saw the right flank of M Company from the 167th swing through the left of his platoon and form a skirmish line at the edge of the clearing. Fisher realized that, when M Company moved forward, the Alabamians might be flanked if he did not also move forward and maintain contact with them.[53]

Still without a signal from Captain Casey, Fisher ordered the remaining twenty-five men from his platoon to step out and join the right flank of the Alabamians. His small platoon was immediately hit by a "terrific fire" from German machine guns both at the farm and in the woods to their right. The men hit the ground and began to crawl forward. Fisher realized that they would be cut to pieces if they stayed where they were, so he pushed the men forward, praying "there would be enough of them left to hold on." Fisher's already small line became thinner and thinner as the enemy fire, which "seemed to cover every inch of land and air," took its toll.[54]

When Fisher saw an Alabama lieutenant to his immediate left, he turned toward him and said, "Lieutenant, my men are about all gone, we will join you." But before the young officer from Alabama could reply, a German artillery shell exploded in his midst, killing him instantly. So Lieutenant Fisher quickly assumed command of both the Iowa and Alabama platoons as they pressed their attack toward the farm.[55]

In the meantime, the other three platoons from F Company were approaching the road. As the 167th made its second attack and the German line began to crumble, these Iowans rose up and pressed forward. When the Germans along the roadbed realized they were about to be flanked by the Americans overrunning the farm complex, they abandoned their machine guns and fled across the field to the east toward the temporary safety of the woods. The three platoons from F Company seized their objective and took cover in the shelter provided by the enemy's abandoned trenches. However, Fisher's fourth platoon did not fare so well. When the combined platoons from the 167th and 168th reached the farm, the only survivors from Fisher's platoon were Fisher and one private. The remainder lay in the open field either dead or dying.[56]

As the 167th was finishing the job of clearing the farm complex of Germans, Lieutenant Sharpe of the 167th's K Company set off with eight men in an attempt to follow the fleeing Germans to the woods east of the farm. Lieutenant Fisher decided to join Sharpe's little group, and they started across the open field toward the woods. They only went a few yards when the Germans opened fire from the cover of the trees, hitting Sharpe in the leg. Sharpe told Fisher to assume command, and they pressed on. But Fisher's period of command was brief. After they had advanced another twenty-five or thirty yards, Fisher, himself, was gravely wounded, hit in the face by rifle fire. For several hours, he laid unconscious in the open as the fighting raged around him. When he regained consciousness, the young lieutenant crawled back to the farm where some men from the 167th found him and helped him to the nearby aid station.[57]

As the 168th's 2nd Battalion made their attack, men from Major Worthington's 1st Battalion moved forward behind them in support. But like many others, some of Worthington's men became lost amid the smoke and artillery fire. As Lieutenant John Taber later remembered, "Anyone who was fighting in the Forêt de Fère that day can swear to it that it was not a difficult matter to lose oneself. It was only slightly less dense than a tropical jungle, and the smoke and gas, the latter requiring the wearing of masks, did not make it easier to find the way about."[58] The B Company platoon led by Lieutenant William Witherell had no decent maps, and Witherell had nothing but his army compass to guide him. Soon, however, Witherell was able to determine his location when he and his men reached the Le Charmel road. However, Witherell realized that, instead of being behind 2nd Battalion, he had reached the front line.[59]

As he was trying to figure out his best course of action, he saw French infantry a short distance ahead. The French had found the German defenses along the road too tough to overwhelm, and they had been stopped before they could attempt their turning movement. So Witherell decided

These ruins are all that remains of La Croix Rouge Farm today. (*Major William Carraway, Historian, Georgia Army National Guard*)

to join forces with the French. The combined French and American forces then made a series of rushes forward, driving the Germans out of their position.[60]

As Witherell was stumbling through the smoke and gas, the B Company platoon led by Lieutenant Arthur Whittemore advanced near the opening where the Le Charmel road entered the forest. Like Witherell, Whittemore thought he was behind 2nd Battalion and continued to lead his men into the open with little caution. The German gunners carefully tracked the platoon's movement until the Iowans were right where they wanted them. They opened fire, and Whittemore's men scrambled for cover. The lieutenant rounded up his men, reorganized, and prepared to fight back. Whittemore gathered Sergeant Luis Gonzales and several other noncommissioned officers and started across the road. Sergeant Gonzales was cut down by machine gun fire after taking just a few steps into the open. The remainder of the platoon provided suppressing fire with such an intensity that their rifles were soon almost too hot to grasp, and they quickly ran out of ammunition.[61]

The men from A Company had also become scattered and confused during their advance. Lieutenant James Breslin's platoon found itself with

H Company at the edge of the woods and, while they did not actively engage in the fight, the platoon took numerous casualties from artillery fire and enemy machine guns. The 1st Battalion's rather disorganized efforts stemmed partly from the fact that, throughout the fight, no one could find the battalion commander, Major Worthington. Further, nobody in 1st Battalion knew what their orders were or, in fact, if the Germans "were 500 or 5,000 yards away."[62]

Lieutenant Colonel Bare from the 167th later told the division historian that he had a "rather interesting experience" as Lieutenant Espy's men were mopping up the enemy machine gun nests. Bare was moving forward toward the trenches when he heard a series of single bullets go whizzing past his head. Since the bullets were striking the ground behind him, Bare knew that a German sniper must be in a nearby tree. Bare moved his head backward and forward in an attempt to determine where the shots were coming from and, in the process, the right side of his face came close to a birch tree. As he did so, another shot from the German rifle came whizzing by, striking the tree about six inches from Bare's right jaw and sending bark fragments into his face. His skin was badly blistered and Bare thought for a moment that half his face might be gone. About that time, Espy came running up, telling Bare that he could see the sniper. Without saying another word, the lieutenant raised his rifle and shot the German out of a large oak tree about 100 yards away. Speaking of the incident, Bare said, "That German was a poor shot because he wasted no less than a half-dozen shells trying to hit me."[63]

As the Alabamians and Iowans tried to consolidate their hold on La Croix Rouge Farm, the Germans continued to make trouble. The machine guns in the woods to the east continued to fire on anything in a khaki uniform that moved, and all efforts to silence them failed. The French were in the best position to take them out, but they were unable to do so. The doughboys in the ditch along the road had some protection and could keep their heads down. Those men inside the farm buildings were also fairly safe, but anyone who ventured into the open was literally taking their life into their own hands. So the men in exposed positions or in the woods dug foxholes "feverishly scooped out with tops of mess kits, bayonets, and bare hands"[64] as the enemy bullets whizzed furiously around them.

As the sun began to fall below the western horizon, Lieutenant Colonel Bare of the 167th received a report that the enemy appeared to be moving in on the left flank north of the farm and forming for a counterattack.

He sent a patrol out to confirm the reports, but after about an hour they returned, saying they not only did not see any Germans but they could also not find any sign of the French 167th who were supposed to be holding the left flank. However, not long after the patrol returned and it was dark, the men could clearly hear troops moving in the woods to the north. By this time, many of the men who had been detailed to carry the wounded to the rear had returned and were reporting in to Bare, who had taken up a position at a crossroads about a half mile north of the farmhouse. Bare called for officers to join him and these soldiers to form a provisional company that would defend against any counterattack.[65]

However, he could only find two officers, Captain Mortimer Jordan and Lieutenant Royal Little. Fearing the Germans might be close by, Bare whispered to Little to take charge and form the company as quietly as possible. Almost without a sound, the lieutenant organized the men, and they moved off as though "they had been drilling together for months." After Little's group had gone about a hundred yards, they could see Germans moving in front of them, outlined against the dark, open skyline to the north. Little ordered his men to open fire, and they began to blast away with their rifles at the dim figures ahead of them. The Germans, caught by surprise, immediately fell back, retreating in disorder toward the Ourcq River.[66]

Around 8:00 p.m., Major Stanley of the 168th's 2nd Battalion sent the first of several brief status reports to Colonel Bennett, the regiment commander. "French on the right were held up," he reported, "No advance made." He continued, saying, "Men are digging in. Company E reports 30% casualties. No report from Company F." Forty minutes later, Stanley sent a second report relaying the news that his men had taken the road around 6:00 p.m., adding that the information came from a wounded soldier, as he had still not heard from Captain Casey. The message also said, "Casualties of E, F, and G are quite heavy. Company H was not engaged. I think it impossible to hold the present position."[67]

Stanley's concerns about being able to hold the farm and the road were well founded. The French on the right had withdrawn to the rear about 500 yards, leaving the American right flank completely exposed. While enemy machine gun fire had slackened as it got dark, the Germans once again began to lay down artillery fire over the whole area. As a result, Colonel Screws had withdrawn the men from the 167th back to the edge of the woods west of the farm. This left the 168th holding a salient about 500 yards in advance of the friendly troops on both his right and left. This probably was not a problem as long as it was dark, but when morning came, Stanley's men would not be able to hold the position. So, at 9:30 p.m., he sent another message to Bennett that said, "Captain Casey just here. Reports 50% casualties. Troops should be relieved or withdrawn. Let me know."[68]

Around 11:15 p.m., Stanley got his answer. Colonel Bennett told him, in no uncertain terms, "Brigade directs you to stay where you are, and to inform the 167th of your action and position."[69] Around 1:30 a.m., Stanley moved C Company to protect the battalion's left flank in the gap between F Company and the 167th. Everyone else remained in place with the 2nd Battalion along the road and in the edges of the woods, Major Brewer's 3rd Battalion along the first unimproved road south of the clearing, with D, F, and A Companies about 200 feet forward of the 3rd Battalion. B Company remained with the French off to the right.[70]

It proved to be a long, dark night. German artillery continued to fire throughout the night with a mix of high-explosive rounds and phosgene and tear gas shells. The ground around La Croix Rouge Farm was littered with the bodies of American and German soldiers. Amid a slow, drizzly rain, the moans of the wounded filled the air. Remembering that awful night, John Taber would write that the rain made it seem "as if the skies were weeping in commiseration at their lot."[71]

Lieutenant Colonel Bare described the ground around the farm as being "literally covered with killed and wounded, both American and German. For some distance you could actually walk on dead men."[72] So, as soon as the lines seemed secure for the night, all energies focused on getting the wounded to the closest aid station, which was located by the side of Étang de la Logette, almost three miles to the rear. The Pioneer troops and members of the regimental bands took on much of this job, doggedly trudging over "narrow paths, deep in mud and dissected by water-filled shell holes" to get the stretchers carrying their precious cargo to the aid station. For hours on end, they made round trips to Étang de la Logette amid the rain and enemy shelling, their hands and shoulders blistered and sore from carrying the heavy loads. But not a single man dropped out or asked to be relieved.[73]

Major John Watts, the 16th's regimental surgeon, later provided a written report about the night of July 26–27:

> Night came on and with it rain, the terribly wounded men staggering along through the deep mud and cold water, stretcher bearers slipping and falling with the mutilated and sometimes lifeless bodies they

THE BATTLE FOR LA CROIX ROUGE FARM

carried. . . . The wounded accumulated in great numbers, the aid stations were literally full of them, both Americans and Germans. Those who were unable to walk to the rear were made as comfortable as possible. Many of the wounded lay on the wet ground with practically no protection. The Germans had located us and seeing an ever increasing crowd started a heavy shelling, making two direct hits on the regimental aid post and killing one of the Hospital Corps men while he was in the act of administering morphine to one of his wounded comrades. The wounded were being brought in during the entire night and were evacuated to the rear as rapidly as possible. The assault battalions advanced about a thousand yards and gained their objective at a cost of approximately one casualty for each yard gained. For when the casualty list was completed the following morning, we sent a list to Regimental Headquarters of over 1,100 names of wounded who had passed through the aid stations from 5:30 P.M. July 26 to 7:00 A.M. July 27.[74]

The aid station at Étang de la Logette was located at an old farm by the lake. The surgeons from both regiments worked together with Alabama getting the carriage house and Iowa occupying the four horse stalls. Standard combat triage procedures were the order of the day, with serious cases being treated first as the "walking wounded" stood nearby or sat on the wet ground. Those on stretchers were covered with blankets or raincoats to protect them from the rain and the cold night air, as men were shuttled on and off operating tables. The most serious cases were to be sent by ambulance to the field hospital at Épieds, but there was a serious shortage of ambulances, and the muddy roads between the old farm and the town made the process of getting the critically wounded to the hospital a nightmare. Naturally, the chaplains from both regiments were very busy comforting the wounded and dying. Hearing about the desperate situation at the aid station, the chaplain from Ohio's 166th even came to help out in any way that he could.[75]

It was a hellish night that followed a truly hellish day.

On August 13, 1918, I Corps issued its official report to AEF Headquarters regarding the actions that took place in its command from July 4 to August 14, 1918. Its description of the fighting at La Croix Rouge Farm was shocking in its brevity: "The 84th Brigade attacked at 5 p.m. La Croix-Rouge Farm and machine guns along the Jaulgonne Road were taken. The infantry dug in under heavy fire of gas and H. E. shells as they were unable to go into Vente-Jean-Guillaume Woods."[76]

The fighting at La Croix Rouge Farm had cost the 167th and 168th Infantry Regiments hundreds killed and many more wounded. The 167th's 3rd Battalion lost one of its company commanders killed and two others badly wounded. I Company alone lost 30 men killed and 100 wounded, a casualty rate of more than 50 percent. The three companies of the battalion suffered so many casualties that Major Smith had to reorganize the battalion into two small companies.[77] Major Carroll's 1st Battalion was in even worse shape.

In the 168th, the main assaulting battalion, Major Stanley's 2nd Battalion, there were very few officers left when the sun rose on July 27. Every officer in G Company with the exception of one lieutenant had been either killed or wounded, and there were only seventy men out of more than 200 left standing. In E and F Companies, meanwhile, Captain Casey and four lieutenants were badly wounded, and Captain Springer of H Company was sent to the hospital in Épieds. In total, Stanley's casualties amounted to 13 officers and 292 men, with about 50 of them being killed in action.[78]

While the 1st Battalion was supposed to have been in reserve, it too had been badly hit as its units stumbled into the middle of the fight. One platoon of D Company had sixty-five men when they started out, but roll call on the morning of July 27 showed only nineteen survivors, with the company suffering a total of sixty casualties. B Company had two killed and fifty-nine wounded, A Company suffered two killed and twenty wounded, and C Company had thirteen wounded. The regiment's total losses at La Croix Rouge farm totaled over 500 men.[79]

Yet, for the staffs at I Corps, 42nd Division, and the French Sixth Army, the battle seemed hardly worth noting, and it certainly did nothing to change their minds about the enemy they were pursuing. It is little wonder, therefore, that even years later, many of the officers from the 167th and 168th continued to express their anger at how everyone from the French Sixth Army to the 84th Brigade had mismanaged the fight. The single biggest complaint was the lack of artillery support, which, had it been provided, might have saved many American lives. Lieutenant Colonel Bare later said this about the absence of any artillery support:

> We had expected artillery fire as the order provided that the 51st Field Artillery Brigade would support the attack of the 84th Infantry Brigade and the 101st Field Artillery would support the 167th Infantry. Also, that the artillery preparation for the attack would begin at 2:50 P. M., and that the Infantry would be preceded by an accom-

This dramatic sculpture of an American doughboy carrying the body of a dead comrade was erected next to the ruins of La Croix Rouge Farm in July 2018 as a memorial to the men of the 42nd Division who fought there. (*Major William Carraway, Historian, Georgia Army National Guard*)

panying barrage which would move 200 meters in advance of the Infantry, at the same rate of advance, and that it would be held stationary beyond the normal objective. Apparently, the artillery never received their orders as there was no American artillery fired on the Croix Rouge Farm positions.[80]

Bare would add that he believed the "orders for the attack on the Croix Rouge farm were prepared too hastily and apparently without definite knowledge of the location and strength of the enemy." Further, he stated that there was not sufficient time allowed from the issue of the attack order to the jump-off time, which led to poor coordination among the assaulting units. Also, he again raised the fact that, while General Brown's orders called for artillery preparation, there was none. "Had they secured the artillery support as provided for in the order," he said, "no doubt the casualties would have been very materially lessened."[81]

Major Dallas Smith was even more succinct: "It is difficult for me to comment on the Croix Rouge Farm for the reason that I have always felt, and I know that our own Regimental Commander, as well as Colonel

Bennett, who commanded the Iowa Regiment, felt that it would be a sacrifice of troops to make an attack through these woods without some artillery."[82]

The losses at La Croix Rouge Farm would have been bad enough in and of themselves had it not been for the fact that there would be no respite for the men who survived the fight. Now, they and the rest of the Rainbow Division would be dispatched to continue the pursuit of the Germans, who had fallen back to prepared defensive positions on the high ground north of the Ourcq River.

There was nothing ahead but more brutal fighting and much more death.

6

THE ADVANCE TO THE OURCQ

July 27, 1918

"Through the long, shivering hours the enemy batteries on the heights across the river searched the hillside and valley for victims. Wherever the men lay, scattered over that big field, the enemy seemed to find them. German shells, shrieking like Valkyries come to bear their dead off to Valhalla, crashed in endless succession, until the constant hammering shook the nerves to the point of madness."
—John Taber, *The Story of the 168th Infantry Regiment*

The Iowans arrived in the wheat fields south of the Ourcq River first, with one battalion of New York's 165th coming up on their left shortly thereafter. What they saw shocked them. The Germans were not running across the river in a desperate attempt to escape the American advance as the Rainbow's men had been told. Rather, they were ready for a fight—a blind man could see that.

While one could not make out the Germans' precise locations, they could clearly be seen moving about the ridges and hills above the river as they scurried among their well-concealed machine gun emplacements. But worst of all, from those heights, the enemy had a clear view of the fields and roads approaching the river that stretched for miles. Every move the Iowans and New Yorkers made could be seen by German artillery observers who quickly called in massive barrages from their heavy guns—guns the French and American command staffs were convinced had been withdrawn north of the Vesle River and out of range.

As a result, when the Iowans came into view moving northeast toward the river and Hill 212 beyond, the German's "long arm" opened fire with both ferocity and accuracy. The advancing Americans were ripped apart as they scattered to find whatever cover there might be, which was not much—a shallow indentation in the ground here, a stream bed there, or the holes made by the incoming shells. Cries and screams for stretcher bearers filled the hot afternoon air as the German high explosives rained down.

The fight for the Ourcq River had begun.

The firing had barely died down at La Croix Rouge Farm when I Corps issued a field order at 1:10 a.m. on July 27, informing its units that an attack across the Ourcq River was anticipated for the night of July 27–28 using elements of the 42nd Division, which, after the 83rd Brigade moved into place to relieve the French 164th Division, would soon be responsible for the entire front of I Corps. At that time, the staff at I Corps believed the main axis of attack would be made by American columns that would move both to the east and to the west of the Château-de-Forêt and the Forêt-de-Fère.[1]

Just over eight hours later, the corps headquarters disseminated General Order 51, which was based on guidance from the French Sixth Army and provided a further detailed plan of attack. It directed that the 42nd Division be prepared to attack "under cover of darkness on the night of July 27/28" at a time that would be communicated later. The objective of the attack was to capture the area north of the Ourcq River from the Meurcy Farm southeast to Hill 212, a distance of about two miles. At the same time, the French 52nd Division of the French VII Corps would attack to the right of the Americans, and the French 39th Division from the French XXXVIII Corps would advance on the left. The boundaries between the 42nd Division and the 39th Division would be on a line just east of the town of Fère-en-Tardenois, which lay about a mile and a half west of the Meurcy Farm. In contrast, the eastern boundary with the French 52nd Division ran along a line just to the east of Hill 212.[2]

The alignment of the Rainbow Division's two brigades was to be the 84th Brigade on the right with the 168th Infantry to the far right and the 167th Infantry on its left. The 83rd Brigade, meanwhile, would move on the left of the I Corps front with the 165th Infantry just to the left of the 167th and the 166th Infantry coming up on the far left. I Corps also pro-

Casualties from the fighting at La Croix Rouge Farm being processed at the division field hospital in Épieds on July 27, 1918. (*National Archives*)

vided the 149th Machine Gun Battalion and 51st Field Artillery to support the 84th Brigade, while the 67th Field Artillery Brigade supported the 83rd Brigade.[3] However, once again, while these orders prescribed artillery support, the artillery would not be on the scene when it was needed most.

However, the most infamous part of the order called for an infantry attack using only the bayonet: "This attack will be in the nature of a surprise and consequently, troops in the attack will not fire during the assault but will confine themselves to the bayonet."[4] Not long after General Order 51 was sent, 42nd Division Headquarters issued a secret memorandum at 10:45 a.m., postponing the attack and directing the 83rd Infantry Brigade to complete the relief of both the 157th and 164th French Divisions. But the most intriguing part of the memorandum followed in a paragraph that read, "The statements of captured prisoners would seem to indicate that the enemy is withdrawing. Those elements of the division now on the line are directed to follow up his retirement with the greatest possible energy and to establish contact."[5]

In other words, the 42nd Division, I Corps, and the French Sixth Army were still operating based on the delusion of a beaten enemy fighting only with rear-guard forces. This despite all the information on the stiff resistance of the enemy at Épieds and La Croix Rouge Farm. The Germans were still making a carefully planned and executed withdrawal, defending positions selected for their natural advantages. As one historian would write, "Nature had made the Ourcq as if to order for a defensive position. The Germans with the keen eyes of well-trained soldiers had not failed to notice it, even before they found the necessity to use it."[6]

The Germans still intended to fall back to a new front line of resistance on the heights above the Vesle River. In fact, on July 27, the German Supreme Headquarters was already planning a final withdrawal for the night of August 1–2.[7] The positions along this line had stopped Allied attacks before, particularly in the spring of 1917 when the French and British suffered more than 300,000 casualties assaulting the Germans there. But they still needed a few days to get the men and supplies behind this new line on the Vesle, and they hoped the hills above the Ourcq River would give them that time.[8]

The hills that confronted the Rainbow Division extended from Hill 212 on the right to Hill 184 on the left. The defensive front on these hills followed the curve of the Ourcq River, which changed course from running almost due north to practically due west after it passed Fère-en-Tardenois. This meant the German defensive line curved inward, causing two problems for the Rainbow Division, both of which were unfavorable to the Americans.

First, German machine guns would not only be able to fire to their immediate front and flanks but would also be capable of engaging targets at a considerable distance to either their right or left. For example, the enemy's guns on the crest of Hill 212 could not only fire on the approaches to the town of Sergy but also engage American infantry moving south of the river well to either their right or northwest of Sergy.[9]

The other problem for the men of the division was that, even if all four regiments advanced at once, the inward curve of the German line meant they could not move forward in parallel, covering each other's flanks. Instead, they would have to attack in different directions as if they were starting from the hub of a wheel down four different spokes. So the farther they advanced, the more separated the regiments would become, allowing the Germans to pour an enfilading fire into their flanks.[10]

This all was worsened because the Germans skillfully employed everything they had learned about using the machine gun during four years of war. They placed every weapon to take advantage of the terrain and the fact that the gunners would have an unobstructed view from the high ground of the attacking American infantry, watching them approach for hundreds of yards. They also hid their guns using the wheat fields, woods, and undulating terrain along with extensive camouflage in the form of straw and tree branches. It was an almost perfect defensive position.

While the 84th Brigade had been so heavily engaged at La Croix Rouge Farm, their comrades in the 83rd Brigade continued the process of moving forward to replace and relieve French units on the left of the I Corps front. The 166th Infantry began its advance to fill in the left flank of the Rainbow Division in the early morning hours of July 25. Earlier on July 24, Colonel Benson Hough, the regiment's commander, received orders from the 83rd Brigade to form the regiment and await further orders. The colonel apparently decided to wait as long as possible to interrupt the men's reverie because Leon Miesse from the 3rd Battalion's L Company recorded that he was not told about the orders until he was awakened and told to get his company ready to move at 4:00 a.m. on July 25.[11] When the regiment was prepared in the early afternoon, Hough was told that trucks would arrive shortly to take them to a point just south of Épieds, some five miles to the northeast of Château-Thierry. However, the trucks did not arrive until 4:00 p.m., and the congestion caused by men and vehicles made for a slow trip.[12]

Corporal Dana Daniels of E Company in the 2nd Battalion described the trip to Épieds in his diary, writing, ". . .we passed thru a country here that was badly torn up and had been hard fought for. Here is where we began to see the real horrors of war, dead horses, cattle, & dogs and a number of dead Germans lying on the battlefield." He recorded that the regiment passed thru Château-Thierry about 7:00 p.m. on July 25 where "barricades were still in the streets," and German weapons were scattered everywhere.[13]

Another soldier wrote about passing through Château-Thierry, saying the traffic was worse than any he had seen, including New York City. "I never saw such traffic in any city," he wrote. "New York at its busiest corner could never produce the traffic that one corner of Château-Thierry had that day! Lines of motor trucks miles long, filled with men—miles and miles of big tractors pulling the big guns up—miles of wagon trains— miles of ammunition trains." At one point, all the roads into the town converged. It took three military policemen to keep things moving. But, like Dana Daniels, he also noted the signs of destruction, which he called "ghastly." There were "ruined homes and "ruthless destruction" that left the town "a scene of desolation." "Household goods all over the streets," he wrote, "trees down, buildings torn to pieces, marks of rifle and machine gun bullets on everything, old barricades built in every alley and narrow street—everything pointing to a terrible struggle that ended with the hurried departure of the German army."[14] The regiment was finally offloaded just outside Bezu-Saint-Germain, about two miles west of Épieds, and, as the rain began to fall, they marched through the forest of Bois de l'Hermitage where the men camped for the night.[15]

The next day, July 26, after Colonel Hough and his three battalion commanders made a reconnaissance, the 166th relieved the 170th French Infantry, who were in reserve positions in the Bois de Beuvardelle Moucheton and Bois de l'Hermitage. Colonel Hough then established his PC at Courpoil, but he moved it later that evening to Beuvardes.[16]

That night, orders came in from the brigade, telling Hough to move his men forward toward the front as part of the 42nd Division's relief of the French 164th Division. The regiment's 1st Battalion marched along the Beauvardes-Preaux Farm road until it reached the northern edge of the Forêt-de-Fère around 10:00 p.m., with 2nd Battalion and 3rd Battalion forming lines behind them.[17] The night was extremely dark, and the battalions traveled cross-country for the most part, using nothing but the stars and the compass to find their way. Colonel Hough was very relieved to find them where they were supposed to be the following morning.[18]

Meanwhile, Colonel Hough and his orderly left Beuvardes to establish a forward PC at the Château-de-Forêt where the brigade PC was located. The night was extremely dark, and Hough later said the trek to the Château-de-Forêt "was made with great trepidation and uncertainty." At one point, Hough stopped to ask directions and was told to continue on the same road until he and his orderly arrived at a crossroads whose identifying marks would be "nine dead horses." Then, they should turn left for two or three kilometers, where they could find the château on the left. Hough and his orderly did, indeed, find the dead horses in the dark and arrived safely at the château around 2:00 a.m.[19]

Just before sunrise on July 27, Hough conferred with General Lenihan in the yard outside the château. Lenihan told Hough that the 165th Infantry was deployed directly in front of the château to the north toward the Ourcq, which was about two miles away. The general then waved his left arm to the northwest and said, "Put your regiment in over there."[20]

Years later, Hough would tell historian Henry Reilly that Lenihan's almost causal wave of his arm was "the sum total of the operations orders

Soldiers from the division march past the Château-de-Forêt where the Post of Commands for both the 83rd Brigade and 166th Infantry Regiment were located. (*National Archives*)

received by me and conveyed to the battalions of my regiment" during the entire eight days of the Aisne-Marne Offensive.[21] Given the scope of operations and the intensity of combat that would cost Hough's regiment alone more than one thousand casualties, this seems absolutely incredible. It also says something about the lack of experience and military knowledge among American commanders that the entire AEF was forced to deal with.

So Hough headed to find his men and tell the 1st Battalion to move in "over there" in the general direction of where Lenihan had waved his arm with the 2nd Battalion about 500 yards behind them in support. What lay ahead as they neared the Ourcq was uncertain, and their move toward that uncertainty began late on the night of July 27 amid a driving rainstorm. Company B of the 1st Battalion led the way and halted at the edge of the Forêt-de-Fère. Unknown to them, the Germans had left a few soldiers behind to act as observers. Hidden in the dense woods, when these Germans saw B Company moving forward, they called in artillery fire. Suddenly, the men of B Company heard the frightening shriek of enemy shells streaming toward them. Explosions began to erupt everywhere because, since the Germans had used the forest to store their own supplies and ammunition a few days before, every inch of the woods was carefully registered—they knew exactly where to place their shots.[22]

One of the first incoming shells exploded amid a group of soldiers, knocking one of them unconscious. When that soldier managed to shake off the buzzing in his skull, he stood up and found that he was uninjured. However, the other twenty-one men in his group had been killed by the blast. Another soldier, Sergeant Paul Jackson, showed remarkable courage and leadership. While everyone else was looking for cover, he took charge and led efforts to make sure the wounded were attended to and sent to the rear. His coolness under fire led to a battlefield commission. In total, the company would suffer 125 casualties that night.[23]

The next morning, as the first fighting was beginning far to the 166th's right, the 1st Battalion could finally see the Ourcq River some two miles away. From the edge of the forest, the ground sloped gently down to the river's edge. During those two miles before reaching the riverbanks, there were no hollows, no natural features of any kind to provide cover against observation by the enemy, much less protection from artillery and machine gun fire. Therefore, when the regiment's men would be asked to attack across the river, the Germans would see them coming immediately and could begin mounting a defense long before they reached the riverbanks.[24]

As the Ohioans were moving up, the New Yorkers of the 165th Infantry were going through a similar process. The regiment spent the night of July 26 at Courpoil while their commanding officer, Colonel Frank McCoy, established his PC at Épieds. On the morning of July 27, McCoy was informed by French officers that their cavalry had detected the Germans withdrawing to the other side of the Ourcq. The colonel immediately made a telephone call to Colonel MacArthur, the division chief of staff, who told McCoy that all the general officers in the division had gone to a conference at French Sixth Army Headquarters, which made McCoy the senior officer in the Rainbow Division at that moment. McCoy responded by telling MacArthur that he would order the 165th to begin moving toward the Ourcq immediately. He asked the French cavalry and armored cars to keep in touch with the Germans as they withdrew to the north.

Around 2:00 p.m., all three battalions of the 165th were heading up the road toward Villers-sur-Fère, with two on the right and one on the left. The road north from Épieds went through the Forêt-de-Fère to the Ferme de l'Espérance and the Château-de-Forêt. Just north of the château were the adjacent villages of La Folie and Villers-sur-Fère. In the 3rd Bat-

THE ADVANCE TO THE OURCQ 121

Men from the 165th Infantry Regiment move forward toward the Ourcq River. (*National Archives*)

talion, Martin Hogan recalled that the road was "almost untravellable" that day because it was jammed with trucks and artillery. As they marched, the men passed "dead Germans, dead horses, and ruined villages and farms all along the line." Finally, about 6:00 p.m., the 3rd Battalion stopped for the night by a lone house on a hill near Villers-sur-Fère. The men were amused by the fact that the Germans had left a sign on the house saying, "*Munchener Bier hier*," or "Munich Beer here."[25]

The Germans must have noticed Hogan and the rest of his battalion on the hill because they began to lob artillery shells at them. Major James McKenna, the battalion commander, ordered the men into a battle formation of platoon columns, and they set off at a quickened pace down the hill toward the shelter of some nearby woods. As they neared the tree line, the German guns slowed their firing, and soon, "the whole countryside seemed all at once to take on quite a peaceful air." Once the battalion was in the woods, McKenna ordered them to dig foxholes and settle in for the night. As the enemy guns drew silent, Hogan and his comrades crawled into their respective holes and rested.[26]

The 1st Battalion, commanded by Major William "Wild Bill" Donovan, had initially relieved the French west of Beuvardes before advancing through Forêt-de-Fère to the crest of a small hill overlooking the river between Villers-sur-Fère and Sergy. Donovan, who would later command the regiment and then go on to serve as the head of the American Office of Strategic Services in World War II, advanced his men out into the open to the Ourcq River's edge. Here, they found themselves alone except for some French cavalry. The Germans opened fire on the cavalrymen, who immediately fell back to the cover of some woods. Seeing the French taking fire convinced Donovan that remaining in the open was not a good idea. So the major wisely pulled the battalion back to the far side of the slope where it was protected from observation by trees and the terrain and ordered the men to dig in for the night.[27]

With the 1st Battalion dug in northeast of Villers-sur-Fère and the 3rd Battalion in place just outside the town in the woods, the 2nd Battalion was held in reserve in the woods to the left of the road leading into the town. As night fell, Colonel McCoy established the 165th's PC in a church near the northern end of Villers-sur-Fère and awaited orders.[28]

On the far right of the corps front, the morning of July 27 found the 167th and 168th recovering from the previous day's brutal fighting at La Croix Rouge Farm. Lieutenant John Taber of the 168th recalled that the morning brought a "sudden stillness" to the fields around the farm. The Germans seemed to have disappeared, and French cavalry scouts pressed forward to the northern end of the Vente-Jean-Guillaume woods, sending back reports that the Germans were moving steadily across the Ourcq River. With this news, Taber later wrote, "The stage was set for the curtain to rise on the second act of the drama."[29]

The first part of the morning was spent reorganizing both regiments and continuing the evacuation of the wounded. The stretcher bearers, who had worked all night, continued their duties by searching the trampled grain in the fields around the farm for any wounded that may have been missed and carried those they found back to the aid station. Finally, by the afternoon, the last patients at the aid station were loaded onto ambulances and sent back to the field hospital in Épieds. That left only the living and the dead, the latter of whom were scattered about the woods and the fields. Those who had been killed were gathered together, and the two regimental chaplains oversaw their burial next to the farm complex.[30]

At 10:30 a.m., Colonel Bennett, the 168th's commanding officer, sent his three battalion commanders a message telling them that the regiment would soon be moving forward again. Around noon, Bennett arrived at the farm to meet with his battalion commanders. He told them that the 1st Battalion would lead the regiment, followed by the 3rd and 2nd Battalions.[31]

At 2:00 p.m., the regiment was ready to move out, and the battalions were formed in a column of twos at the point where the Le Charmel Road entered the forest south of the farm. At first, there seemed to be some delay getting Major Worthington's 1st Battalion moving. General Brown, the 84th Brigade commander, rode up on horseback about this time, and, seeing the delay, ordered Major Guy Brewer's 3rd Battalion to move into line to the left of the 1st Battalion and lead the regiment. As the men came abreast of the farm complex, Brown told Brewer, "Push on as fast as you can. You are to gain the Ourcq, secure the heights beyond and hold them."[32] Unknown to Brown or any other Allied soldier, the Germans were already dug in on those heights in force and waiting for the Americans.

As the first two battalions moved out, they found the fields next to the road muddy from the recent rainfall. Even though the men were only carrying their own weapons and ammunition, it was hard going as they plodded through the mud. So far, however, there had been no German reaction to their presence on the road. But everyone could hear the distinct rumble of German artillery off in the distance to the east where the French and the American 3rd Division were moving on Courmont and Ronchères, and they expected the enemy would open up on them soon. For now, however, the men laughed and joked, which was, of course, "mere camouflage to conceal uneasiness."[33]

As the regiment turned on the road that led northeast toward Sergy and the Ourcq, they passed the La Croix Blanche Farm and moved into a long stretch of open, rolling prairie with the hills beyond the Ourcq now clearly visible. For some reason, the 3rd Battalion found itself moving ahead of the 1st Battalion. Whether this was because orders had been changed or, as usual, Major Worthington of the 1st Battalion "didn't know what he was about," no one will ever know. No sooner had the the 3rd Battalion passed the farm when a line of flashes was seen on the hills above the Ourcq. The men soon heard the "shriek of speeding steel, and then the sound of tearing flesh, louder even, it seemed, than the explosion of the shells" as they landed in their midst. The regiment began to move faster now as the German guns continued to hammer them.[34]

The Germans, of course, had a clear view from the high ground north of the river, and their shells seemed to have the "range down to an inch." When the first shell landed, it killed ten men. John Taber later wrote about these terrifying moments as the 168th kept pressing forward:

One would see the blinking flame from the gun, hear the approaching shell, and drop to the ground to avoid the force of the explosion. If he were lucky, he received nothing more than a shaking-up and a shower of mud. But the cries of the wounded and the appeals for stretchers that were taken up and passed to the rear told tragic stories. At each burst the soldiers' gaze would stray to the smoking spot. What comrade had gone this time? That was the question that always came first. Khaki figures darting to the newly made crater, a limp form lifted on the canvas litter, and another perilous journey commenced—then eyes again to the front.[35]

One shell that landed in the wheat fields wounded Private Floyd Wallace. His corporal, Vinton Bradshaw, who John Taber said was "an exceptionally fine man," ran to Wallace's aid. But just as he reached the private, another incoming shell exploded nearby, killing them both.[36]

The French cavalry was also taking fire from the German artillery above the river. A detachment that had been reconnoitering ahead of the 168th began receiving fire. One of the first shells exploded next to a chasseur à cheval. The explosion blew the Frenchman off his horse but, miraculously, neither he nor his horse was injured. He calmly remounted and continued on. However, another German shell then exploded, severing the legs of another horse, a "magnificent black charger." As the horse fell, the rider leaped from his back, and then, risking his life as the shells continued to fall around him, the French cavalryman stayed to mercifully end his mount's life by shooting him in the head before proceeding forward on foot.[37]

The 1st Battalion and 3rd Battalion continued their parallel advance, but soon, a low ridge separated the two columns. As the 1st Battalion approached the crest of a hill near the La Cense Farm, a German aircraft appeared overhead. It dived down on the Americans, who immediately scattered for cover. The plane began dropping bombs on the battalion, with the first one exploding just ahead of D Company and the second bomb hitting the 1st Platoon. As the company commander, Captain Haynes, watched in horror, Lieutenant Peyton was blown high into the air by the blast. Remarkably, Peyton was not killed, only wounded. However, the 3rd Platoon was not so fortunate. The third bomb landed squarely in their midst, killing an entire squad of eight men.[38]

The 3rd Battalion tried to gain some cover by shifting to the left on the road that cut through the northern tip of the forest. To their left, they could see Major Donovan's battalion from the 165th advancing across a plateau. The Germans were also firing on them, but their gunners were having a more challenging time hitting a moving line in open formation.[39]

Major Brewer now led the battalion toward the La Favière Farm, which was less than a mile from the bridge across the Ourcq where they were to cross. Despite the nearby danger posed by the Germans, some of the men could not help but notice how beautiful the countryside was. John Taber described it as being filled with "rippling seas of burnished wheat, in what the French call *un paysage riant*—a smiling landscape—variegated fields of grain, brightened with touches of poppies, corn flowers, and daisies; feathery, Corotesque trees lining the streams that cut in between the full-breasted hills." In the distance, he could see a "chaste spire" here or there, "peeping over the bosom of the rise" beneath "an azure sky flecked with fleecy clouds." [40] It was probably hard to believe there was a war raging amidst such pastoral beauty.

But there was a war on, and the 3rd Battalion's immediate objective in the war was to secure the bridge over the Ourcq. Major Brewer sent Lieutenant John Christopher of M Company ahead with some scouts to see if the bridge was still intact and, if not, to determine if the river could be forded. It was approaching dusk as Christopher and his scouts moved forward. At the same time, the remainder of the battalion halted about 300 yards from the bridge. As they waited for Christopher's report, Brewer noticed Major Donovan's battalion from the 165th falling back from the river.[41]

About that time, the lieutenant returned after having drawn heavy artillery and machine gun fire as he approached the river crossing. He told Brewer that the Germans had demolished the bridge but that the river was fordable. However, he added, based on the fire he received at the crossing, any attempt to ford would be "difficult and costly." Brewer thought for a moment and then said, "We will cross." The major ordered the rest of the battalion forward with M Company in the lead, followed by K Company, then I and L Companies bringing up the rear.[42]

The German observers on the high ground north of the river saw the American battalion deploying to advance across the Ourcq immediately and opened fire with both artillery and machine guns. As they cut swaths through the waist-high wheat, Brewer's men began to fall. "The whole valley was reverberating with the crash of explosions," John Taber remembered, "flying pieces of steel tore through the air and buried themselves in the soft earth with dull thuds, and wounded were struggling back." The battalion's Chauchat riflemen crawled forward to provide covering fire, and the men prepared to cross the Ourcq.[43]

But before they got into the water, Major Brewer received a message from Donovan telling him that the New Yorkers were withdrawing so American artillery could lay down a barrage on the hills beyond the Ourcq and silence the enemy's machine guns. While the American artillery support never materialized, Brewer realized that Donovan's withdrawal would leave his entire left flank exposed, making his position untenable. He ordered his men to withdraw about 500 yards to a position behind a hill opposite the La Favière Farm and sent a dispatch to Major Worthington to let him know his plans.[44]

As Brewer's battalion had been trying to force a river crossing, the 1st Battalion was getting nowhere. The enemy had hit them hard with a ceaseless artillery barrage just as they approached the La Cense Farm. Worthington's men had taken cover along the banks of a small creek, the Rû de la Goulée, and in the smoking shell holes being created by the enemy's artillery fire. Once again, no one could find Major Worthington at this crucial moment. Captain Haynes called a conference of company commanders. With the major missing, they had neither maps nor orders. So they decided to fall back fifty yards where they could hide from the enemy's view in a wheat field.[45]

The Germans followed the retreat with a fusillade of high-explosive and gas shells, the latter sending two of the 1st Battalion's officers to the rear, badly gassed. At that moment, as the battalion found some shelter, Major Worthington appeared out of nowhere, seeming "exhausted and terrified." Major Brewer, who had been trying to get Worthington's battalion in some sort of order, had been yelling at Lieutenant Taber to get his company together. Upon seeing Worthington and noticing his befuddled behavior, Brewer ordered Taber to dig a foxhole for Worthington. Taber said nothing in reply, but as Brewer walked away, the lieutenant, clearly disgusted with his battalion commander's apparent cowardice, decided to "let Worthington hunt a hole for himself."[46]

While the other two battalions had been advancing, Major Stanley's 2nd Battalion had remained in the woods southeast of La Croix Rouge Farm until nightfall. They moved under cover of darkness without difficulty, reaching a point along a creek in the Vente-Jean-Guillaume woods, where they camped for the night.[47]

Colonel Bennett moved his PC forward as well, and the regiment remained dug in for the night of July 27–28. The men had not slept for the better part of three nights, and no one would get any sleep this night, either. Some men would later say that this night was the worst one of the war. The

German artillery continued its barrage all night long. Their shells hammered the fields south of the Ourcq, shaking men's nerves "to the point of madness." Men huddled in either shell holes or hastily dug fox holes as the explosions seemed to creep nearer and nearer to where they lay. John Taber described the experience by saying, "First one in front, hurling bits of mud and stone into the shallow foxholes; then one just beyond. An eternity of agonized suspense until the next one broke." Every few minutes, they would hear someone call out frantically for a stretcher bearer, making them "shudder with its piercing note of anguish and terror." Some of the men became so desperate for protection that they abandoned their foxholes for the bed of the nearby creek. It may have been cold and muddy, but it appeared to offer more shelter. Just before dawn, the Germans seemed to tire of their game and ceased fire, giving the Iowans an "ephemeral respite."[48]

Like the Iowans of the 168th Infantry, the Alabamians of the 167th were a badly damaged group of soldiers at dawn on July 27. Their unit historian would later say that, as the sun came up that day, "after a miserable night, everyone felt so dejected and let down it seemed that any further advance on the regiment's part would be impossible."[49] But like the 168th, they would soon receive orders to move north from La Croix Rouge Farm toward the Ourcq. During the morning, Major Carroll and Major Smith set about combining the survivors of the 1st and 3rd Battalions into a single battalion. Things were so bad that one officer, Lieutenant Maurice Howe, had to take command of the remaining soldiers from I, K, and L Companies, a total of only 210 men from what normally would have been a combined total of over 600. At the same time, Captain Ravee Norris took command of another unit that consisted of M Company and everybody else who remained standing.[50]

Around 2:00 p.m., Colonel Screws received the same orders as Colonel Bennett from the 84th Brigade, telling him to move his tired and demoralized soldiers toward a new round of fighting. Their march turned out to be a little less hazardous than that of the 168th to their right. Major Everett Jackson's 2nd Battalion led the way, as they had seen the least fighting at La Croix Rouge Farm, with the tattered remains of 1st and 3rd Battalions coming up behind them. They marched up the Le Charmel-Fère-en-Tardenois road, but Screws had his men peel off to either side and trek through the Forêt-de-Fère, which gave them some cover from enemy observers. The Germans did send a few shells in their general direction around dusk, but no one was hurt. Once the regiment was past the Forêt-de-Fère, they turned slightly to the northeast and continued onward.[51]

Lieutenant Colonel Bare led the advanced regimental PC team and pushed forward toward the river until orders came in from division headquarters telling them to stop short of the Ourcq. So the 2nd Battalion made camp in the open fields east of Villers-sur-Fère along a small creek, while the 1st and 2nd Battalions encamped in the northern edge of the Forêt-de-Fère.[52] Officers from brigade headquarters soon arrived to tell Colonel Screws that the 167th's sector was the wheat fields directly north of L'Espérance Farm, with his right flank boundary about 600 yards west of Sergy. The left flank, meanwhile, would connect with the 165th Infantry, meaning that the entire wheat field to the Alabamians' front was theirs to clear.[53]

As the men made camp in the fields and woods near Villers-sur-Fère, most of them were getting their first rest in days. Private Hayes of I Company later wrote, "For the first time in three days and nights we had the chance to stretch out on the ground for much needed sleep and rest. We had no sleep from the time we boarded trucks near Paris to go to the front until we reached the Ourcq River. Thus, we had no sleep from the morning of the 24th of July till the early morning hours of the 28th."[54]

But while the regiment was bedding down for the night, Sergeant Sidney Blasingame of E Company made a most interesting discovery. His lieutenant had sent him and a small patrol of five men to reconnoiter through the wheat fields toward the river. As they left the safety of the woods, Blasingame heard someone moving nearby. He signaled his men to advance toward the sounds cautiously. In a few minutes, they came upon fifteen men sleeping in several shell holes. Figuring they were Germans, the sergeant and his patrol decided to capture them. However, to their great surprise, when they rushed the shell holes, the first soldier they encountered cried out at them in English. It turned out they were soldiers from New England's 26th Division. How they got all the way to the Ourcq River is anyone's guess. Blasingame told them that their division had been relieved two days before at LaCroix Rouge Farm, and they better get on back to their units as soon as possible. Hearing that, the New Englanders immediately gathered up their gear and headed for the safety of the rear.[55]

A new day was coming, one that would see the worst bloodshed of the war for the men of the Rainbow.

7

CROSSING THE OURCQ

July 28, 1918

"With the night came rain. The woods and valleys were drenched
with gas. The troops established bridge heads and hung on. . . ."
—Major Walter B. Wolf, *A Brief Story of the Rainbow Division*

Just after dawn on July 28, 1918, the sun was beginning to rise brightly
over the eastern horizon behind Hill 212, a "dome-like eminence"[1] that
stood about 300 feet above and to the northeast of the little valley formed
by the Ourcq River. Calling the Ourcq a river was quite a compliment
from the French because it was, in reality, little more than a stream. The
Germans had destroyed the small bridge that had once crossed the river,
so the men of the 3rd Battalion of the 168th Infantry would have to cross
the river by fording it on foot. Quietly and slowly, they crept into the
waist-high waters of the Ourcq with their rifles held at high port.

Shortly before dawn, the battalion commander, Major Guy Brewer,
had received a single-sentence order from Colonel Bennett, the regiment
commander. Bennett had written the order, such as it was, on the back of
a piece of paper in pencil. All it said was, "Cross the river and seize the
heights beyond."[2] Brewer had immediately formed the battalion, placed
K Company in the lead, and began advancing to the riverbanks near the
old bridge. Luckily, as the men crept across the river, the little river valley
was filled with a dense early morning fog, which screened their movements from the German machine gunners who waited for them on the
far side on the crest of Hill 212. However, at the same time, Brewer and

his men could see "the surrounding country as one standing concealed in the dark looks into the light." As a result, they saw the Germans moving about the top of the hill, carrying ammunition to the guns on the hill's forward slope. They "seemed feverish in their haste." This indicated that, while they might not be able to clearly see the advancing Americans, they sensed their presence and were preparing a deadly greeting.[3]

As the Iowans started to emerge from the mist enveloping the Ourcq, the rising sun caught the men's bayonets, glinting brightly and signaling the Germans to open fire. At first, one only heard an isolated "rat-tat—rat-tat-tat" sound. But, within only a few seconds, that sound changed into an "overwhelming crackle that sounded like a wind-whipped forest fire striking dry timber."[4] There should have been American artillery support to help silence the enemy machine guns, but, once again, there was none. Most of the artillery was miles to the rear, mired in the muddy roads leading to the Ourcq, and the rest had received conflicting orders on where to go and which units to support.

The attack could have waited, but General Degoutte was still insisting on pressing the supposed fleeing enemy. However, Major Brewer and his men could plainly see that these Germans were determined defenders, not a broken, retreating foe.

As soon as the Germans began firing, Brewer's men immediately dropped to the ground, returning fire with their Chauchats and Springfield rifles. As the German machine guns swept the little valley at the foot of the hill, the 3rd Battalion began to take casualties, leaving the ground "dotted with fast stiffening forms."[5] But the Iowans never hesitated as they crawled and clawed their way up Hill 212.

The bloody advance across the Ourcq River was underway.

During the night of July 27–28, orders began to filter down to the four American regiments now facing the Ourcq River. General Lenihan at 83rd Brigade received a message from Colonel MacArthur that contained an order from I Corps to make an attack across the river before daylight. The attack was not going to receive any artillery support, and it was hoped that the assault would have the advantage of surprise. Lenihan immediately relayed the orders to his regiments, and the same process occurred in the 84th Brigade.[6]

About midnight, Colonel Blanton Winship from I Corps arrived at the 165th's PC and gave Colonel McCoy the orders. McCoy later said that the

This contemporary photo shows the view looking south from Hill 212 and clearly shows the German's commanding view of the approaches to the river. The line of trees in the foreground indicates the location of the Ourcq River. (*Major William Carraway, Historian, Georgia Army National Guard*)

orders from the French Sixth Army specified that the attack would take place that night, regardless of the conditions. The objective was to seize the high ground north of the Ourcq between the towns of Seringes-et-Nesles and Nesles. Since the 165th was the only regiment in the 83rd Brigade positioned to immediately cross the river, General Lenihan gave Colonel McCoy the orders to lead the advance.[7]

McCoy pointed out to Winship that, while the 167th was nearby on his right, there was no one to support his left. So he requested that the 166th be ordered forward to cover the regiment's left flank. He also insisted on artillery support but was told that the orders had to be carried out immediately to keep the Germans moving and prevent them from digging in on the heights above the river.[8] Of course, unknown to anyone at higher headquarters, the enemy was already dug in across the river. As for keeping the Germans moving toward the Vesle, they were still doing that all on their own.

Since the 3rd Battalion was closest to the river, McCoy decided it would lead the attack with the 2nd Battalion in close support and the 1st Battalion in reserve. He then ordered the Supply Company, Sanitary Detachment, and Headquarters Company to move forward to the Château-de-Fère. He sent orders to the 2nd and 1st Battalions via messenger and left with Colonel Winship to deliver the orders to the 3rd Battalion in person.[9]

When he arrived in the woods outside Villers-sur-Fère where the 3rd Battalion was camped, he discovered almost the entire command sound asleep. He woke Major McKenna, his captains, and a French major who was attached to the battalion. Once they were all awake and gathered, McCoy told them their orders and then gave them all the information he had, which was not much. This would be yet another attack made with almost no information about the German defenses, their disposition, or their strength. McKenna told McCoy what information he had been able to gather about the river crossings. While the major thought the water was fordable, the French officer added that his own cavalry had found the river strongly defended, and a successful crossing without proper artillery support was highly unlikely. At this, McCoy turned to Colonel Winship and questioned the soundness of the orders once more. Winship's answer was chilling—General Degoutte was determined to keep the Germans moving and that, if necessary, the regiment must be sacrificed in the effort.[10]

While there might certainly be some military value in harassing a retreating enemy and inflicting losses upon him in the process, any such value was absolutely not worth the lives of nearly three thousand men. To suggest it had such value was both unprofessional from a military point of view and undeniably inhumane. Even from a cold, clinical, analytical perspective, losing valuable military resources in the form of an entire infantry regiment made absolutely no sense whatsoever. But, perhaps, after four years of bloody, seemingly endless butchery, Degoutte and others in command were insensitive to such considerations. After all, Field Marshal Douglas Haig, commander of the British Expeditionary Force, had referred to the loss of more than fifty-seven thousand dead or wounded on the first day of the Somme Offensive in July 1916 as "normal wastage."[11] So sacrificing a mere regiment of American National Guardsmen would seem acceptable by such standards.

However, what is perhaps most disturbing is that, from the available information, it seems no one in the American chain of command at I Corps, 42nd Division, or either brigade protested or even pushed back against these orders from Degoutte and his staff at the French Sixth Army.

Furthermore, it does not appear that anyone even tried to press for or propose a saner alternative to attacking without the benefit of reconnaissance or artillery support.

Upon hearing what must have been a deeply disturbing reply from Winship, Colonel McCoy began to prepare for the assault. He went over the map with Major McKenna and the French liaison officer. They decided that their Stokes mortars would support the attack, and their fire would be the signal for the attack across the river. Looking closer at the map, they saw a small unimproved road at the base of a hill on the far side and chose it for the battalion's assembly area once the crossing was effected. As McKenna and his officers hurried off to assemble the men and prepare for the attack, McCoy moved his PC to the orchard at the northern edge of Villers-sur-Fère and ordered the Sanitary Detachment to establish their field hospital in the cellars of some of the sturdier buildings in the village. Finally, he brought up the Machine Gun Company, placing its guns in a position to support the 3rd Battalion, and established liaison with the supporting and reserve battalions.[12]

The ground that lay ahead of the New Yorker along their narrow part of the I Corps front was daunting, as was the entire front line the Rainbow Division was assigned to assault in the gray, early morning hours of July 28. The 165th would move forward from the area around Villers-sur-Fère, whose appearance on the map looked like a "thin curved caterpillar" in the words of Father Duffy. The church and the buildings that surrounded the village square looked like the head of this caterpillar. From there, a short, steeply curved street led north to the cemetery on the right and an orchard on the right. There, the street stopped at a T-intersection where the road roughly paralleled the course of the Ourcq. To the left, the road led to Fère-en-Tardenois, which was just under a mile and a half away to the northwest. As the 165th prepared to advance over the Ourcq, the French were trying desperately to fight their way into Fère-en-Tardenois. To the far right of the regiment's small sector was the village of Sergy, which was just over a mile and a half distant.[13]

But the first objective, the banks of the Ourcq, was directly ahead, about eighty yards to the northeast across open ground with a few clumps of trees scattered about. There was a small bridge to the left and another to the right near the Moulin Vert (Green Mill) on the far bank. Just beyond the river was a small valley formed by a little stream, the Rue du Pont Brûle, that led northeast to the cluster of stone buildings at the Meurcy Farm. The ground around the stream was marshy and heavily wooded near the Ourcq with small patches of underbrush. About 200 yards west of the Meurcy Farm was a very thick patch of woods, the Bois Colas, with another smaller woods, the Bois Brûle, to the north of the farm.[14]

All of the terrain on both sides of the Ourcq sloped toward the river. Still, the biggest challenge facing the soldiers of the 165th was the slopes that formed on both sides of the little valley formed by the Rue du Pont Brûle. On the northwest side of the stream, the ground rose gradually toward Seringes-et-Nesles, about one thousand yards away. To the immediate east of the intersection of the stream with the Ourcq, the ground rose away from the valley in two different slopes, the first one very sharp and the second more gradual. About 600 yards north of this terrain was the Forêt-de-Nesles, which formed a "thick green wall" across the northern approaches to the river.[15]

What made the attack up the little valley of the Rue du Pont Brûle toward the Meurcy Farm so tactically challenging was that the valley became a trough that would funnel the infantry through a gauntlet of machine gun fire from both sides as well as from the farm and the Bois Colas. Once any attacking force reached the eastern crest of the hill, they would face 500 yards of upsloping open ground between themselves and whatever defenses the Germans had devised near the Forêt-de-Nesles. However, these challenges certainly could have been overcome with artillery support, of which there was none.[16]

What added to the dangers posed by the terrain all along the I Corps front was the Germans' effective placement and employment of their machine guns. The men of the 167th and 168th had learned the hard way that assaulting hidden machine guns in the standard line formation standing upright invited slaughter, and the word quickly spread throughout the division's infantrymen. As one veteran later recalled, "rushing through the open up to the concealed German machine guns in the hope of frightening the gunners into surrender, or of catching them off guard, was sheer suicide."[17] So rather than attack standing upright and advancing at the double-quick, they would make the assault at a pace characterized by one 42nd Division officer as a "crawl."[18]

The idea behind this "crawling" pace tactic was to minimize exposure, complicate the enemy machine gunners' task, and allow each machine gun emplacement to be neutralized in turn. The advance would be made by short burst squad rushes and even rushes by individual soldiers when necessary. For example, from the machine gun crew's perspective, they

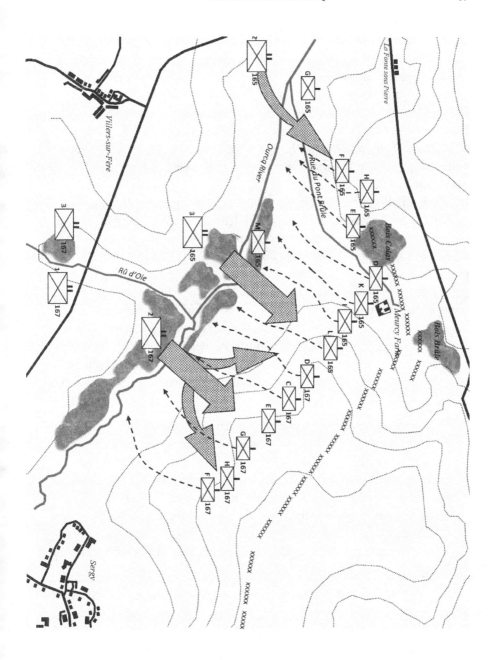

Map 4. The assault across the Ourcq River on July 28, 1918, by the 165th and 167th Infantry Regiments.

would suddenly see a few men in khaki jump up from the wheat to their right, run ahead for a few yards, and then disappear from view just as the gunner shifted his weapon and opened fire. For a moment, the field would be still and quiet. Then, off to the left, another small group would rush forward before taking cover, again just as the gunner was able to shift his fire to the left. Next, there would be a group rush into the center, then another to the right, and one to the left, advancing in a continuing process and taking quick dives for cover whenever the German machine gun would turn to them.[19]

Soon, a half-dozen Americans would be converging on the machine gun emplacement, and now their attack had supporting cover fire from their comrades' rifles. The process might take thirty minutes, or it might take an hour, but, eventually, the Americans would close in. Once within range, they would toss hand grenades into the emplacement and charge forward to kill any surviving Germans with rifles and bayonets.[20] So while the opening moments of the 165th's attack would include the standard infantry formation, they would quickly take up crawling along the ground with quick tactical rushes by small groups as their primary tactic.

Forty-six years later, Douglas MacArthur described this tactical approach and the action that characterized the fighting along the Ourcq River:

> We reverted to tactics I had seen so often in the Indian wars of my frontier days. Crawling forward in twos and threes against each stubborn nest of enemy guns, we closed in with the bayonet and the hand grenade. It was savage and there was no quarter asked or given. It seemed to be endless. Bitterly, brutally, the action seesawed back and forth. A point would be taken, and then would come a sudden fire from some unsuspected direction and the deadly counterattack. Positions changed hands time and again. There was neither rest nor mercy.[21]

At 3:45 a.m., the 3rd Battalion, known in the regiment as the "Shamrock Battalion," was ready to begin their attack. The plan was for I and L Companies to leapfrog K Company, which was on the south bank of the river "exchanging shots in the dark." I and L Companies would then cross the Ourcq and seize the heights on the far side with K Company right behind them. M Company was to be held in reserve, and D Company from the 1st Battalion would guard the right flank. The Stokes mortars that Captain Merle-Smith from L Company had collected opened fire, signaling the advance. As their shells crashed into the woods across the river, they produced "dramatic flashes lighting up the countryside," which was in Merle-Smith's words "somehow comforting." As the men stepped off, they advanced in a "thin and jerky line" down through the fields south of the Ourcq. However, before I and L Companies could reach K Company's position to leapfrog them, the men of K Company had become too eager and began their own advance. They shifted to the left of I Company, pushing L Company farther to the right toward the 167th's sector.[22]

The Germans saw the 3rd Battalion sweeping toward the river in the dim light just before dawn. Later, captured Germans who were there that morning said they thought the Americans must be crazy to make this attack.[23] They reported the coming attack, and German artillery and machine guns quickly sprang into action. The first German shells went roaring over the Americans' heads, chewing up the little woods where they had camped the night before. Martin Hogan of K Company recalled, "Each particle of the air over our heads was alive with a typhoon of shells. . . . and the strength of the fire grew until hell seemed to be moving in layers right over our heads."[24]

As the intensity of the enemy's artillery fire increased, his machine guns began their deadly work. As the red flame from their guns burst out in a "continuous sheet," the men pressed on. "One felt a queer uneasy sensation in the pit of the stomach as one ran to think of the myriads of steel needles streaming through the air around him, and one felt from minute to minute that the end could only be a matter of the next step or so," wrote Martin Hogan. Men seemed to fall all around the young private. "Almost at every stride some comrade fell," he later recalled. Stretcher bearers rushed forward to the aid of the wounded amid the machine gun fire. "I saw these incidents," Hogan wrote, "little nightmare incidents, flashed upon the screen of my vision in jumbled, jerky fashion, and I ran on feeling that the whole thing was just a dream, stopping to aim and fire as some chance gray uniform showed, and then blindly running on. . . . It was," he said, "suicide to stay and certain death to go forward."[25]

K and L Companies arrived at the Ourcq first, and, as he reached the banks, Captain Merle-Smith noted the river was only about thirty feet wide. But it looked deep. As a result, many of his men hesitated at the edge of the river, and some were cut down as they decided whether or not to jump into the water. The captain had an "awful thought" at that moment—while he knew he must be the one to lead, he also "never liked a cold bath in the morning." Quickly dismissing this thought, Merle-Smith jumped into the water, prepared to swim. But his feet almost immediately hit bottom, and he was standing in waist-high water that was not cold at all. Seeing their captain moving forward across the river now, the rest of the company jumped into the Ourcq and followed him.[26]

To Merle-Smith's left, K Company had also reached the riverbanks. They, too, paused for a moment before jumping into the river to make their way across. Captain John Hurley, the company commander, had been wounded crossing the field south of the river, leaving Lieutenant Patrick Dowling in command. Like Merle-Smith in L Company, Lieutenant Dowling led the way, leaping into the water while holding his Chauchat above his head and calling for the men in his company to follow. Dowling's platoon sergeant, Frank Doughney, was right behind him, but German machine gun fire killed him midstream. Corporal James McGovern, the senior noncommissioned officer of the platoon, followed Doughney into the water. He and the lieutenant were the first to pull themselves up from the water at the opposite bank, as the river was now filled with men and the "splatter of enemy steel."[27]

As L Company emerged from the river to the right of K Company, they pushed forward through intense enemy fire to the woods that bordered the river and the small unimproved road that ran along the bottom of the hill beyond. They quickly overran a small German detachment in the woods, shooting two German snipers out of the trees in the process. The hill ahead was covered in wheat fields, providing a completely open field of fire for the Germans who had five machine guns in foxholes on the side of the hill about 100 yards away. Captain Merle-Smith deployed his men to assault the guns using small rushes. The enemy continued to fire until Merle-Smith's men were right on top of them before throwing up their hands and shouting "Kamerad!" in surrender. In most cases, they were given quarter, but in others, they were not.[28]

In K Company, the men found every tree and woods manned by German machine gunners who "poured. . . a rain of bullets" at the advancing American infantry. Some Germans fell back from the riverbank, but others stayed in their positions, firing from behind stumps and rifle pits. The men from K Company were rapidly among them, overrunning their positions, and a "brisk fight" ensued. Some Germans were killed with the bayonet, and others were "picked like ripe fruit out of the trees by rifle and revolver fire." K Company had suffered heavy losses, but the riverbank was secured.[29]

Back to K Company's right, as L Company subdued the German machine guns on the side of the wheat-covered hill ahead of them, three Germans rose up and fled to the rear at least 200 yards in the open. Some of Merle-Smith's men opened fire on them, but all their shots missed. The captain got the men moving up the hill again as heavy enfilading machine gun fire erupted from both their left and right and front and rear. His men began to fall, but the line continued to move on just as a new German artillery barrage began. Rather than taking cover, the captain decided to hurry the men forward in an attempt to get through and inside the artillery fire. As Merle-Smith raised his arm to give the signal to double-time, he was shot through the arm. Knowing how much the men had hated seeing the double-time signal during training, he wondered if his wound brought them some perverse satisfaction. Despite the wound, the captain kept going on to the top of the hill with his men.[30]

Right behind the advance of K and L Companies came I Company, which was led by a veteran of the Boer War, Captain Richard Ryan. They swept across the river, losing only one man killed in the advance, and joined K Company. The left platoons of K Company were to move up the little Rue du Pont Brûle valley to take the Meurcy Farm, but that would be impossible until either one of the valley's slopes was cleared of enemy machine guns. Even in their current position just across the river, one group of enemy guns was directing fire on their flank. So Captain Ryan dispatched five men led by one of his best, Sergeant Edward Shanahan, to silence the guns. Shanahan, while Irish, was the odd man out in the company, as he hailed from Cleveland, Wisconsin. But he seemed a natural leader. While Ryan did not have much hope of success, Shanahan and his small detachment came through, silencing the enemy machine guns.[31]

Not realizing that Captain Hurley had been hit, Lieutenant Dowling of K Company asked where he could find the company commander. Upon learning that Hurley was wounded and out of the fight, young Dowling set about getting the company moving forward. Seeing that I Company had subdued that one set of enemy guns, he gave his men orders to move on the Meurcy Farm. While the left of his line moved up the stream's valley, the remainder of K Company along with I Company would move up the smooth, bare slope of the hill to the right, clearing the enemy machine guns placed there and an "almost unbearable enemy pressure." He led them up the slopes, well in advance of his men, shouting words of encouragement and firing his Chauchat. However, he had not gone far before he was shot through the heart and fell mortally wounded on the side of the hill. One of his men ran to his side, gently lifting the lieutenant in his arms. Dowling looked up at the soldier and asked, "Did they get that machine gun on the right?" The soldier replied, "Yes, sir." Dowling said, "Thank God," and died in his comrade's arms.[32]

Meanwhile, as K Company and I Company struggled against the German guns around the Meurcy Farm, Captain Merle-Smith's L Company reached their objective, the top of the hill opposite the farm, while I Company now covered their immediate left. The captain looked about their position and assessed the situation. The top of the hill was "smoothly rounded" and had nothing to provide any cover from enemy fire. Ahead lay between 1,500 to 2,000 yards of open fields that gently sloped down to the Forêt-de-Nesles. To his right, Merle-Smith saw the ridge that ran southeast toward Sergy, which lay in a hollow that hid it from his view. He could not make out any German positions toward the edge of the Forêt-de-Nesles, and just a few German helmets kept popping up over the ridge toward Sergy. A few of his men opened fire on them, and they quickly ducked out of sight.[33]

To the left, he could make out two German machine guns in the direction of Seringes-et-Nesles, and, using his field glasses, he could see two ammunition carriers continually supplying the guns there. One of his platoons opened fire on the guns, but they were over 1,600 yards away, and their rifles had no effect. All the while, however, the company was taking heavy fire from enemy guns skillfully hidden in the wheat to both their left and right. While trying desperately to locate these guns, one of Merle-Smith's men crouched to run forward but was immediately shot through both legs. He dropped to his hands and knees to be hit again, this time in both the legs and arm. Then, as he lay flat against the ground, one final burst of machine gun fire struck him in the head, killing him instantly. As he watched this horrible scene play out, another German bullet ripped through the captain's coat on the back of his shoulder, but he was unhurt.[34]

About this time, Merle-Smith later said that he began to have a "terrible feeling of helplessness." All but one of the men from his headquarters section were hit, and, because he could not clearly locate any enemy positions, there seemed to be no one to fight back against. Instead, all he saw was "180 degrees of emptiness," and all he could do was have his men fire at every potential source of cover for the enemy, which was terribly futile because there were so many. He barked out the order to dig in, but, as his men rolled on their sides to use their spades, many exposed themselves to enemy fire and were hit. Merle-Smith countermanded the order

This contemporary photo taken from just northwest of the village of Sergy (which can be seen in the foreground) shows Hill 212 in the distance beyond the village. (*Major William Carraway, Historian, Georgia Army National Guard*)

and instead sent a request to the rear for artillery fire on the hollows and woods north of the Meurcy Farm and the edge of the Forêt-de-Nesles. However, he soon learned that there was no artillery in position to provide the much-needed supporting fire. About that time, a German spotter plane appeared overhead, and it began directing artillery fire on L Company's position atop the hill. This quickly became something of a blessing because the incoming rounds produced shell holes that his men could use for cover.[35]

Merle-Smith was sure that I Company to his left was getting hit as hard as his men were, and he received a report that Captain Ryan had been wounded twice. But, when he looked in that direction, he could see the old Boer War veteran shouting orders and encouragement to his men. Some of L Company's men managed to get a machine gun mounted and opened fire on the German guns around Seringes-et-Nesles. But within minutes, five of them were killed, and the gun was disabled. While some men moved to try to repair it, the captain ordered it abandoned as "its operation seemed pretty futile in any event." As he looked around, Merle-Smith could see that, while the men were "very steady," there were "only a pitifully few left." The 1st and 2nd Platoons had taken the highest casualties, but the 3rd was doing better and had some cover from the enemy fire in a shallow depression in the ground.[36]

Just then, a runner brought a message from Colonel McCoy telling him that L Company was way over into the 167th's sector. However, the good news in the message was that some of the Alabama units were moving up from behind his position to relieve him and his men. German fire began to slacken, so Lieutenant William Spencer made his way "very coolly" over to the captain and started to bind up his wounded arm. As the lieutenant attended to Merle-Smith, the two men discussed exactly how they might fall back and reorganize the company once the 167th arrived. They decided to move all the survivors from the 1st and 2nd Platoons to a hollow behind the 3rd Platoon's position, carrying all the wounded that they could. In the meantime, he told the lieutenant to try to get a few patrols out to protect their right flank. With that, Spencer went back to his platoon and carried out the captain's orders.

Once most of the 1st and 2nd Platoons had fallen back, Merle-Smith gave the arm signal to Lieutenant Spencer to withdraw as well. The captain stayed behind with a few men to make sure all the wounded had been moved. He saw Lieutenant Spencer turning his platoon over to his sergeant so he could go gather in his patrols and confer with the 167th men who were moving up. Merle-Smith then fell back thirty yards with the rest of his men to the cover of the hollow, where he learned that Lieutenant Spencer had been wounded while withdrawing and had been taken to the rear.[37]

Not long after the fighting had begun, Major McKenna wanted to extend his flanks as far as possible to prevent them from being rolled up by the enemy. Colonel McCoy had given him D Company from the 1st Battalion to use if needed. So McKenna sent half of the company to the right of L Company and the other half to the left rear of K Company, where they could support K Company's advance up the valley toward the Meurcy Farm.[38]

With Lieutenant Dowling's death, command of K Company, or what was left of it, had fallen to Lieutenant Howard Arnold. Arnold kept pushing the company forward, with some of them moving up the hill to their right while the rest continued their advance toward the Meurcy Farm. The men tore their way through dense thickets and up the hill and the valley, subduing enemy machine guns wherever they could locate them, shooting snipers out of the trees, and "cleaning up patches of advanced covered fighters, here and there, with bayonets." They made steady progress, but "the trail of the Shamrock Battalion up that hill was marked out clearly by its losses."[39]

As K Company struggled to advance, a runner brought word to Lieutenant Arnold that, despite his wounds, Captain Hurley was trying to follow the company "as fast as failing strength would permit." Arnold told the runner to go back to the captain and tell him the company had suffered serious losses and that the enemy opposition seemed to be increasing. The lieutenant added that he did not think much of the company would be available to defend the crest of the hill once it was taken. The runner dashed off to deliver the message to Captain Hurley, but no response came back.[40]

Fearing the runner had not made it back to the captain, Arnold temporarily turned command over to Sergeant Herbert McKenna. He then headed off to find Captain Hurley and deliver the message himself. Arnold soon found the captain, who was in a shell hole "exhausted from loss of blood, and where he was resting to gather strength" so he could follow the company. As the lieutenant approached the captain to report what was happening at the front of the company, a German machine gun bullet struck him in the heart, and he fell dead next to Captain Hurley. K Company had now lost three commanding officers in the attack. Hurley painfully pulled himself out of the shell hole and began staggering up the hill to reach his men. He had not gone far before another German bullet hit him in the leg, and he fell, unable to go any farther.[41]

Sergeant McKenna, meanwhile, continued to lead the company in what seemed to be a somewhat futile effort. Martin Hogan later wrote, "We could see plainly that the enemy was getting the best of us—that is, gaining in strength and in fresh men. Most of us were winded, and a great part of the battalion was scattered all over the trail behind, struck down and out of action." The Germans would try to advance themselves, and there would be brief periods of hand-to-hand fighting with the bayonet before the Germans fell back. As a result, the lines would sway, sag, and bend before the company resumed its advance.[42]

At one point in the fighting, Sergeant Sidney Da Costa was moving up the hill in advance of the line when he passed a section of the hill that was very steep and covered with underbrush. Out of the corner of his eye, he saw something move in the brush. The sergeant immediately rushed headlong into the thicket. When he emerged on the other side, he found a German machine gun emplacement with a six-man crew only a few feet away. Before the Germans could react, Da Costa killed four of them with his sidearm, causing the other two to throw their hands up in surrender. Da Costa sent them to the rear with a guard and continued up the hill in pursuit of his men.[43]

While most of K Company struggled up the hill to the right, the left of the company, along with men from D Company, had better luck moving up the valley toward the Meurcy Farm. One platoon from K Company led by Sergeant Francis Meade and two platoons from D Company led by Sergeant Stephen Crotty worked their way up the valley along the Rue du Pont Brûle until they reached the old stone walls of the farm. A sharp fight ensued until the men could thrust their rifles through the windows, allowing them to fire on the German defenders. This caused the Germans to abandon the farm buildings and retreat rapidly from the farm. The doughboys paused briefly to grab some apples from the trees in the farm's orchard before Sergeant Crotty moved some of them into a skirmish line to fire on the Germans in the Bois Colas. At the same time, Sergeant Dick O'Neill and his men from D Company held the farm. The grip on the Meurcy Farm, however, did not last long. As soon as the Germans learned the farm had fallen into American hands, they began to shell it heavily, forcing the New Yorkers to fall back.[44]

To the right of K Company, I Company found itself in the middle of the battalion's line, taking heavy losses on the hillside. Many platoons lost their officers, so sergeants took command. But many of them also fell within minutes of taking the lead. As Captain Ryan looked over his company's situation, he and his men could clearly see the field ahead of them. The terrain to their front was level and open with no cover. Five hundred yards away was the Forêt-de-Nesles, where Ryan could see prepared emplacements protected by barbed wire. The veteran officer knew it would be useless to advance toward those woods, as not a single man might survive the effort.[45]

At that moment, Captain Ryan was hit as a bullet passed through his left side. One of his lieutenants tried to move him to the rear, but Ryan threatened to shoot anyone who might attempt to take him from the field. Luckily, as a company from the 167th appeared to I Company's right, Captain Merle-Smith from L Company arrived to tell Ryan that they had been ordered to fall back through the 1st Battalion, which had now occupied the lower slopes of the hill.[46]

As I, K, and L Companies moved back down the hill, the sights the men saw were disheartening. Father Duffy wrote, "The ground was littered with the bodies of the brave, and the slopes of the Ourcq were dotted with the wounded, helping one another to the dressing station across the river in Villers-sur-Fere." More than half of the 3rd Battalion was either dead or wounded. Of the six officers in K Company, three were killed, and the others were wounded, which meant not a single officer was left standing. In L Company, Captain Merle-Smith and three of his officers were wounded, and a fourth was dead, leaving Sergeant Eugene Gannon as Merle-Smith's second in command. I Company, however, was in the worst shape in terms of officers. Captain Ryan was the only officer left in the company, placing his first sergeant, Patrick McMiniman, "a rock-ribbed old-timer" in command.[47]

But the worst news for the battalion, perhaps, was that Major McKenna had been killed. Around 5:15 a.m., General Lenihan sent word to suspend the assault because the 84th Brigade might not be ready to support the attack. McKenna rushed forward, trying to recall his men, but quickly realized there was no way for them to pull out of the fight safely. Seeing the situation, he headed back across the Ourcq to meet with Colonel McCoy. As McCoy and his adjutant walked to the rear, a German shell exploded nearby, knocking both of them to the ground and wounding McKenna's adjutant. When the adjutant stood up and ran to McKenna, he discovered the major was dead with no wounds on his body.[48]

All three of the battalion's company commanders met and agreed that their position on top of the hill was untenable. German artillery and machine gun fire continued unabated, sweeping the open ground where their thin line tried to hang on. But they were being told that they had to hold as long as possible to support the other units from the division who were also attacking across the Ourcq. What was needed was artillery support, which was still nowhere to be found.[49]

While D, I, K, and L Companies had been battling their way up the hill and toward the Meurcy Farm, another fierce fight was raging on the western slopes above the Rue du Pont Brûle. The 165th's 2nd Battalion, led by Major Alex Anderson, had been brought forward as a reserve. Just before the general attack was made, Lieutenant Colonel Harry Mitchell from regimental headquarters arrived to tell Anderson that the battalion would not remain in support. Instead, at 5:45 a.m., they were to make an attack to the left of the 3rd Battalion. Anderson immediately woke his men up and organized them for an advance. He placed E and F Companies in the front with E Company on the right and G and H Companies right behind them. The four companies marched forward under heavy artillery fire until they reached the southern slope of the hill just south of the Ourcq.[50]

Here, Anderson was told that the battalion was to cross the Ourcq just west of its intersection with the Rue du Pont Brûle and advance up the hill toward the Bois Colas and the ground east of Seringes-et-Nesles. Anderson's battalion, led by E and F Companies, splashed across the Ourcq and began moving up the slopes to the west of the Meurcy Farm and the Bois Colas. As they came over the crest of the hill, German gunners hiding in La Fonte sous Pierre, a small group of three houses east of Fère-en-Tardenois, opened fire on them. Anderson's men returned fire on the houses using their 37mm one-pounders. However, the French delivered a coup de grâce when their 75mm guns blasted the houses at point-blank range, killing all the Germans hiding there.[51]

That provided some temporary security to the left flank of F Company, led by Captain Michael Kelly. But his company had the toughest assignment in the battalion. They were to sweep up the hill east of Seringes-et-Nesles while the village itself was assaulted by the 166th, which was moving up toward the river. The French were consumed with the task of taking Fère-en-Tardenois, which left Kelly's flank entirely in the air. Once his company reached a point directly opposite the village of Seringes-et-Nesles, they would likely be subjected to a devastating enfilading fire. Already, the fire from enemy machine guns hidden throughout the wheat fields on the slopes south of the village was taking a severe toll.[52]

Kelly could see that if the Bois Colas on his right turned out to be heavily defended, he would be leading his men into a deadly funnel where they would be fired on from left, right, and front. So Kelly sent a runner to E Company on his right to see what resistance they had encountered from the Bois Colas. As it turned out, they found the woods had been abandoned by the Germans, and Lieutenant Conners, commanding E Company, took possession of the woods up to its northern edge. F Company, meanwhile, was being hit hard by both artillery and machine gun fire, forcing Kelly to have his men take cover in a partially sunken road between Fère-en-Tardenois and the Bois Colas. Seeing the 166th crossing the river to his left, Kelly sent a request for two Chauchats from the Ohioans, which they provided. He also asked for reinforcements from Major Anderson, who dispatched men to F Company's assistance. These men worked their way out from the Bois Colas toward Kelly's men, supporting F Company's right flank in the process.[53]

Major Anderson soon realized what the leaders of the 3rd Battalion had learned—while they had taken the initial German lines of resistance, they could not advance, nor could they hold their ground without artillery support. To continue the attack as ordered by the French Sixth Army would mean moving across thousands of yards of open ground against a well-planned enemy defense, which would be suicidal. If they simply tried to stay where they were, they would be gradually destroyed by German artillery and machine gun fire.[54]

It was now approaching 10:00 a.m. To the right, across the Rue du Ponte Brûle, Major Donovan's 1st Battalion had successfully relieved the 3rd Battalion. Donovan could see that trying to hold the top of the hill by placing his men there would be useless. So, instead, he placed Chauchat automatic riflemen and sharpshooters in the wheat fields on the crest of the hill. At the same time, the rest of the battalion took position behind the high inner bank of the river road at the base of the hill. This way, Donovan figured he could at least prevent the Germans from returning to their positions on the top of the hill. As noon approached, the 165th was deployed from the riverbank and marshy ground to the left and along the river road to the right, where their flank was linked with the men from the 167th.[55] They had suffered severe losses and taken the initial objectives assigned. Still, they could neither advance farther nor hold their ground without more support.

Not long after the 165th began their advance, the 168th Infantry started to move forward on the far right of the I Corps front. After the initial orders for an advance had come during the evening of July 27, Colonel Bennett, the 168th's commander, notified his three battalion commanders to be ready to move across the Ourcq during the night. However, as midnight approached, Bennett had not heard anything more definitive. A little while past midnight on the morning of July 28, Major Cooper Winn from the 84th Brigade staff arrived at Bennett's PC on a hillside near the La Favière Farm with a message from General Brown. Winn told the colonel that Brown was ordering the 168th to resume their advance at daylight with the same objective as the day before—the heights above the Ourcq River.[56]

It was about 4:00 a.m. when Major Guy Brewer, commander of the 3rd Battalion, received a scrawled, handwritten note from Bennett saying, "Cross the river and seize the heights beyond."[57] Brewer had seen the terrain on the approaches to the river and the high ground beyond firsthand the previous afternoon when his battalion attempted a crossing near the demolished bridge. As usual, the Germans had used their considerable military talents to, first, choose positions that took maximum advantage of the natural terrain. Next, they had arranged them in a manner that allowed their machine guns to command every possible approach, provide mutual support, and afford them excellent concealment. The guns themselves were placed in pits dug in the wheat fields that covered the hills and camouflaged them with fresh straw, making them almost invisible to the naked eye. Just as with the situation the other regiments faced across the I Corps front, the 168th was forced to face a battlefield that the enemy defender could control.[58]

Hill 212 dominated the ridge above the river. All the surrounding hills rose in a gradual slope to a height of about 130 to 260 feet above the small valley made by the Ourcq. Behind Hill 212 were three wooded areas, the Bois Pelger, Bois de la Planchette, and Les Jomblets, which the Germans had filled with artillery and machine guns. One historian considered an expert on the fighting here said that these positions were "by far the most serious obstacle encountered on the front of the [French] Sixth Army."[59]

The approaches to the hill, like much of the surrounding area, were covered in wheat without a tree in sight to provide cover or concealment. The little Ourcq River flowed to the northwest about 100 yards from the base of Hill 212, where it was only about two feet deep and eighteen feet wide with small willow trees along its banks. While the river might have been narrow and shallow, the banks on the far side were quite steep, which would make it difficult for soldiers carrying weapons and ammunition to climb out of the water while under fire. On the right of the regiment's sector, just a few yards north of the ruins of an old mill, the Moulin Caranda, the Ourcq merged with a stream called the Ru de Coupè, which led to the town of Cierges. On the left of Hill 212 was the village of Sergy, which sat in a hollow at the hill's base with a ridge just beyond it that would make it a formidable defensive position.[60]

At about 4:15 a.m., Brewer accompanied two squads of automatic riflemen from K Company to the crossing where the bridge had once stood. He ordered them to take positions securing the crossing for the remainder of the battalion, which would advance around 5:00 a.m. Then Brewer took another look at the battalion's objective. What caught his attention the most was the thick bank of ground fog that blanketed the river, making the little valley on either side invisible to the enemy's view. If he were lucky, the mist would hold long enough for his men to silently approach and cross the river to reach the hill's base undetected.[61]

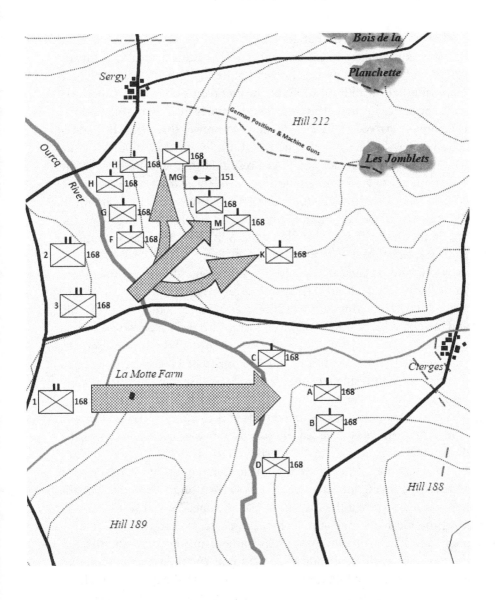

Map 5. The attack across the Ourcq River at Hill 212 on July 28, 1918, by the 168th Infantry Regiment.

Brewer returned to his battalion PC, where he met with Captain Percy Lanison, commander of L Company. He told Lanison that L Company would lead the assault and, as Brewer pointed to Hill 212's location on a map, said that the hilltop would be the company's objective. As Lanison left to organize his men, Captain Glenn Haynes from the 1st Battalion's D Company arrived at the PC. Haynes told Brewer that, while he had received orders for the advance, he could not locate Major Worthington, who had been missing all night. As a result, Haynes told Brewer that he was prepared to lead his battalion but needed instructions on how he could support the attack by the 3rd Battalion. Brewer gave the captain all the information he had and told him his job would be to move up on the 3rd Battalion's right and cover that flank. With that discussion complete, Haynes sped off back to his own battalion.[62]

A few minutes later, at 4:50 a.m., the squads guarding the crossing sent word that the way ahead was clear. Brewer ordered Captain Lanison to move out with his company, cross the river, advance 500 yards up the hill, and then hold his position.[63] Lanison formed his men in platoon columns with the 1st and 2nd Platoons as the assault group with the 3rd and 4th Platoons in support. As his men quietly approached the river, he signaled them to break into smaller squad columns with scouts in the lead. They held their weapons at high port as they cut through the "damp, bowing wheat" toward the banks of the Ourcq. At 5:15 a.m., still bathed in fog, Lanison's company succeeded in crossing the river on the stones of the destroyed bridge, unseen by the Germans atop Hill 212.[64]

The men of L Company were soon climbing up the banks of the river and slowly moving into the line of willow trees on the far side. Captain Lanison then formed the men into a "fan-shaped" skirmish line. Up to now, the Germans had not seen the Americans advancing, but they seemed to know something was happening. Lanison could see through the now-diminishing shroud of fog, and he saw the Germans moving about the top of the hill, carrying ammunition to the guns on the hill's forward slope. They appeared to be hurrying to resupply their guns, indicating that, while they might not be able to clearly see the Iowans, they might sense their presence.[65]

Major Brewer's plan was to have the ends of his line swing left and right in a double envelopment maneuver as the center of the line pushed directly up the hill. With everyone in place, the line began to advance, emerging from the fog. Almost at once, heavy machine gun fire erupted from Hill 212, ripping into Lanison's men as guns in Sergy to the left and

Moulin Caranda on the right also hit L Company's exposed flanks hard. Lanison ordered his 3rd Platoon, led by Lieutenant James Christopher, to move against the Germans in Sergy, while Lieutenant Mahlon Wallace's 1st Platoon advanced in the center of the line up the slopes of Hill 212. As these two platoons moved to the attack, Brewer had Lieutenant George Noble's 2nd Platoon flank the hill on Wallace's right, as Lieutenant Theodore Jones's 4th Platoon attacked the hill on the right flank. The entire line advanced to the sunken road at the hill's base, driving the Germans' forward positions back up the hill and taking about fifty prisoners. Lanison then reorganized his company and consolidated their position as more support from the battalion arrived.[66]

While Major Brewer watched Lanison's progress, he had sent a message back to Colonel Bennett saying, "We are advancing." A few minutes later, Brewer sent another message telling the colonel that all his men were across the Ourcq, followed by a third that said, "Advanced to the base of Hill 212. Casualties heavy. Advancing." But the advance would be slow and, as John Taber would record, "For every yard gained a life was given."[67]

As for the Germans, they quickly realized the scale of the assault and dispatched reinforcements from their reserve forces in the Bois Pelger. Major Brewer now sent the order, "Off the road and up the hill." With that, Lanison's men adopted the tactic of crawling forward and making small rushes under covering fire from the company's Chauchat automatic rifles. Realizing the danger posed by the Chauchats, the Germans began to focus their machine guns on the automatic riflemen, causing numerous casualties among those Iowans. But whenever one rifleman fell, another man would come up to replace him and continue to lay down heavy fire. A squad would rush one way, a couple of men would run in another, moving the line steadily up the side of the hill and closing in on the main line of German machine gun pits. Suddenly, a few Germans could be seen racing to the rear and up the hill while others at the top of the hill seemed to be breaking up. Steadily, Lanison's men surrounded individual machine guns, tossed in hand grenades, and then finished off the surviving gunners with their bayonets.[68]

On the far left, Lieutenant Christopher's platoon moved against the enemy's flanking fire. Despite heavy resistance, they managed to capture six enemy machine guns and thirteen of their surviving gun crews. As more German prisoners were taken, the Americans began using them as stretcher bearers for the battalion's wounded.[69]

About this time, I Company moved up and took control of some of the outlying buildings in Sergy, and Lieutenant Charles Brigg's M Company came forward, plugging its platoons into any gaps in L Company's line. Lieutenant James Cotter's K Company also advanced and swung to the right to cover the battalion's flank. As Lanison's men reached the top of the hill, the Georgians from the 151st Machine Gun Battalion arrived and dashed up the hill with their guns. However, they lost a number of both men and weapons in the process. So their commander, Lieutenant John Olson, told his men to take the German machine guns that were left on the hill, turn them around, and use them to fire on the retreating Germans.[70]

The Germans now began to lay down a heavy artillery barrage on the hill, but Brewer told his men to hold their ground and consolidate their positions. I Company held the outskirts of Sergy while L and M Companies held the top of the hill. K Company, meanwhile, held the ground immediately east of the hill.[71] While Brewer and his men had pushed the Germans completely off Hill 212, they could go no farther. While the Iowans paused to consolidate after the exhausting and costly attack up the hill, the Germans reorganized and reinforced their troops in the nearby Bois Pelger and Les Jomblets. They also still held the entire ridge running between Hill 212 and Sergy, from which they continued to pour a deadly enfilading fire.[72]

The advance by the 3rd Battalion had seen far too many casualties but also many instances of courage and heroism. As I Company was moving around the left flank and L Company was struggling up Hill 212, German resistance stiffened. Amid that desperate fighting near the crest of the hill, Lieutenant George Noble was hit by a bullet that pierced his arm. He resisted going to the rear but eventually went down the hill to receive aid. However, instead of remaining behind, as soon as his arm was bandaged, he climbed back up the hill and fought with his platoon. He did not finally go to the rear until late afternoon when Major Brewer expressly ordered him to do so.[73]

In M Company, Corporal George Boustead led four men from his squad in rushing a machine gun nest held by twelve German soldiers. He killed one of the enemy, captured the other eleven, and then had his squad turn the gun about to fire on the retreating Germans. Meanwhile, after assaulting and capturing an enemy gun, Sergeant Byron Hamilton of M Company found himself well in advance of his men and bleeding so badly from wounds that he could no longer stand. Hamilton sank to the ground, turned around, and started to crawl back toward his men. However, he suddenly saw a large group of Germans rapidly approaching him.

Members of Georgia's 151st Machine Gun Battalion, which participated in the assault on Hill 212 on July 28, 1918. (*Major William Carraway, Historian, Georgia Army National Guard*)

Hamilton forced himself up onto his knees, aimed his rifle, and proceeded to coolly shoot several of them before the rest turned and fled just as his rifle's ammunition clip fired its last round. The Germans' decision to retreat before Hamilton's sharpshooting turned out to be a good thing because the sergeant had now lost so much blood that he could not even reload his rifle.[74]

The longer the 3rd Battalion remained on top of Hill 212, the more precarious their situation became. The German shelling was raining down on them, and Brewer decided he needed to reduce the battalion's exposure. So he ordered most of the battalion to fall back and dig in on the reverse slope of the hill while he established a small group of outposts to hold the crest of the hill and prevent the Germans from reoccupying the top of the hill. About 8:00 a.m., he sent a message to Colonel Bennett that said, "Objective reached. Have taken up position on the reverse slope of Hill 212. Machine guns to our front. Artillery support imperative. We are being heavily shelled."[75]

After his early morning meeting with Major Brewer, Captain Haynes rushed back to the 1st Battalion, where he met with all of the battalion's officers. He explained Major Brewer's plans and how their battalion should attack in support of the overall assault. He then told Lieutenant Witherell to take a squad and scout the crossings over the Ourcq to see if they could successfully ford the river. In this portion of the regiment's sector, the Ourcq turned almost directly south, passing between Hills 189 and 188 before eventually flowing roughly halfway between Ronchères and Courmont. Witherell returned to say that the approaches to the river were clear, adding that he could see the 3rd Battalion was fighting their way up Hill 212. So Hayes began forming up the battalion for the advance when, suddenly, Major Worthington appeared from nowhere to reassume command.[76]

It was just a few minutes after 8:00 a.m. before the 1st Battalion finally got moving. Hayes had placed A Company and B Company in the lead with A Company on the left. C Company and D Company followed in support. Lieutenant Donald Mackay from the battalion's headquarters staff took a squad forward to scout the way. As soon as they reached the crest of Hill 189 and began going down toward the Ourcq, German machine gunners across the river on Hill 188 opened fire on them and the lead companies that followed.

As the battalion approached the La Motte Farm, Major Worthington moved the line to the east to protect the 3rd Battalion's right flank. As he did so, German machine gun fire increased, and then artillery was added to the deadly mix. The battalion halted on the northwest slopes of Hill 189 and began to frantically dig in. Then the slow crawl and rush tactics began, with men moving in small groups to subdue the enemy's gun emplacements. Worthington kept sending back calls for artillery support, but just as everywhere else, none came, at least at first. Finally, about noon, the American artillery came to life, laying down a heavy barrage on the German positions across the river.[77]

At 12:45 p.m., Worthington signaled for the battalion to move forward across the river. But just as the men were splashing across the Ourcq, the friendly artillery support suddenly and inexplicably ceased. The battalion deployed into thin skirmish lines and kept advancing as German artillery continued to rain down, causing heavy casualties. Soon, they were moving up the slopes of Hill 188 and approaching the main line of enemy guns, which were hidden in a hedge line. A and B Companies worked their way forward in small rushes, eventually flanking the line of machine guns and closing in on their gun crews. As soon as the Germans realized what was happening, they abandoned their guns and rapidly retreated toward the town of Cierges, where a large Red Cross flag flew from the steeple of the village church.[78]

The 1st Battalion continued to advance over the hill and toward Cierges until they began to receive heavy machine gun fire from the hills just northeast of the town. Worthington sent back a request for his own machine gun support to come forward along with the 37mm one-pounder. The Machine Gun Company made it to the front, but the one-pounder was damaged, and many of its crew were killed or wounded by artillery fire as they moved across the river. The Hotchkiss machine guns were quickly placed into action, "spraying the edge of the woods" where the German machine guns were located. But the enemy fire was too great for the battalion to cross the open ground between them and Cierges. A and B Companies dug in where they were, while C and D Companies fell back to the base of the hill. D Company, meanwhile, moved to the extreme right of the battalion's line and pivoted, so they faced to the southeast. This way, they could protect the battalion's right flank, which was in the air because the American 28th Division had not yet advanced.[79]

Back on Hill 212, the 3rd Battalion was still holding, but Major Brewer was deeply concerned about their situation. First, he had extended his front as far as he could to the left, but there was still a large gap of about 250 yards between his left flank and the right flank of the 167th. This situation was worsened because Sergy sat in the middle of this opening in the American line. The Germans still held the village. If they decided to counterattack, they could exploit the gap between the 167th and 168th and possibly roll up their exposed flanks, which could be disastrous. Brewer sent a message to Colonel Bennet explaining the situation and requesting reinforcements. The 2nd Battalion had remained in reserve because it had been so severely battered at La Croix Rouge Farm, but the time had come for them to get into this fight.[80]

Major Stanley's 2nd Battalion had spent the morning moving into position to potentially provide that support. They had followed the Rû de la Goulée past the La Cense Farm until they were opposite the La Motte Farm. The battalion stopped about 9:30 a.m. amid heavy German shelling. Stanley could see the 3rd Battalion up ahead on the slopes of Hill 212 and sent word to Major Brewer, letting him know where the 2nd Battalion was positioned. In response, Brewer asked for support to help him shore up the gap on his left. Stanley immediately ordered H Company, now commanded by Lieutenant George Hoar, to move to the aid of the 3rd Battalion. Hoar and his men ran forward, crossing the Ourcq

Nine German prisoners (sitting on the ground in the front two rows) taken captive by men from the 168th Infantry Regiment during the fighting on July 28, 1918. (*National Archives*)

under heavy fire and moving up the hill. Brewer ordered Hoar to send three of his platoons to the far left of the line while using the fourth to plug a gap that had appeared between I and M Companies. [81]

About 11:00 a.m., once Hoar's men were in position on the left, they could see German reinforcements moving into Sergy. The counterattack feared by Major Brewer seemed to be imminent. Brewer sent another request for help to Major Stanley, and, as soon as he received it, Stanley came forward to Brewer's PC to discuss the situation in person. The two men talked and determined that it made no sense to keep feeding Stanley's men into the line piecemeal. So they decided to have Stanley move his entire battalion into the left of the line and assume command of the area between the 3rd Battalion and the 167th. Stanley ordered the remainder of his men to move up on the left and, while they rushed forward under terrific artillery fire from the enemy, the time for them to get into position made for "a tense few minutes."[82]

The 2nd Battalion initially stopped at the base of the hill under cover of the slope. Stanley ordered E Company to lengthen the line to the left, while G and F Companies remained along the road as a reserve. E Com-

pany's 3rd Platoon entered the line near the crest of the hill while the 2nd
Platoon under Lieutenant George Vaughn moved farther left down the
slope toward Sergy in an attempt to establish a link with the 167th. However, he immediately discovered he did not have enough men to close the
gap with the Alabamians. Further, the 3rd Platoon was exposed to heavy
fire from an enemy machine gun posted in the steeple of Sergy's church,
and Vaughn was forced to turn his line downhill at a right angle to that
of the 3rd Battalion. Vaughn had a runner take a message to Major Stanley
and Major Brewer explaining the situation. Stanley then committed half
of G Company to move in on Vaughn's left and close the gap. When the
men from G Company arrived on the left, they effectively eliminated any
chance for the Germans to drive the Americans off Hill 212 with a counterattack from Sergy. Upon seeing the new forces arrive, the Germans in
Sergy ceased firing and apparently pulled out of the village in favor of the
high terrain of the ridge just north of the town.[83]

However, this withdrawal did not allow the Americans to actually take
control of Sergy. In fact, the situation was quite to the contrary. From
above the village, the Germans could continue to pour heavy machine
gun fire into the 168th's lines and still control the approaches from below
the village. They also could quickly dispatch men down to Sergy in response to any move by the Americans to enter the village, as shown by
their response to a patrol sent into Sergy from E Company.[84]

To determine if the Germans were still in the village, that patrol, consisting of five men and led by Corporal Pierce Flowers, was dispatched to
scout the town. The men entered the village from the east and worked
their way silently toward the center of the town, hugging the walls of the
buildings as they went. There were no signs of the Germans, and all was
well until they reached the town square. Suddenly, a large group of Germans emerged from the buildings where they had been hiding in wait
and surrounded the patrol. Instead of surrendering, Flowers and his men
fought back, and a brief but intense firefight ensued. Corporal Flowers
fell dead, shot through the head, and Private Howard Turnbull went
down, as well. Private Charles Miller, meanwhile, was wounded and taken
prisoner. The Germans would attend to his wounds but left him in a
nearby cellar where he was later found dying. Private Warren Booth, who
had been bringing up the rear of the patrol, was able to open fire on the
Germans as his buddy, the gravely wounded Private Emil Johnson, tried
to crawl to safety. Booth's covering fire allowed Johnson to escape only to
die a few days later in the hospital in Épieds. As for Booth, the Germans

pursued him to the edge of the village, and he ducked from shell hole to shell hole until he made it back to American lines.[85]

As the afternoon progressed, Major Brewer and Major Stanley assigned snipers to pick off enemy machine gun crews on the edge of the Bois de la Planchette and Les Jomblets whenever they exposed themselves to view. They also assigned the 151st Machine Gun Battalion to positions on the crest of the hill to engage the German guns in the woods. The two sides exchanged fire until late in the day when the Germans apparently tired of the harassment, bringing down a massive artillery barrage on the Americans on Hill 212. This forced Brewer and Stanley to pull their men back below the crest of the hill, where they dug in for the night.[86]

The only remaining duty to be done was to take care of the numerous men who had been wounded. There were so many casualties that there were not enough litters for the stretcher bearers to use. So duckboards and blankets were pressed into service as the sunken road at the base of Hill 212 filled with the day's bloody carnage. The stretcher bearers worked tirelessly going up and down the hill despite continued heavy shelling by the Germans. One man who was assigned to care for the many wounded from the regiment was Sergeant Maxwell Farley. Farley's reputation was that of a fearless and able soldier who was dedicated to his comrades. John Taber remembered Farley, saying, "No one was in too exposed a position for 'Doc' Farley to go to his aid, no hand more gentle than his." At one point in the late afternoon, Farley had brought in and was taking care of forty-six wounded men. Farley's courageous actions were believed to have saved many an Iowan's life that day. Another soldier, Private Andy Thomsen, who was characterized as a "big, brawny, brave" man, spent the day crawling up along the front line, bandaging the wounded and then lifting them up on his broad shoulders to carry them down the hill to the nearest available litter.[87]

As the day ended, the 168th held a line from near Hill 189 on the right to just below Sergy on the left. In the center, they held a vulnerable salient formed by a thin line up Hill 212 to just below the crest. The cost of seizing that line had been severe. The three days of fighting that began at La Croix Rouge Farm had cut the 168th's strength in half to just over 1,500 effectives. B Company of the 1st Battalion had only 100 men left standing that night. Major Stanley reported the 2nd Battalion's strength to Colonel Bennett, saying, "Effectives in my battalion as follows: E 81; F 54; G 61; H 106; attached M.G. [Machine Gun] Company (Company C 151st M.G. Bn.) 51. Total 353." It had been a terrible and unnecessary price to pay for so little gain.[88]

As the New Yorkers of the 165th fought their way up the hill near the Meurcy Farm and the Iowans of the 168th struggled to hold Hill 212, the Alabamians of the 167th began their own advance. The regiment's 2nd Battalion, plus C Company from the 1st Battalion, took the lead with the 1st and 3rd Battalions in support. Like with the 168th, the lead battalion was chosen because it had suffered the least at La Croix Rouge Farm. They advanced down the Rû de la Taverne toward the Ourcq before turning slightly east. Colonel Screws established his PC at the l'Espérance Farm while Lieutenant Colonel Bare set up a forward PC at an abandoned German shelter in a small, wooded area along a tributary of the Ourcq, the Rû d'Oie. The shelter sat next to a spring, which the Germans knew the Americans might use. As a result, they had carefully registered coordinates for the spring and proceeded to shell Bare's advance PC heavily throughout the day. Most of the shells contained gas, so Bare and his staff had to don their gas masks. Unfortunately, Bare had to use his field telephone a great deal, which meant that he had to lift his mask briefly whenever he talked. As a result, he "suffered considerable burns and nausea from the effect of the gas."[89]

The 167th was assigned to take the heights above the Ourcq in the wheat fields "directly north of l'Espérance Farm," which would allow them to connect with the 168th to their right near Sergy and the 165th on the left near Meurcy Farm.[90] It was about 10:00 a.m. when the 2nd Battalion and C Company forded the river. C Company moved off to the left to establish contact with the 165th's right flank, while 2nd Battalion moved up the hills to their front. As with the other regiments of the Rainbow Division, the Alabamians began to receive heavy German artillery fire from the moment they approached the Ourcq. Then, as they crossed the river, 2nd Battalion began to take flanking machine gun fire from Sergy and the ridge above the town.[91]

From the 3rd Battalion's position just south of the Ourcq, Private John Hayes could clearly see the attack develop and go forward. He said that "whole companies rushed forward in the initial attack, but recoiled from the fierce fusillade of machine gun fire." The 2nd Battalion immediately shifted to the crawl and rush tactics. Hayes later wrote, "the attack after then was pressed by smaller contingents—squads, groups, and platoons— who held their ground and pressed slowly forward by taking advantage of features of terrain, such as patches of trees, clumps of bushes, and ground elevations and depressions." "I remember watching group after group as they attacked through the wheat fields," he added. "An entire group would begin a rush together, but in a matter of minutes, men would start taking head-long falls. From where we were, it looked like their feet were being snatched out from under them." [92]

The 2nd Battalion finally reached the crest of the hill and made contact with the 165th on their left. However, once they consolidated their position, they continued to receive flanking fire from the direction of Sergy and could not link up with the 168th to their right. So Colonel Screws sent the 1st Battalion across the river and to the right to fill the gap between his regiment and the Iowans on Hill 212. The 1st Battalion made contact with the 168th and succeeded in clearing out the last remaining German snipers and machine guns in Sergy. Once that was done, two of their platoons actually entered the village. Still, they, too, were forced to fall back when the Germans laid down a heavy artillery barrage on them. [93]

During the attack up the slopes by the 2nd Battalion, Corporal Sidney Manning of G Company took command of his platoon when his platoon commander and sergeant went down. The platoon was near the center of the line and was taking severe machine gun fire. Though already wounded himself, Manning led the remaining thirty-five men until they gained a foothold in the wheat fields. By the time the platoon had managed to secure their position, Manning had been wounded a second time, and he only had seven men left in his little command. Manning consolidated what remained of the platoon and held off a large group of Germans only fifty yards away using his Chauchat. All the while, the corporal refused to take cover until the platoon's position was firmly secure. By the time he finally dragged himself to shelter, he was suffering from nine different wounds. Manning would receive the Medal of Honor for his actions that morning. [94]

Colonel Screws later complained that he received a series of contradictory orders from the 83rd Brigade during the fighting on July 28. He told division historian Henry Reilly, "There were a number of attack orders issued and countermanded. On two occasions my regiment advanced a considerable distance when we received orders to come back. In coming back, we suffered more casualties than in going forward." [95]

The last regiment to go into action on July 28 was Ohio's 166th. Their movement forward had begun the evening before in a driving rainstorm. Later that night, Colonel Hough received the similarly disturbing orders as his counterparts in the division. 83rd Brigade Headquarters wanted the 166th to advance across the Ourcq in the morning toward the village of Seringes-et-Nesles. But while the brigade told him where the other regiments were located, there was nothing indicated about the enemy's strength or position. Like every other regimental commander along the I Corps line, it would be up to Hough to direct his men. "There were no battle orders except as before stated," he later commented, "and the entire engagement was carried out by verbal orders of the regimental commander, which met all local tactical situations. The careful preliminary reconnaissance which the technicians teach to be absolutely imperative, was not had, nor could it have been had under the circumstances."[96]

All Hough's orders really said was to "leap-frog the French and take up the advance."[97] Again, like everyone else, the brigade was essentially telling the regiment to develop information about the enemy's positions by actually establishing and maintaining contact with them. Once the fighting started, the regiment was essentially on its own. Hough's officers and men would have to develop attack plans and tactics on the spot to press the Germans and hurry their continued retreat.

At 1:00 a.m., the 1st Battalion was ordered to advance down the slopes to the riverbank, cross the river at 3:45 a.m., and take the village of Seringes-et-Nesles. The ultimate objective was to take and hold the town as well as the Forêt-de-Nesles just beyond it. The orders also explicitly told Hough that his men would receive no Allied artillery support. As one soldier from the 166th said bitterly, "Only God can tell where those machine guns are located—and there isn't any artillery to drive them out!"[98]

Just before dawn, the 1st Battalion began to move out of the Forêt-de-Fère but had some difficulties. As a result, instead of crossing the river at 3:45 a.m. as scheduled, they did not emerge from the woods and begin their approach to the Ourcq until almost 7:00 a.m. As they descended the gentle slope to the riverbanks, their advance went without incident, as both German artillery and machine guns remained silent. The Ohioans quietly waded across the river, but they could clearly hear the Germans firing at the 165th to their immediate right. As they crawled up the far bank, it was their turn for similar treatment. As soon as the battalion had crossed the river, they were hit with withering machine gun fire from numerous hidden emplacements, as well as carefully placed German artillery fire. As the sun came up and the morning wore on, forward progress was measured in feet or even inches.

As soon as the enemy engaged them, the men dropped to the ground and began to crawl forward. The C Company commander, Captain Oscar Koeppel, was hit in the back by a jagged piece of shrapnel from a shell that exploded just above him as he crawled across the open ground. The shrapnel almost severed his spinal cord, but Koeppel refused to leave his command until the new line was established. Finally, Private Harry Leonard was able to drag him back across the river to safety amid a rain of enemy artillery shells. Lieutenant Milton Latta took command of C Company and tried to keep the men moving. But he soon discovered that one of the other platoon commanders, Lieutenant James Moseley, had been hit in the head by a machine gun bullet and killed, leaving only Latta and Lieutenant Sinclair Wilson plus Sergeant William Farrar in command. Between the three of them, they found there were only about fifty men in C Company still alive and able to continue. They moved to their final position 300 yards north of the river, where they dug in with those 50 men. Meanwhile, two platoons from D Company made it as far as La Fontaine-sous-Pierre, about 500 yards north of the river. But murderous machine gun and artillery fire forced them back to where the tattered remnants of C Company had finally dug in. Moving forward to support the left flank of the 165th was simply out of the question. The 1st Battalion had no choice but to dig in where they were and hold on.[99]

Their Machine Gun Company support was in similarly dire straits. They had lost three lieutenants and six sergeants in the fighting and continued to fight with one officer, Lieutenant Frank Radcliffe, who had just joined the company a week before and had no previous experience employing machine guns. But faithful to their task, his remaining sergeants came forward, took command of the company's three platoons, and continued the fight.[100]

As 1st Battalion held on for dear life, a French infantry unit managed to advance through the wheat fields toward the village of Fère-en-Tardenois, which was about a half-mile to the west of 1st Battalion's position. They were able to force the Germans out of the village, clearing the battalion's left flank. The Germans fell back to the crest of the ridge above the town and dug in. The French moved cautiously up the slopes of the ridge until they too were struck with heavy machine gun fire that drove them back to the east-west road leading from the town.[101]

The lack of Allied artillery support allowed German artillery to operate without fear of counter-battery fire, and they made the most of it. Just like the positions in the Forêt-de-Fère, the Germans had carefully registered every road leading to the Ourcq River, making movement by the regiment's Supply Company impossible during daylight. The only option was to take food and water forward at night, an operation that could be quite hazardous on unfamiliar roads using unreliable maps. But the Sup-

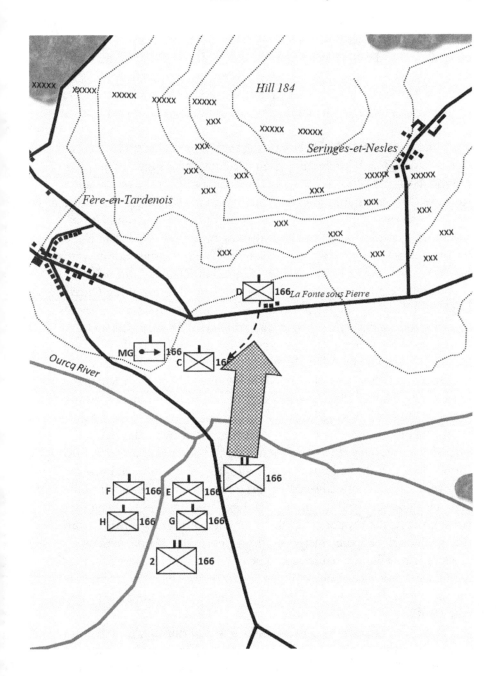

Map 6. Crossing of the Ourcq River by the 1st Battalion of the 166th Infantry Regiment on July 28, 1918.

ply Company did its best, as always. They sent ration carts carrying cooked food and water carts filled with hot coffee as far forward as possible under cover of darkness. From there, groups of men from the Pioneer and Stokes mortar sections of Headquarters Company and members of the regimental band carried the meals and water forward under cover of darkness.[102]

As the 1st Battalion had been moving to the crossing, Captain George Geran followed with his 2nd Battalion. He deployed his men in the open ground just north of the Forêt-de-Fère while waiting for the 1st Battalion to move through them. Once they had arrived and started down the slopes to the river, Geran followed about 500 yards behind. E and F Companies led the way with G and H Companies in support. Geran had E and F Companies form into two platoons in line, with the men at one-yard intervals, while G and H Companies followed in squad columns.[103]

When the lead companies reached a small ridge south of the Ourcq, Geran could see that the 1st Battalion was having a tough time against determined resistance. At that moment, a runner arrived with orders for Captain Geran from Colonel Hough to pull his men back until they were at least one kilometer behind the 1st Battalion's position. As his men were in the process of falling back, the brigade adjutant suddenly appeared on the scene and demanded that Geran turn his men around and move forward. "Colonel Hough considered we were jammed up too close to the 1st Battalion and ordered me to retire until I had one kilometer distance," Geran replied. The adjutant shot back, "Show me the order." Geran tersely informed him that the order was verbal, and the adjutant insisted that the major turn around and advance. At this point, Geran had enough of the adjutant's nonsense, telling him that he refused to do so unless the order came through the proper chain of command, which was directly from Colonel Hough or, in an emergency, from General Lenihan in person.[104]

Geran's battalion remained a kilometer from the beleaguered 1st Battalion, who were desperately holding on across the river. He ordered his men to dig in, as they were subjected to heavy artillery fire and strafing and bombing by German aircraft.[105]

As the 1st Battalion held its perilous position during the afternoon and night of July 28, the 2nd Battalion entrenched in positions south of the Ourcq. The 3rd Battalion, meanwhile, spent most of the day in the Forêt-de-Fère. Then, at 6:00 p.m., they were ordered to move forward to a new position just west of the chateau in the Bois de Villemoyenne and about two miles south of the Ourcq.[106]

At sunset, the fields around the Ourcq became quieter, with only the occasional German shell or the brief rat-tat of a machine gun disturbing the peace. John Taber later described the scene as darkness approached:

> The blood-red sun, balancing for a moment before plunging over the brink of the farthest hill, bathed the field in a rich glow. In brilliant color, like a flaming Remington canvas, it painted the valley of the Ourcq and its furrowed heights. Never was there a more vivid picture of the dreadfulness and brutality of war than that picked out by the carmine light on the trampled wheat. . . . Dead bodies, pitifully strewn about in grotesque attitudes of supplication, surprise, despair; some pitched forward on their faces, others crumpled up on their knees as death had caught them trying to struggle to their feet; some in repose, as if asleep; one or two still clenching in lifeless fingers, lifeless cigarettes; a few unrecognizable. Shells falling on men already dead. Everywhere, the debris of battle; here a blood-soaked shoe, there a pierced helmet; ravelled puttees, dented canteens, torn blankets, gory litters. Not a pleasant sight to view, horrible to remember. On the hill a motionless line of khaki figures huddled close to earth to escape the deadly bursts that momentarily dust the sky.[107]

It had been a hellish day for the Rainbow Division, but there were more to come.

8

THROUGH THE WHEAT FIELDS

July 29, 1918

"Tomorrow we must continue to push the enemy back by energetically concentrating our artillery fire on the points of resistance and by operating against these points with mixed infantry and cavalry advance guards. Close contact must be maintained both day and night, to prevent the enemy from slipping away. This is the duty of all."

—General Orders No. 3,627, French Sixth Army,
7:00 p.m., July 28, 1918

On July 29, 1918, two small French villages became the center of bitter fighting along the Ourcq River. Their names were Seringes-et-Nesles and Sergy. After over a thousand years of a peaceful, tranquil existence, that they would become the scenes of so much death and destruction would never have been imaginable to their residents. But that would be their fate this summer day.

Seringes-et-Nesles sat atop a ridge above the Ourcq just east of what the Allies called Hill 184 and one mile east of the larger town of Fère-en-Tardenois. Seringes-et-Nesles had a small church, ninety houses, and twelve water wells. Most of its 293 residents farmed the large fields of wheat that surrounded the village. However, since the Germans had arrived in force a few weeks earlier, almost all of them had fled.

Nothing important had ever happened in Seringes-et-Nesles, but on this day, hundreds of Americans and Germans would die to possess the village and the ridge on which it was located. The village was certainly nothing special in the grand scheme of things, but, no doubt, the people who lived there loved their homes, the small village church, and the small shops. By the end of the day and the next, virtually all of the homes and even the church would be rubble, and the streets and surrounding fields would be littered with the dead and dying.

Sergy, meanwhile, sat in a hollow atop a ridge north of the Ourcq about two miles southeast of Seringes-et-Nesles. Like its sister village, Sergy had always been a pastoral and peaceful place. It was slightly smaller than Seringes-et-Nesles, with a population of 256 souls living in seventy-eight small houses. They also had a church, a town hall, a school, and one café. John Taber, who visited the village as part of the 168th Infantry, described it as not being "noteworthy for its beauty nor was it overly clean, but it was picturesquely snuggled in between two hills rounded from the lovely countryside of orchards and checkered fields upon which it drew for its existence."[1]

The Germans had overrun the village in September 1914 before being pushed out by the French Army. From then until just two months earlier, the war had not intruded on the villagers' doorsteps. But on May 29, the Germans returned to take the town. At first, no battles raged nearby, but seemingly unending columns of German soldiers moved through the village on their way toward Paris. Then, in July, the French and Americans counterattacked. The rumbling of artillery could be heard in the distance, but with every day, it came closer. Then, during the last week of this fateful July, the Germans returned and began digging trenches and setting up artillery batteries on the hills behind the town.[2]

On July 26, the German commandant ordered all young women and boys to move north out of the path of impending danger. The next day, the war truly arrived in Seringes. The German artillery around the village fired incessantly as new columns of German soldiers appeared. But these were headed north, and many of the men had a "dejected, sullen look." The people heard that the Americans were coming, which surprised them. All along, the Germans had been telling them that there were only a few Americans in France because most of their ships had been sunk by U-boats while they attempted to cross the Atlantic.[3]

On this day, the Americans would liberate the village and be greeted with thankful tears by the few people who remained. But, sadly, repeated artillery barrages by both the warring factions would destroy the tiny village. By the end of the day, Sergy would be nothing but a "smoking heap of battered masonry."[4]

July 29, 1918, would be a day that saw the destruction of these two small villages that had lived in peace for a thousand years. The people who lived there had done nothing to deserve this fate. And hundreds of men from distant, foreign places called Alabama and Iowa would live their last moments in their streets and the surrounding fields. Like the people of Seringes-et-Nesles and Sergy, their fate was undeserved as well, and they never dreamed their all-too-short young lives would end here.

Such was the tragedy of this "war to end all wars."

The orders to the 42nd Division for July 29 seemed to reflect the same misguided view of the situation along the front as all the days that had preceded it. The General Orders from the French Sixth Army and Field Orders from I Corps issued during the evening of July 28 began with similar statements that the enemy had given way under pressure from attacks by the Rainbow Division.[5] They had, in fact, given way, but that progress could only be measured in hundreds of yards that cost thousands of American lives. It was hardly the resounding success the language in the orders seemed to suggest. Perhaps worse, Field Order No. 10 from the 84th Brigade to the 167th and 168th Infantry, which ordered a continuation of the attack for the morning of July 29, stated the need for maintaining contact with a retreating enemy. "The higher authorities seemed bound to view the situation with optimism," wrote John Taber, "but if any of them had come within three kilometers of the front they would soon have perceived that the enemy was in anything but retreat. He was, on the contrary, firmly lodged in positions of almost impregnable security."[6]

However, perhaps the most insane part of the orders for the day was the objectives stated in the I Corps field order. They directed that the main body of the division's assault forces should reach a line from Chéry-Chartreuve along the Chéry-Chartreuve-Bruys road to the western edge of the Bois de Dole. At the same time, advance units would move forward to reach a line between Mont-Notre-Dame and Mont-Saint-Martin. The first line was over five miles from the division's current position, and the latter line was almost seven miles away. Given that thousands of men had fought to gain a few hundred yards the day before, such goals were clearly beyond ludicrous.[7]

However, interestingly, these objectives likely reflected the desires of the French Sixth Army and not those of I Corps. That same evening, Gen-

This watercolor painting made by Ernest Clifford Peixotto after the battle shows the ruins of the small church in Seringes-et-Nesles. (*National Archives*)

eral Liggett, the I Corps commander, sent a message to General Degoutte that detailed the situation along the front. In it, Liggett told Degoutte that, while the 42nd Division had reached its initial objectives, it had come at an estimated loss of about 4,200 casualties. He also told the French general that the continued advance contemplated would be impossible if the 28th Division and the French 154th Division did not advance as ordered on the 42nd Division's right and left, respectively. Liggett said such an attack by the Rainbow Division would be "hardly practicable" even if it met "with little resistance." He went on to bluntly say, "In the meantime, pursuant to operation orders No. 3,627 the advance will be ordered as you direct, and every attempt will be made to carry it out with the certainty that if the enemy is retiring contact will be maintained, and with the equal certainty that if resistance is serious and the units on the right and left do not perform their full part in keeping abreast, the move will be stopped almost on its inception."[8]

Just before dawn, Colonel Bennett received a warning order from the 84th Brigade that there would be an attack made around 7:00 a.m. with the objective of reaching a point about one mile north of their present position near the town of Nesles. Bennett decided the 2nd Battalion would lead the attack with the 1st Battalion in support and the 3rd Battalion in reserve. He let the battalion commanders know what information had been provided and awaited more detailed orders to arrive from the brigade. When Major Stanley received the message from the colonel, he replied with a message asking what routes his battalion should use in moving forward and called attention to the fact that his battalion was very weak. As he waited for a response from Bennett, he sent a patrol out to reconnoiter Sergy and determine the German strength there.[9]

Stanley was correct about the condition of his battalion and, in fact, every battalion in the regiment. In K Company of the 3rd Battalion, John Taber noted in his diary, "It's July 29th and we've had no food since leaving the Forêt-de-Fère, reserve rations gave out some time ago, and most of us are getting weak. The men look haggard and sunken eyed, just when we are most in need of dependable men."[10]

Shortly after receipt of the warning order, Bennett received Field Order No. 10 from the 84th Brigade directing the attack to begin at 8:00 a.m. and saying that supporting forces from the 28th Division would advance to cover their right flank. Bennett sent the updated orders to the battalion commanders by runner and noted to Major Stanley that Sergy would be the biggest obstacle in his path. Bennett also told Stanley that American artillery would shell Sergy and that he should avoid the town unless he found that any Germans there posed no danger to his flank. In addition, the colonel informed all the battalion commanders that 84th Brigade Headquarters was sending two battalions of infantry from the 47th Infantry Regiment of the 4th Division to help shore up their dwindling numbers.[11]

Things got off to a bad start almost immediately. German artillery fire had increased during the night and, just before sunrise, they picked up the intensity of the shelling, sweeping the 168th's positions on the hills. As soon as it became light, German aircraft appeared overhead and added to the Iowans' misery by strafing and bombing their foxholes. Further, the 55th Brigade of the 28th Division had begun their assault to the 42nd Division's right, but heavy German artillery and machine gun fire brought them to an immediate halt. This, of course, meant that the 168th's right flank would continue to be uncovered.[12]

At 8:10 a.m., as Major Stanley watched for any sign of the promised supporting troops on his right, his patrols to Sergy returned. They told him that the main enemy line of resistance was about one thousand yards ahead of the 2nd Battalion's line. But, they added, there were isolated machine gun emplacements placed closer and the Germans had positioned cross-firing guns to cover the open space between the 2nd Battalion and the Germans' main line. As for the situation to Stanley's left, scouts he had sent to find the 167th returned to report that the Alabamians' 1st Battalion had been moved into position to try to fill the gap between the two regiments, but they had been unable to completely close it.[13]

Twenty minutes later, Stanley decided he could not wait any longer for support on his right and ordered his scouts to advance, followed by G, H, and I Company with F Companies in support. The men had gone only a few yards before German machine guns and artillery began to sweep across their ranks from Sergy and seemingly every direction. As they hit the ground for cover, American artillery finally showed itself. However, rather than striking the Germans, the friendly shells fell on Stanley's men. The major immediately sent word back for the artillery to shift its fire to the coordinates he had previously provided for the German positions and for additional machine guns and fire support from the unit's 37mm gun be sent forward.[14]

Just a few minutes later, as Stanley's 2nd Battalion tried to survive the intense German fire, Major Worthington from the 1st Battalion notified Colonel Bennett that he had contacted the 110th Infantry, which was one of the 55th Brigade units trying to advance on the right. He told Bennett that the 110th informed him that they not only were no longer moving forward but that they were actually falling back. If Stanley's battalion were going to make any progress, they would have to do it independently.[15] So, within just thirty minutes, the situation for the 168th had gone from bad to worse.

Meanwhile, Stanley's battalion was being raked by machine gun fire from Sergy on their left, the ridge above the town in their front, and from enemy guns placed in the church steeple in Cierges about a mile away. Perversely, the large Red Cross flag still flew from the steeple where the German guns were located. At 9:00 a.m., the American artillery fire shifted but not forward on the 2nd Battalion line toward the Germans. Instead, it was now falling behind Stanley's men on the 3rd Battalion position where one of the shells mortally wounded Lieutenant Van Hof. Major Brewer wrote a hurried, desperate note to Colonel Bennett: "Our 155's [155mm artillery guns] opened up on our line just now, and the first shell fell 100 yards within my line and the next three on it. Lieutenant Van Hof is either killed or badly wounded, and his platoon is shot all to Hell. Cannot we have effective liaison with the artillery? The Boche are shelling me on one side, and our artillery on the other!" At the same time, the 1st Battalion was being pounded by German artillery, and Major Worthington requested that friendly artillery shift to counterbattery fire.[16]

Major Stanley now realized that, given the dozens of machine guns hidden in the Bois Pelger and the Bois de la Planchette, trying to move toward Nesles from the east side of Sergy would be impossible. Furthermore, the enemy continued to fire from concealed machine gun emplacements in the wheat fields that lined the Sergy-Nesles road and the ridge just above Sergy, overlooking it from the right. While he had been told not to enter Sergy because of American artillery fire planned for the village, not a single American shell had fallen anywhere near the village. So Stanley decided he would take the village and try to advance from there.[17]

Stanley immediately went to find Lieutenant Kirt Chapman of F Company, the leader of the 2nd Battalion's scouts. The major found Chapman at an observation post to the left of the battalion line where he was watching German movements around Sergy. Stanley told Chapman that he planned to take Sergy and that Chapman and Lieutenant George Vaughn from E Company would be the ones to capture the village. The major also said that he would leave the size of the attacking force and the plan for the attack to Chapman and Vaughn's best judgment. With that, Stanley left to go back to the battalion PC, leaving the two young lieutenants to make their plans. They decided that, since Chapman and his scouts had operated east of the village and knew the terrain there best, he would lead a frontal attack from that direction with his eighteen scouts. Vaughn, meanwhile, would take a force of twenty-five men from the 3rd Platoon of E Company following the course of the Ourcq until they could make an assault directly from the south of the village. With the plan in place, Chapman took his men toward the east side of Sergy, where he waited for Vaughn to get into position.[18]

Once Chapman could see that the E Company contingent was ready for their advance from the south, the lieutenant signaled his men to move out. They crept forward at a deliberate pace until they neared the edge of the village. Remembering what had happened to the earlier patrol that had been surprised and surrounded in the center of Sergy, Chapman sent his men forward in small groups of two or three men, spaced a minute or two apart. They came to a sudden halt at the sight of what appeared to be a German machine gun nest until one group went forward and discovered it had been abandoned. Chapman then gave another signal, and the entire group of eighteen men rushed forward to the edge of the village, where they took cover behind the stone walls that bordered the town.[19]

Lieutenant Vaughn's team had simultaneously been using similar tactics to approach Sergy from the south. Once both groups were in place, they carefully observed what they could of the village and detected no evidence of German activity. Chapman's scouts then entered the village, darting from house to house and wall to wall. When they reached the town church on the eastern side of Sergy, Chapman detailed Corporal Paul Dixon and Private Arthur Kirchoff to remain there and guard the rear. Then Chapman sent the other men forward into the village in groups of three.[20]

As they crept through the rubble along the streets, it appeared that the Germans had withdrawn completely, as not a single shot was fired at them. Suddenly, however, they heard the muffled sound of voices. The scouts converged on the location of the sound to discover it was coming from below a securely locked cellar door. With rifles at the ready, they forced it open and found a trembling elderly couple in hiding. As they helped them out of the cellar, another younger couple and a fourteen-year-old girl emerged from their hiding places in the basement. As soon as these people realized who Chapman and his men were, they shouted, "*Américains*," embracing them while weeping in joy.[21]

Chapman and Vaughn's men would soon locate all twenty-three of the town's remaining citizens, but not all of them had fared so well. In one house, they found a young woman sprawled on her couch with a newborn infant. She had apparently given birth without medical assistance in the cellar a few days before as German shells crashed into the streets above. Since then, she and her baby had laid on the couch with only a candle for light and no water or food. The Iowans quickly sent for a stretcher that then took her and her infant to the rear for medical care. Sadly, they both died a few days later, two more tragic casualties.[22]

Meanwhile, Chapman and Vaughn questioned the other citizens about the German presence. They told them that most Germans had left the previous night, leaving just a few rear guards to harass any American advance. Since then, they had not seen or heard any sign of them. However, it soon became clear that the Germans on the slopes above the town had watched the Americans enter the village. As the Iowans moved through Sergy toward the western edges of town, they found less cover and were immediately hit by a new storm of artillery and machine gun fire. They tried to establish outposts and move beyond the village toward the ridge north of Sergy but were quickly driven back. At noon, while Vaughn placed his men in positions just west of Sergy in the relative safety of the banks of a narrow stream that cut through the lower western end of the village and tried to gain liaison with the 167th, Chapman sent word to Major Stanley that they had secured the village and that it was clear of any Germans.[23]

Stanley replied by sending a runner with word that American artillery was about to fire on Sergy. This was the bombardment that had been scheduled for early morning, and the artillerymen were apparently just now starting the fire mission. Because liaison with the American gunners was so bad, Stanley knew he could not stop the barrage from starting. He advised Chapman and Vaughn to have their men take cover quickly. For the next thirty minutes, the small detachment "lived through an inferno" as American 75mm shells combined with the German shelling of Sergy. What was left of Sergy was soon crushed amid "shells crashing everywhere, splinters flying in all directions, roofs falling in."[24]

The American artillery must have learned of their error because they quickly ceased firing, as did the Germans, who probably thought the American guns were doing an excellent job all on their own. With the end of the shelling, Lieutenant Chapman took advantage of the relative quiet to move through the village, checking on his men. All was fine until he reached the church. There, he found a smoking shell hole with Corporal Dixon and Private Kirchoff's bodies nearby, mangled so severely that they were almost unrecognizable. When he located Lieutenant Vaughn, he learned Vaughn had lost twelve men. Chapman and Vaughn then moved out to place outposts fifty yards above the village.[25]

About that time, the men of the 2nd Battalion on Hill 212 saw a large group of troops moving up behind them down the ridge leading from La Croix Blanche Farm toward the Ourcq River. These men were ominously in combat formation with bayonets fixed and scouts in the lead. For a moment, the men on the hill thought the Germans might have gotten in behind them. But as the troops grew closer, they could see they were wearing khaki uniforms and flat steel helmets—they were Americans. The first man from the battalion to greet them was a runner who was on his way to Colonel Bennett's PC. "Where are you fellows going, Buddy," he called out to one of the scouts, "What is your outfit?"[26]

"This is the Third Battalion of the 47th Infantry," came the reply. "We're going to take that town," said the scout, pointing toward Sergy. The Iowan responded in good humor, saying, "Oh, is that so? Our men are out in front of it now. Welcome to our city."[27]

The 3rd Battalion of the 47th was one of the two battalions sent to support the 84th Brigade, and neither had seen any combat. It had been assigned to support the 168th while the other battalion was going into the line with the 167th. The battalion commander, Major Heidt, had reported to Colonel Bennett at his PC at the La Cense Farm around 8:00 a.m. Since Bennett had no specific assignment for the battalion, he had his operations officer, Captain Ross, lead the major to a nearby hollow in the wheat field west of the farm where Bennett wanted the men from the 47th to dig in and wait for orders. He also gave Heidt careful instructions on the path to take when moving his men up to avoid detection by the German artillery observers.[28]

Either Heidt misunderstood Ross's instructions or simply did not know how to read a map because he not only did not take the right approach to the wheat field, but he also led his men directly across the worst possible open ground. They were completely exposed to the Germans, who proceeded to pound them with merciless artillery fire, inflicting terrible casualties. Major Heidt was wounded and taken to the rear as the rest of the battalion continued to a position in the woods just south of the Ourcq.[29]

Everyone in the 168th assumed the new battalion understood that they were to await specific orders. Still, after remaining in the woods for a couple of hours, they suddenly appeared again, moving past La Favière Farm toward the river. With Major Heidt wounded, Major Cole had taken command of the battalion, and he sent Captain Roberts of the battalion's I Company to Colonel Bennett's PC. Roberts told Bennett that they had withdrawn to the woods bordering the river, about 500 yards north of La Motte Farm, and that Major Cole would wait there for further orders. So Colonel Bennett was naturally shocked to see the battalion leave the woods about an hour later and start moving toward Sergy. As they began crossing the river, the Germans rained artillery down on them, inflicting heavy casualties. The 47th's men immediately fled to the rear in panic.[30]

Major Stanley had witnessed the disastrous advance and went to see the battalion commander. He discovered that Major Cole had also been wounded during this second foolhardy advance and that Captain Roberts was now in command. Cole had left for the aid station with all the maps, papers, and orders, so Roberts told Stanley he was unsure of what he was supposed to do. Stanley told him to dig in and stay in the woods and then go see Colonel Bennett again at the 168th's PC. Stanley also told him that his 2nd Battalion had surrounded Sergy with outposts now posted about 200 yards north of the village.[31]

Roberts reported to Bennett, where he was told once more to have his badly battered battalion remain in the woods until ordered otherwise. An hour later, Bennett sent a runner to Roberts with a message saying, "The senior officer of the battalion of the 47th Infantry will assume command and reorganize the battalion. Have the troops dig in for shelter in suitable position. Send one runner from each company to these headquarters until the battalion is reorganized, and then Battalion runners." However, it took almost two hours for the runner to locate Captain Roberts. Roberts acknowledged the order and replied that he would begin reorganizing his command. Unfortunately, Roberts was wounded shortly after that, and another captain took command. At this point, the battalion became essentially useless to the 168th. The plan for their support had been a good one in theory, but this battalion clearly was not capable of executing it.[32]

With Sergy cleared of German forces and outposts established north of the town, Major Stanley got his entire battalion ready to advance through the village and on toward the north, as originally ordered. However, when he consulted with Colonel Bennett, and they discussed the strength of the enemy's machine guns to the east, Bennett decided Stanley's men should dig in where they were until the 28th Division arrived on their right flank. As for the town itself, the colonel told Stanley to keep his outposts in place and put just enough men in the village to maintain contact with the 167th on the left and stop German snipers from returning.[33]

The situation on the right flank had continued to confound the ability of the 168th to advance. The 28th Division, which was made up of units from the Pennsylvania National Guard, had been late in replacing the French 39th Division on July 28. They began their effort to advance through Cierges and then pivot to the north early on the morning of July 29. The unit on their left flank was the 110th Infantry Regiment, which sent a runner about 3:30 p.m. to inform Major Stanley that they were assigned to link up on the 168th's right. Not long after that, the Iowans on the right side of their sector watched the Pennsylvanians try to push across the plateau of Hill 189 to take Cierges. But just like the 168th's 1st Battalion the day before, the intense German artillery and machine gun fire from Cierges swept them away, and they had to dig in on the lower side of the hill.[34]

As nightfall approached, the men of the 168th were a frustrated lot. Yes, they had finally managed to subdue the German threat from the area around Sergy, but they could not advance any farther. Worse, perhaps, was the fact that morale was sinking. The Iowans were "tired, haggard, and worn." They had been subsisting primarily on their individual reserve rations for four days, and now, the polluted waters of the Ourcq added to their misery. The river was the only local supply of water on the right side of the sector, and drinking its waters caused acute diarrhea, making these already exhausted troops feel even worse. Late in the afternoon, the Supply Company was able to get some decent meals sent forward, but the men were so nauseated from the combination of polluted water and the fumes from the enemy's gas shells, most could not bring themselves to eat. But perhaps worst of all, the men found themselves surrounded by dead comrades whose bodies could not be safely buried until nightfall.[35]

To the Iowans' left, the 167th began the day by attempting another assault through the wheat fields directly to their front toward Nesles and the west side of Sergy. However, the Germans' severe artillery and machine gun fire stopped them cold, and not a yard was gained. The rest of the regiment remained dug in just north and south of the Ourcq, where they were subjected to almost constant enemy shelling. I Company was one of the units south of the river, and Private John Hayes recalled that they were in a support position in a small wood near the spring. The proximity to this source of fresh water would have been a good thing except for the fact that men from other companies kept coming to use the spring as well. German observation balloons and aircraft detected this movement and apparently thought it indicated the presence of a troop concentration. So naturally, they directed an artillery strike on the area around the spring that killed and wounded several of Hayes's comrades.[36]

By the evening, the 167th remained in the same position where it had started the day. Because of their heavy losses since La Croix Rouge Farm, the 84th Brigade ordered the 1st Battalion from the 47th Infantry to relieve the Alabamians. After dark, the 167th quietly moved away from the Ourcq to camp in the Forêt-de-Fère. Once there, Colonel Screws decided to combine the 1st and 3rd Battalions into a single battalion under the command of Captain Ravee Norris. However, the move to the forest did not do much to relieve the suffering of the men, as the Germans subjected the woods to a constant bombardment that prevented sleep and wounded several men.[37]

Unlike the 167th, the New Yorkers in the 165th saw considerable action on July 29. On the night of July 28–29, the regiment continued to dig in and consolidate the line they held on the north side of the Ourcq. To ensure the Germans did not reoccupy the ground atop the hill below the

Meurcy Farm, Colonel McCoy sent out nighttime patrols into the area, which had now become a no man's land. They encountered German patrols, and small firefights erupted between the two sides in no man's land throughout the night.[38]

During the night, Colonel McCoy received his orders for the next day, which directed another assault on the Meurcy Farm and the Bois Colas. Initially, the plan was for the 3rd Battalion to make the advance and, at 2:00 a.m., the battalion received orders to expect an assault at 4:00 a.m. Most of the men were exhausted and had not had any sleep. Martin Hogan later recalled hearing the news of the impending attack: "From the moment of the outbreak of the heavy enemy barrage up to the receipt of these orders the men had been going at their best, first fighting a stubborn enemy all day, much of the time at grips with him, and then constructing intrenchments and fighting again in the evening. The orders meant another hard go on top of a sleepless night and possibly on an empty stomach. It was not a cheerful prospect." But thirty minutes before jumping off, new orders arrived, canceling the battalion's attack and ordering them to fall back to the rear.[39]

The change in the 3rd Battalion's assignment came because the attack had been delayed until 8:00 a.m. McCoy decided that Major Donovan's 1st Battalion would take the lead, with Major Anderson's 2nd Battalion supporting their immediate right. The attack was to occur in concert with a renewed attack by the 166th on their left toward Seringes-et-Nesles. Donovan's men were to advance along both sides of the Rue du Pont Brûle with the Bois Colas on the left and the Meurcy Farm on the right while Anderson's battalion supported them by securing the slopes to the right. If all went well, Donovan's battalion would link up with the Ohioans of the 166th to establish a line from the Bois Colas across the hills west to Seringes-et-Nesles and Hill 184 beyond.[40]

In the hours before dawn, the 1st Battalion began shifting to the left, so their line faced up the little valley toward the Meurcy Farm. Major Donovan recalled that this move was not as simple as one might hope. "The [German] machine gunners had climbed in so close to us in the night that it was very difficult to move," he wrote. "I went back to the P.C. of the 167th myself to get some artillery assistance. I thought I should never get back as I had to go up a little draw that was just singing with machine gun fire and heavy artillery."[41]

Luckily, the major was assisted by a soldier from the 167th who had been assigned to provide Donovan with support and who he remembered with great fondness. "I had a liaison man from the 167th outfit," he later wrote to Henry Reilly, "and I shall never forget him. He knew the best course, the shortest routes, and the quickest crossing across the river. He was calm and self-contained and cheerful. I would like to see him again." Donovan, his Alabama guide, and some of Donovan's men had to move up the flank to get to their assigned position, which meant they must cross some open ground where they would be exposed to fire from two German machine guns. Donovan ordered the men to each race across the open ground one at a time, but the Germans were able to get off a burst of fire as each man emerged to make his dash. They managed to hit each of the first ten men who made an attempt, but the others, including Donovan, made it safely across the deadly space.[42]

Major William Donovan, commander of the 1st Battalion of New York's 165th Infantry Regiment in the fighting along the Ourcq River. He would later become the commander of the regiment, be awarded the Medal of Honor, and serve as director of the Office of Strategic Services during World War II. (*National Archives*)

Donovan eventually reached the spot where his men were forming for the attack at a place where the stream made a bend. To the right of the stream was A Company, led by Lieutenant William Baldwin, while B Company, under the command of Captain Thomas Reilly, was nearby in support. Their job would be to advance out from the cover of the trees and up the gentle slope to the Meurcy Farm. To their left, C Company under Captain Herman Bootz took the lead with D Company, led by Lieutenant Edward Connelly, in support. Bootz and Connelly's assignment was to push up the hill above the Rue du Pont Brûle to seize control of the Bois Colas, which Father Duffy described as "a thickly wooded clump of trees about as big as three city blocks."[43]

When Donovan arrived back with his battalion, he found his men improperly forming for combat. "I had found that most of our troops in advancing had taken the formation of the books," he later said. "They had forgotten that these formations were made to advance with protection of artillery fire. I insisted that Company Commanders send their men forward as we used to do in the olden days, which is, one, two or three at a time, moving fast, and when they have advanced a few yards to flop."[44] So, once again, a savvy commander realized that the tactics in which they had been trained would not work in this situation.

When all was ready, the 1st Battalion began moving up the valley around 8:00 a.m. Amid withering German fire, Donovan had his own machine guns open fire on the German positions and assigned a sniper to each of his machine guns so they could pick off German gunners whenever they might reveal themselves. But the going was difficult, as the enemy had moved guns back into the Meurcy Farm, as well as on both sides of the farm complex. The worst fire, however, came from the enemy machine guns on the hill slopes to the right, which were also the most difficult to subdue. One of Donovan's sergeants attacked a machine gun nest with a detachment of twenty men. While they were able to take the gun's position, the sergeant had only four men left when they got there to take the seven-man gun crew prisoner. Later, there were reports of war crimes being committed by members of the Rainbow Division against German prisoners during the fighting on the Ourcq, and Donovan, for one, seemed willing to admit they occurred. He later said, "We took very few prisoners. The men, when they saw the Germans serving machine guns against us, firing until the last minute, then throwing up their hands and crying 'Kamerad,' became just lustful for German blood. I do not blame them."[45]

A Company was in the van of the attack. Advancing against heavy machine gun and artillery fire, young Lieutenant Baldwin urged his men forward, waving his sidearm in the air. The company had not gone far when German machine guns cut Baldwin down, one bullet striking him in the chest. Sergeant Thomas Sweeney ran to his side, kneeling down in an attempt to assist his lieutenant. Baldwin looked up at him and uttered his last words, saying, "Sergeant, carry out the orders." Baldwin was the first of twenty-six men in A Company who would be killed that morning.[46]

As the advance continued, Major Donovan's battalion adjutant, Lieutenant Oliver Ames, came running up to make sure the major was properly looked after, as Ames always did. Donovan was moving up the stream, trying to stay ahead of both A Company on his right and C Company on his left. As German fire increased, Donovan laid down at the edge of the stream with Ames at his side. The major half-turned to say something when a sniper's bullet whizzed past his shoulder, striking Ames in the ear and killing him instantly. As Donovan reached for his adjutant, another

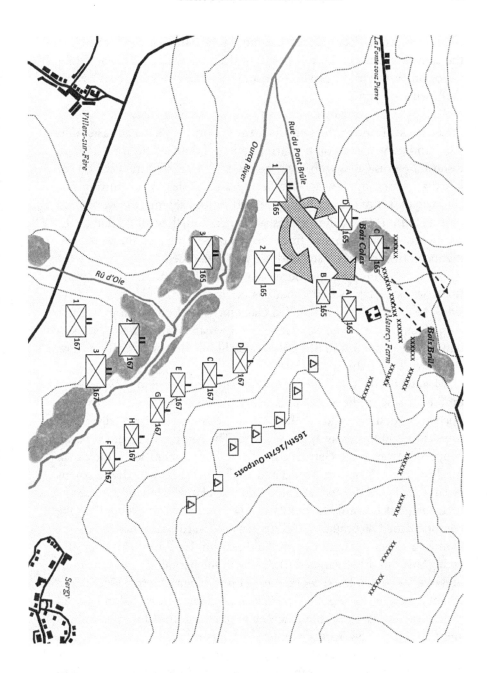

Map 7. The attack by the 165th Infantry Regiment against the Meurcy Farm and the Bois Colas on July 29, 1918.

round from the sniper's rifle struck him in the hand. He then rolled into the creek and crawled up to a group of his men, where he remained for almost forty-five minutes with mud and water up to his waist as German shells fell all around.[47]

While A Company made it to the walls of the farm, they were quickly forced back. However, their efforts made C Company's job an easier one. As A Company moved on the farm, Captain Bootz led his men forward toward the Bois Colas with the brook to their right and their left on the hill that sloped upward toward Seringes-et-Nesles. After putting one enemy gun out of action, they advanced cautiously into the woods, expecting to find strong German resistance. Instead, they found that all the enemy troops had retreated from the woods, leaving just one scared soldier behind who quickly surrendered to Bootz's men.[48]

But the capture of the woods was not totally without cost, as Captain Bootz was struck by a bullet that passed through his chest from side to side. The wound might have killed many men, but Bootz was, apparently, a tough customer. As he was carried to the rear, he smiled, took his signature pipe in hand, and threw it to one of his lieutenants, saying, "Here, son, I won't need this for a while."[49]

Meanwhile, the remainder of C Company proceeded to take positions on the far side of the Bois Colas facing the Forêt-de-Nesles. Across the open ground, they could see the Germans gathered near the edge of the forest some 300 yards away to the north. The company's riflemen began peppering away at the Germans who were in the open. Soon, their own machine guns came forward to add to the mix. Many of the Germans began to fall, and the rest retreated into the relative safety of the trees.

Lieutenant Edward Connelly from D Company was ordered to take command of C Company, and he went forward searching for Major Donovan to get the major's specific direction. He found Donovan still taking cover in the streambed while one of the battalion's machine gunners, with a rifle in hand, worked to get the sniper who had killed Lieutenant Ames. He had spotted the German rifleman move behind a dead horse near the farm. So the machine gunner "cuddled his rifle, waited, and fired." The New Yorker's bullet found its mark, and the sniper was seen standing up halfway before dropping to the ground dead.[50]

In the afternoon, Donovan moved the men along the stream up into the Bois Colas, where they entrenched just above the Meurcy Farm. With the 2nd Battalion firmly in place on the slopes above and to the farm's left, the Germans there were effectively checked and would eventually pull out. As Major Donovan would later relate, "We had advanced some distance. We had done it with rifles, machine guns and bayonets and against artillery and machine guns—one machine gun to every four men."[51] Now, all that was needed was for the Ohioans of the 166th to move up on the New Yorkers' left toward Seringes-et-Nesles.

That final act in the day's fighting was almost certainly the most difficult. The 166th's objective, Seringes-et-Nesles, lay atop gently rising slopes covered in ripe wheat like most of the open ground above the Ourcq. The village itself was manned by a sizable contingent of German infantry who had placed numerous machine guns in the town and along its southern and western boundaries. Farther north of the village on the far side of the hill were multiple pieces of artillery that could provide accurate and heavy fire support, guided by the German artillery observers in the village. But the most challenging obstacle for the attacking Ohioans was the machine guns in the wheat fields. The Germans had deployed layers of machine gun emplacements among the waist-high wheat, which were heavily camouflaged and carefully placed to provide interlocking fire.

On the night of July 28–29, the 166th made plans for the beleaguered 1st Battalion to attempt another assault on Seringes-et-Nesles. Although they were dug in, had been pinned down for most of the previous day, and had taken extremely heavy losses, the battalion began to move forward under intense machine gun fire around 8:00 a.m. as the 165th began their attack on the Meurcy Farm and Bois Colas. However, they got no farther than D Company had the day before and finally dug in at La Fontaine sous Pierre, which was about 700 yards from Seringes-et-Nesles at the edge of the wheat fields. When they were in position, a C Company platoon leader, Lieutenant Eddie Coyle, noticed that one of his men had been severely wounded and was lying out in the open. Coyle climbed out from his shallow trench along the roadway and started to crawl through the wheat field toward the wounded soldier as German shells continued to fall around him. When he reached the wounded man, Coyle grabbed him by the shirt collar and dragged him back to safety.[52]

Seeing the 1st Battalion was now in truly desperate straits, Colonel Hough decided to move Captain Geran's 2nd Battalion across the Ourcq to relieve the 1st Battalion. This time, however, there would be some friendly artillery preparation to at least keep the enemy's heads down while the new battalion moved into place and the 1st Battalion retired to safety. The artillery fire would begin at 4:00 p.m., and while the barrage would be relatively brief, it might be enough to make a difference in the outcome. As the artillery bombardment began, E and F Companies from the 2nd Battalion made their way down the slopes toward the Ourcq. Once at the river's edge, they splashed into the hip-high water and made their way across, even though they were carrying full packs on their backs. After they waded across the Ourcq, they climbed up the steep bank on the far side and into open, flat ground. Captain John Stevenson led F Company and was in overall command of the attacking force, with Lieutenant Herman Doellinger in command of E Company.[53]

The men moved up across the little road that paralleled the river about 300 yards away as the remnants of the 1st Battalion fell back and crossed the river. A few moments later, E and F Companies reached the 1st Battalion's old position, stopping in an orchard behind an old stone wall to rest for a few minutes, drop their packs, and prepare to advance with just their rations, ammunition, and weapon. As the men rested in the orchard, Stevenson quickly moved to the right, searching for Doellinger. In a matter of minutes, he found Doellinger, who was on his way to find Stevenson. The two officers crouched down and discussed how they should execute the attack.

Stevenson and Doellinger decided that E Company would swing to the right and attack the left flank of the Germans in Seringes-et-Nesles. At the same time, F Company would make an assault directly ahead toward Hill 184 and the road leading into the village. From the very start, the two officers wisely concluded that the only viable tactic was to crawl forward and employ the small group rushes that had proved successful elsewhere along the I Corps front. Doellinger returned to E Company, which was on the battalion's right, telling his platoon officers and sergeants to form a skirmish line with the 1st and 4th Platoons as the initial wave. Once the American artillery lifted their barrage, the two companies began their approach. As soon as the Americans emerged from cover, the German machine guns opened fire from positions to their front and from their right flank, the chattering fire of their Maxim guns filling the air.[54]

Corporal Dana Daniels of E Company went to his squad and quickly explained the plan of attack. When the first men rose up to move out, they were met with more machine gun fire, and now, German artillery fire was added to the mix. Everyone dropped to the ground as Daniels tried to determine the position of the nearest enemy machine gun emplacement, a real challenge given that they were well hidden in the waist-high wheat. While they were lying there, one of his men, a newly arrived draftee named Harry Bell from Brownsboro, Alabama, was hit in the leg,

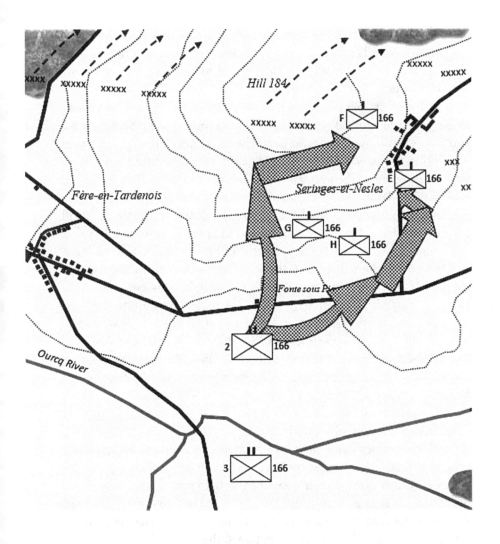

Map 8. The assault on Seringes-et-Nesles by the 2nd Battalion of the 166th Infantry Regiment on July 29, 1918.

and Daniels sent him to the rear. About that time, Daniels was hit in the helmet by a round from an enemy machine gun, making a one-fourth-inch dent in the steel headgear. He decided to change tactics and only send one or two men forward at a time. [55]

As the first couple of men began their rush forward, an unseen machine gun opened fire at almost point-blank range from a position on the squad's right flank. Private Robert Thorn, a young hotel clerk from Marysville, Ohio, was hit immediately and fell dead amid the stalks of wheat. He would be the first man in E Company killed in the attack, but, sadly, not the last.[56]

Daniels continued to send the men from his squad forward in small rushes, as ordered. Despite the machine gun fire and enemy artillery that now resumed its firing, "the boys in khaki never stopped a second." One of Daniels's soldiers, Private George Leffler, was lying to the right of Daniels. When Leffler started his rush forward, he only got a few steps before he was hit by machine gun fire. The bullets hit him on the right side and came out the left. Daniels could see Leffler was gravely wounded, and he assigned another soldier to take Leffler to the rear, where he died in a field hospital the next day. Now, it was Daniels's turn to advance, and, having seen Leffler get hit, he was "pretty doubtful" of his chances. But he got up anyway, knowing any delay on his part would hold up the entire platoon's progress. Daniels ran forward as "Boche bullets went "whiz whiz [underlined in original] around" him.[57]

Both companies made slow but steady progress up the slopes. Small groups of khaki-clad figures could be seen darting left then right as the German gunners swung their weapons trying to put fire down on them. Steadily, these little groups would close in on the nearest enemy gun until they were close enough to toss hand grenades at the emplacement. As the grenades burst amid the German gunners, the Ohioans would rise up, charge the emplacement, and kill any remaining Germans with their bayonets. Across the wheat fields, this drama continued both to the left and right as the German machine guns were subdued one by one.

As F Company slowly moved up Hill 184, E Company reached its position on the village's left flank. By this point, they had lost several men, with most of them wounded. The company now received orders from Captain Stevenson to shift their position to the road leading into the village. Corporal Daniels sent his men running in that direction, where they took cover in a shallow ditch about eighteen inches deep. The enemy turned their fire on Daniels's new position, which, since it provided minimal cover, he described as a "tight place." In fact, while he was lying flat on his stomach in the ditch, a machine gun bullet skidded across the top of his helmet.[58]

With the Americans closing in on the village, the Germans increased the pace and intensity of their artillery fire, and shells began to drop all around E Company's position. Daniels's platoon commander, Lieutenant Joseph McMinimy, jumped up and started running up the road with a few of his men when a German artillery shell landed right next to him. The blast shredded McMinimy and one other soldier, killing them instantly while wounding three others, including Daniels's friend, Sergeant Neal Davis. Davis was severely hit and died on the way to a field hospital. A few seconds later, Daniels's Chauchat gunner, Private William Elliot, was struck and sent to the rear. Another soldier took Elliot's Chauchat forward on the advance into Seringes-et-Nesles.[59]

E Company continued its advance with Daniels's platoon in the lead. When they reached the edge of the village, the corporal formed his squad just inside along a hedge fence, quickly deploying machine guns to cover the town. The rest of E and F Companies continued their advance up the road and into the village but at a great cost. The well-concealed German machine guns continued to fire right up to the moment the Americans entered the village. F Company lost Lieutenant John Hanford during their attack as well as Lieutenant William Hyman, who was killed as he tried to take out an enemy machine gun that had his men pinned down. Both were from the group disparaged at Camp Mills as "Sears and Roebuck officers," but they had proved their worth, just like many other such young officers in the Rainbow Division.[60]

As the men of the 2nd Battalion deployed into the village, they mopped up the enemy in a house-to-house search. They only found a couple of Germans because the rest had fallen back to the crest of the hill overlooking Seringes-et-Nesles. With the Germans gone, Stevenson now positioned the platoons of both companies at strategic points around the village.[61]

The captain could see that his men were in a badly exposed position. The Germans were on three sides of the town with machine guns placed on the left and center at distances from 75 to 300 yards. On the right, the enemy had withdrawn about a half-mile away across the valley. However, these Germans had an excellent view of Seringes-et-Nesles and could observe all of the American defensive positions. Luckily, some of Stevenson's men soon came to him and said they had discovered the attics in a few of the houses that provided a view directly down into the German trenches and gun pits. So Stevenson sent men to each attic where they could watch for signs of enemy movement, and he gave them strict orders not to fire at the Germans. Hence, the enemy remained unaware that they were being observed.[62]

While the 2nd Battalion was moving on Seringes-et-Nesles, the 3rd Battalion was ordered to move up to the Ourcq in support. When the orders were issued, the 3rd Battalion was deployed in Villers-sur-Fère, where they had been sent to support possible operations by the 167th. That attack had been canceled when the Alabamians were withdrawn, so the Ohioans were told to cross the Ourcq and be prepared to help the 2nd Battalion repulse a potential German counterattack.[63]

However, what should have been a simple maneuver became extremely complicated due to a bungling staff officer who mistakenly sent two of the 3rd Battalion's companies back to the Forêt-de-Fère as well as by intense German artillery fire on Villers-sur-Fere. The two missing companies were retrieved, but their commander, Captain Henry Haubrich, wisely decided to get the other two companies moving forward in case the 2nd Battalion needed them. As enemy shells came crashing down on the town, Haubrich had the two companies advance on opposite sides of the street, with each man separated in the column by about fifteen feet. With "fragments of shells, pieces of brick, stone, and tile roofs" raining down on them, the men slowly made their way to the northern side of town, where the artillery shelling finally stopped. From there, they moved up the road leading to Fère-en-Tardenois, crossed the Ourcq, and dug in. The other two companies crossed the Ourcq and joined the battalion late on the night of July 29.[64]

All during that night, the Germans subjected Seringes-et-Nesles and the 2nd Battalion to continuous artillery fire. Because of this, no attempt was made to advance and clear the crest of the ridge of Germans, most of whom had retired to positions on the edge of the Forêt-de-Nesles.[65]

As night fell along the I Corps front, the 42nd Division's line extended from west of Cierges and then up over Hill 212 to Sergy. From there, the line still followed the roadway just north of the Ourcq until it moved northward toward the Meurcy Farm before turning northwest along the northern edge of the Bois Colas toward Seringes-et-Nesles. The line then surrounded that village before leading to the west along the base of Hill 184. As a result, the 166th positions north of the Ourcq and at Seringes-et-Nesles created a vulnerable salient. As Raymond Cheseldine would later say, "Ohio stuck out in front of the sector like a sore thumb."[66]

On the night of July 29, it appeared that some sense of reality was beginning to dawn at French Sixth Army Headquarters. At 8:20 p.m., they issued a general order that encapsulated the situation along the front. It stated: "North of the Ourcq, the army has encountered serious resistance which has made our advance very difficult." For the first time, Degoutte and his staff seemed to admit that things were not as they should be, that the enemy was not in full retreat. However, they also ordered a continuation of the advance as had been ordered on July 28.[67]

The next phase of the fighting would seek to advance the lines to eliminate the salient around Seringes-et-Nesles and continue pursuing the Germans toward the Vesle River. It would prove just as costly as all the other days that had preceded it.

9

SENSELESS SACRIFICE

July 30–31, 1918

"I have received your report, Major Brewer, and have noted what you say of the proposed attack, but it is an Army order. The Corps orders the attack. I have no choice. We shall make it."
—General Robert Brown, Commander, 84th Brigade,
at a 2:00 a.m. meeting on July 30, 1918

The 168th Infantry and the 3rd Battalion of the 47th Infantry had been ordered to attack north from Sergy and take the area around the town of Nesles, just over one mile away. Given the tenacity of German resistance to date, this would have been a daunting task in the best of circumstances. But on the morning of July 30, the circumstances were far from the best.

Even today, someone standing at the northern edge of Sergy can clearly see the impossibility of what was being asked of the Iowans and the men from the 47th. First, the ground slopes upward from Sergy to a low ridge about 700 yards away, where the Germans were posted in strength with massive machine gun support. The land between Sergy and the ridgeline is almost entirely open. There is no cover except for a shallow streambed about 300 yards to the north of the town. On this July morning in 1918, the ground was covered in wheat and clover, much as it is today, allowing the machine guns atop the ridge to sweep the fields before them, mowing down anyone who showed themself.

However, the frontal fire would not be the greatest threat. That threat came from the three sets of woods to the east—the Bois Pelger, Les

Jomblets, and Bois de la Planchette. These woods were filled with German machine guns and mortars that were only 700 to 1,100 yards away, giving their gunners a clear field of fire against the advancing Americans' exposed right flank. The plan from the 84th Brigade promised an intense preparatory artillery barrage on these woods along with continuing artillery fire support during the attack. Major Brewer, the man designated to lead the assault, flatly told the regiment and brigade commanders that there was virtually no chance of success if the artillery fire did not suppress the German forces in the woods along his right flank. Up to this point, American artillery support had been almost nonexistent for a variety of reasons, one of which was the complete inability of the brigade to provide effective command and control of their artillery. The artillery always seemed to either never open fire, fire on the wrong target, or fire on American positions.

As a result of all these obstacles, Major Brewer and the other battalion commanders had little hope of success. At an early morning meeting with General Brown, the 84th Brigade commander, Brewer presented his plan and analyzed the challenges to its success. Despite all the issues, the general said, "You are to attack at nine o'clock tomorrow morning." As John Taber would later write, "At that time, he [Brewer] was to take the auctioneer's hammer of battle and force the best bargain he could for the lives of the men under his command. It was a sacrifice sale at the best. He understood that."[1]

All during the night of July 29–30, the Germans subjected Seringes-et-Nesles and the 2nd Battalion of the 166th Infantry to a continuous and violent artillery bombardment. As a result, while the next step for the Ohioans was clearly to advance and clear Germans from the crest of the ridge north of the village, it was simply impossible to do so given the ferocity of the enemy shelling. Dana Daniels wrote in his diary that the "big shells were falling like hail all around us, and our faces were black with powder and smoke." At one point, as he and two other men took shelter in a shell hole, it became clear that an enemy observer had decided to focus the artillery fire on their position. So Daniels ordered his men to follow him and relocate to a post on the far end of the village. After a mad dash through the shellfire, they dropped down behind a stone wall to catch their breath. As they took cover there, a German shell came roaring in, exploding just beyond the wall while a second shell blasted a building less than twenty yards away. So Daniels decided the wall was also not a good place to be, and he led his men on a run through a garden toward one of the stone buildings left standing in the village.[2]

As they raced across the garden, more shells fell close by, and one of Daniels's men, Private James Odensoff, was hit in the leg by shrapnel. Odensoff shouted to Daniels over the shellfire that he could keep going. So the men entered the building, where they found a cellar in which they could take refuge. Once below ground level, Daniels tended to Odensoff with his first aid kit. Soon, another man entered to take shelter in the cellar. He had been wounded in the hip, so Daniels did his best to bandage the wound. When the artillery barrage slackened slightly, Daniels went back upstairs and outside, where he learned that another of his men had been hit by shrapnel in the head and throat, dying instantly.[3]

The enemy shelling increased in intensity again, and around 8:00 p.m., it got even worse. The pace and ferocity of the German artillery fire convinced Colonel Hough that the enemy might be about to stage a counterattack designed to regain control of Seringes-et-Nesles. Therefore, he ordered the 2nd Battalion to withdraw to prepared positions about 300 yards southwest of the village and wait for the German barrage to lift. At the same time, American artillery finally came to the regiment's aid, opening fire on the German batteries and the open ground between the crest of the ridge and the village. This proved to be critical because, as it turned out, the Germans were, indeed, attempting an infantry assault on the village. However, the American artillery fire was so effective that only a few Germans managed to reach the village.[4]

At 9:30 p.m., Hough ordered A Company and B Company of the 1st Battalion to advance from their positions near La Fontaine Sous Pierre. They were to attack the Germans who had made it into Seringes-et-Nesles and drive them out. They swept into the village with fury, killing most of the Germans there and forcing the rest to retreat back to the Forêt-de-Nesles. By 10:30 p.m., the village was secured, and E and F Companies returned to their positions.[5]

To the right of the 166th, the New Yorkers of the 165th's 1st Battalion held their positions in the Bois Colas and around the Meurcy Farm on the night of July 29 and into the morning of July 30. C Company held the line west of the woods, maintaining the regiment's connection with the Ohioans, while D Company and its machine gun support remained along the upper edge of the Bois Colas. A and B Companies, meanwhile, were entrenched on the approach to the farm. During the night, some food finally made its way to the front line, which improved morale, as the men had long since exhausted their reserve rations.[6]

Major Donovan had established his battalion PC in a shell hole near the southern edge of the Bois Colas. Having lost his battalion adjutant, Lieutenant Ames, during the previous day's fighting, Donovan was glad to see the position filled by a volunteer and a very able member of the regiment's intelligence staff, Sergeant Joyce Kilmer. Kilmer, the famous poet and author of "Trees," could have remained in the rear at the regimental PC, but he was not the sort to shrink from frontline duty. Father Duffy would later say of Kilmer, "The Major placed great reliance on his coolness and intelligence and kept him by his side. That suited Joyce, for to be at Major Donovan's side in a battle is to be in the center of activity and in the post of danger. To be in a battle, a battle for a cause that had his full devotion, with the regiment he loved, under a leader he admired, that was living at the top of his being."[7]

The 165th's orders for the day were to hold their position but, as the day progressed, Donovan had what he later referred to as a "poker hunch." He sensed that the German machine gun position at the edge of the Bois Brulé, about a half-mile away, might be vulnerable to an attack. He had worked his way to a place in the right rear of the Germans and, while his men were now in a very tight salient, they had a clear view of the German position. Donovan hid in a wooded knoll armed with an extension telephone and a map. From there, he would plan and coordinate the attack.[8]

A fifteen-man platoon from D Company under Sergeant Richard O'Neill would make the assault. Donovan divided them into three groups of five men and began the attack with a barrage from the battalion's Stokes mortars and 37mm one-pounder. The ground to their front was rough and filled with slight depressions for about 200 yards, followed by two rows of trees that led up to the Bois Brulé. To their right, the terrain sloped down to the brook where it ran past the Meurcy Farm. Unseen, however, was a deep and irregular sandpit on the edge of the woods.[9]

As Sergeant O'Neill led his men forward, he saw the sandpit. He had started to move around it when he realized a group of twenty-five German infantrymen was in the pit. He yelled a warning to his men before leaping into the sandpit with his sidearm drawn and at the ready. Before the Germans realized what was happening, O'Neill had shot and killed three of them. Some of the other Germans tried to flee the pit while the rest opened fire on O'Neill, hitting him seven times. But the sergeant refused to go down and continued firing, an act for which he would later be awarded the Medal of Honor. The Germans who tried to leave the pit ran headlong into the other members of O'Neill's little attack force, and a fierce but brief firefight ensued. Three of fifteen New Yorkers were wounded, and four were killed as the remaining Germans fled across the open ground toward the Bois Brulé. At this point, some Germans emerged from the woods, and a cry went up among the 165th that a counterattack was being launched.[10]

Back in the woods, Major Anderson heard about the counterattack and sent his 2nd Battalion storming forward with reinforcements. His men and the 1st Battalion's machine gunners opened fire, cutting down the Germans. But it would turn out that the enemy was not attacking. The firing ceased in just a few minutes, and a "few bedraggled prisoners in dirty field gray uniforms" were its only byproduct. But in the process, the Germans abandoned their positions in the Bois Brulé, and Donovan was able to establish outposts there.[11]

Major Donovan would later say that he and his men had a "hard time" in the afternoon. During the afternoon's fighting, he was hit by shrapnel in the chest, left heel, and leg, and his entire battalion staff was either killed or wounded. Among those killed was Joyce Kilmer. When the warning was received about a possible counterattack, Donovan sent Kilmer forward to the edge of the wooded knoll where Donovan had positioned himself. He told Kilmer to reconnoiter and report on the situation. Kilmer grabbed Privates Edwin Stubbs and Jack McDonald and told them to come with him.[12]

The three men crawled in the open ground just along the edge of the woods as German machine gun bullets zipped right above their heads, using the many foxholes and shell holes along the way as cover. Stubbs was in the center with Kilmer on his right about five to ten paces away and closest to the woods. Kilmer would signal the others to advance, and all three men would continue to crawl forward until they reached the top of a gradual slope in the ground about 100 yards from their starting point. Once in position there, Stubbs and McDonald waited for the signal to continue forward but none came. Stubbs looked toward Kilmer's position and saw the sergeant slumped with his head and shoulders somewhat exposed. Stubbs called out to him, but there was no response. So he and MacDonald crawled over to Kilmer. There they found the brave soldier-poet was dead. He had been struck in the head and chest by enemy bullets, and, as they could find little evidence of bleeding, Stubbs and MacDonald believed he must have died instantly. Kilmer was buried the following day next to the regiment's PC with Father Duffy performing the burial rites.[13]

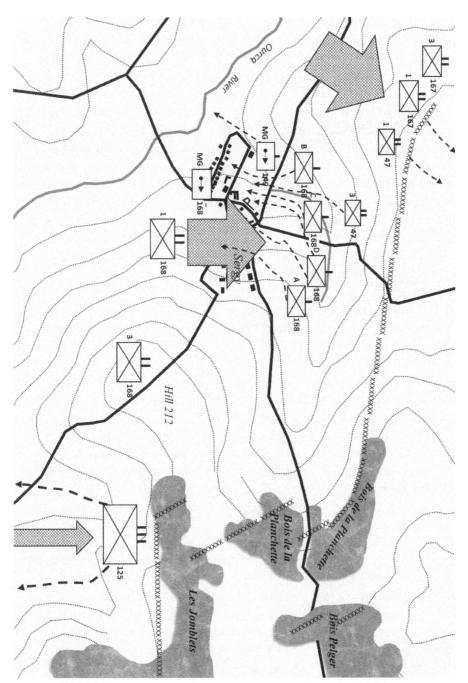

Map 9. The assault on the ridge above Sergy by the 167th and 168th Infantry Regiments on July 30, 1918.

While the 166th held its position and the 165th made some small gains into the Bois Brulé, the day's real drama would play out on the far right. Once again, it would be the Iowans of the 168th who would be called upon to play the leading role. This time, the drama in which they would participate would genuinely be a tragedy.

Around 6:00 p.m. on the evening of July 29, Major Brewer, who still led the 3rd Battalion of the 168th, received a message from the regiment's commander, Colonel Bennett. The message said that the 84th Brigade commander, General Brown, was placing Brewer "in command of all the troops in the line of this organization." Bennett went on to say, "It appears that there is some dissatisfaction with the situation." He added that Brewer should reorganize the men and provide a report as soon as possible as to their disposition.[14]

Needless to say, it was a very odd message. Brewer, a battalion commander, had just been told to take command of all the troops in the regiment and those assigned to the regiment from the 3rd Battalion of the 47th Infantry. There had been rumors during the day that Brewer would lead an attack from Sergy to capture Nesles, and many believed this message merely confirmed that rumor.[15] But this message also meant that, somehow, Colonel Bennett had been effectively removed from the chain of command for this attack. This would prove to be the opening move in a series of events that would see significant changes in command of both the 84th Brigade and the 168th Infantry.

As soon as he had digested the order from Colonel Bennett, Brewer met with the other two battalion commanders, Major Stanley and Major Worthington. The three men reviewed the situation carefully and agreed that the enemy was not about to give up the heights above Sergy without a "bitter fight." They discussed the challenges of advancing over a mile of open ground toward Nesles, with the first half-mile being uphill against strongly defended German positions on top of the hill. They were also unanimous in their view that, unless there was some support on their right that could suppress the German guns in the Bois Pelger, Les Jomblets, and Bois de la Planchette, they stood no chance of success. One historian accurately described these woods as the "Keep or Citadel" of the German position above the Ourcq. The three battalion commanders then drafted a message for General Brown informing him that, given the strength of the German positions in the woods to the east and the supporting German artillery located in the Forêt-de-Nesles, any attack made from Sergy toward Nesles "was doomed to failure" unless American artillery could subdue both the enemy forces in the woods and their artillery support.[16]

Later that night, a messenger on a motorcycle arrived with an order for Major Brewer to report to the 84th Brigade headquarters at La Croix Blanche Farm. Brewer walked down to the Ourcq, crossing to find Colonel Bennett waiting for him in a car. Together, they drove to the headquarters where they went into a 2:00 a.m. conference with General Brown, his adjutant, Major Winn of the 151st Machine Gun Battalion, and Brigadier General Dwight E. Aultman, commander of the 51st Artillery Brigade of the 26th Division, which had been assigned to support the 84th Brigade.[17]

Sergeant Joyce Kilmer of New York's 165th Infantry Regiment, the famous soldier-poet and author of "Trees," killed at the Bois Colas on July 30, 1918. (*National Archives*)

Brown kicked off the meeting by telling Brewer that he had received the report drafted by the three battalion commanders, and he had noted their concerns. However, Brown told Brewer that he had no choice but to order the attack, regardless of the enormous barriers to success. As John Taber would later write, "In spite of the protests of every field officer in the regiment, and against the better judgment of the Brigade Commander himself, the weakened remnants of the 168th were to be thrown against the gun-bristling woods held by the Prussian Guard. Major Brewer had absolved himself of all responsibility. He had counseled against it and had gone on record in writing."[18] This was another example of the irresponsible and unprofessional conduct of both the French Sixth Army staff and the American I Corps. Brown, who would soon pay the price for pushing back against orders like this one, had little choice, and the results would be disastrous.

Amid a grim atmosphere, the men bent over a map as the attack plan was outlined for them. The inexperienced and badly battered 3rd Battalion of the 47th Infantry was tasked to lead the attack with the 1st Battalion of the 168th in support. They would also receive support from the 168th's Machine Gun Company and a company from the 149th Machine Gun Battalion. Of course, what was really required was artillery support, and

General Aultman told them his guns would bombard the three wooded areas with heavy fire before, during, and after the assault. They agreed that a high-tension electric line that ran slightly east of the road from Sergy to Nesles would mark the boundary of the infantry assault and that Brewer's men would stay west of the line. At the same time, the artillery would pound everything east of it. Both Brewer and Bennett made their feelings about every aspect of the plan abundantly clear, but they were assured that the artillery support would be provided, and there would be no serious issues providing it. With that, the meeting ended about 3:00 a.m., and Major Brewer and Colonel Bennett headed back for the Ourcq.[19]

The first order of business upon their return was to inform the battalion from the 47th of their role in the coming attack and get them organized. Bennett had called ahead, telling his operations officer, Captain Ross, to find the 47th's battalion commander. But when Bennett and Brewer returned, they were astounded to hear that no one could find any trace of the battalion. A short while later, a lieutenant from the missing battalion arrived and told them that even he could not find it. For two hours, Captain Ross continued his search until daybreak when he found a captain from the battalion. That officer told Ross that the battalion was so badly scattered and disorganized that it could not be assembled in time for the attack.[20] Needless to say, this was not an auspicious start to the assault.

While Captain Ross was searching for the 47th's battalion, Major Brewer went back to his PC on the slopes of Hill 212. The brigade's promise of substantial artillery support had made him slightly more confident. Still, given how so many pledges of artillery support had been broken during this campaign, he found it difficult to believe in any real chance of success. For the time being, he laid down, adjusted his helmet to serve as a pillow, and tried to get a little sleep before the time came for the assault.[21]

At 6:00 a.m., Brewer was awakened by a soldier who was delivering a message from Colonel Bennett. The message told Brewer about the disorganized state of the 47th Infantry's battalion and expressed doubt that they would be ready for the planned attack. Bennett said that if Brewer thought the attack could go forward without their support, he suggested that Brewer use the 1st Battalion to lead the attack. Conversely, if Brewer believed the attack would not succeed with the 47th's men, he should immediately forward a report stating so directly to General Brown.[22] Beyond the facts stated in Bennett's message, the subtext was clear—Bennett was clearly operating in only an advisory capacity and had no power to direct Brewer in any way.

Brewer got up and immediately sent word for the 1st Battalion to move up to the base of Hill 212 and prepare to lead the assault. Once word reached them, the battalion's men began to make their way slowly across the valley toward the hill. But sadly, they no longer had the "appearance of a battalion." Instead, they were "but a remnant of the strong force that once had paraded on Hempstead Plain" at Camp Mills.[23]

At 8:30 p.m., only thirty minutes before the time to jump off for the attack, the 3rd Battalion of the 47th arrived on the west slope of Hill 212. Their captain reported to Brewer, telling him he had about 300 men and was ready to lead the attack. It was remarkable that they had been able to gather themselves, much less come forward to lead the assault. Brewer gave final instructions to all his officers, and the men moved out to get in position on the northern edges of Sergy. The 47th would step off first with two companies, so they made sure they could establish contact with the 167th's men, who would also make an advance on their left. The staff at 42nd Division Headquarters was apparently confident about this highly ambitious plan because they sent word that the 84th Brigade should begin moving their headquarters to Sergy.[24]

As the two lead companies made their way through Sergy, the outpost on the northern edge of the village withdrew to allow the attacking force to advance. Lieutenant Francis Pearsall, the leader of the outpost force, told the officers moving to the attack that, while everything was clear to the outskirts of town, they should expect resistance as soon as they advanced beyond the village. Within minutes, the first line of the assault force was in place, and, as the clock ticked 9:00 a.m., they moved forward. As soon as the first line had cleared the village, German artillery opened fire, and shells began to fall around them. They picked up the pace of their advance, quickly moving past a German sign that said *"Nach Nesles"*—To Nesles.[25]

As the attack began, the question on everyone's mind at the front was, "Where is our artillery support?" Brewer had been promised preparatory and supporting fire that would "smother" the Germans in the woods to the east of the attacking force, but no American shells had been seen landing in the woods. Now that the attack had begun, a few rounds were hitting the German positions in the woods. However, the level of artillery fire did not even come close to that required. And after just a brief period, that weak artillery support stopped completely. In a formal investigation made after the attack, it was alleged that the American guns ceased firing because they received an erroneous message from General Brown indicating that American troops had been seen entering the targeted woods. Brown called the 168th's PC twice to confirm the veracity of this reporting and was told it was incorrect and that no friendly troops were in the woods to the east. Brown then requested confirmation from the 167th lookout who had reported seeing these Americans and was told the information was accurate. So Brown ordered the guns to cease fire despite protests from General Aultman.[26] However, while this explains why the American artillery stopped firing altogether, it does not explain the complete lack of the promised preparatory barrage.

Without artillery support to subdue the enemy guns in the woods, the attack was doomed from the very start. As soon as the men from the 47th were in the open, they were hit by a blast of machine gun fire from both their front and the right flank, "bowling over the first line like tenpins." Major Brewer ran to the 47th's battalion commander and told him to move his men as fast as possible, saying, "it is your only hope." But no matter how quickly the men tried to advance, it would make no difference to the outcome. The Germans were ready for them and now had every possible advantage. The enemy enveloped the Americans "in a cyclone of high explosive and shrapnel" and a hurricane of machine gun bullets. John Taber, who witnessed the assault, later said, "The slope of the hill north of Sergy was to be their Calvary. They were not long in finding out that no infantry could make it."[27]

The 47th's advance quickly stalled under the fury of the German resistance. The men of the 168th's I and M Companies crawled forward from their outposts on Hill 212 in an attempt to provide some supporting fire. Their snipers began picking off those German gunners who showed themselves, but the effort was like trying to bail water with a bucket after the dam has burst. The German fire continued unabated.[28]

Brewer now hurried the 1st Battalion from his own regiment forward, hoping to get the line moving again as the battalion from the 47th melted away in the wheat fields. But as the 1st Battalion rushed through the streets of Sergy, the enemy rained artillery shells down on the village, their fire "boiling and seething like an angry volcano" as the village streets filled with choking clouds of red dust made by collapsing tile roofs. The 168th's Machine Gun Company was hit by the enemy bombardment as they entered the village, and an entire squad was taken out of action, their men left dead and wounded in the streets and their guns turned into mangled piles of useless metal.[29]

The bodies of German machine gun crews killed on the ridge above Sergy. (*National Archives*)

Once the 1st Battalion reached the northern side of Sergy, D Company moved to the right, lined up along an old sunken road, with A Company a few yards behind them. C Company then took up the position on the left of the line, and B Company formed in their rear in support. For a few moments, the men were forced to take cover because the surviving members of the 47th blocked the way some sixty yards to the front. About 10:30 a.m., the way was clear, and C Company began moving ahead. Instantly, as they cleared the village, they met the same flood of machine gun and artillery fire from the front and right that the men of the 47th had experienced. Lieutenant Elmer Silver, leading the 4th Platoon, ordered his men to hit the ground just as one of his privates was shot and fell dead on top of him. The rest crawled forward, returning the enemy's fire with their rifles and Chauchats. Now, the Germans added a hail of Minenwerfer mortar shells to the deadly mix, "sending over jarring bombs whose concussion bruised the body and forced the blood to the nose and deafened ears."[30]

About the same time, Captain Haynes told D Company to advance on the right of the line. He had already lost all of his runners to enemy fire, and he feared what was about to happen to the rest of his men, who had already been reduced in strength to two platoons. The time to make an advance at the double-quick was gone. Like Silver, he ordered his men to the ground. Haynes said later, "We had to crawl from the start. The bullets were just skipping over the top of the ground, in a seemingly solid wave. Shells were falling thick and fast all around us, and they had the range to a foot. We crawled along as best we could. Ahead of us in a draw was a small stream lined with a few trees. To this bit of shelter—all that was of-fered—300 yards away, we determined to go."[31]

With the July sun beating down mercilessly, the heat was fast becoming suffocating. Below the sun, the men of 1st Battalion scratched their way forward, now having gained a distance of about 100 yards. Captain Haynes realized they would never reach the top of the ridge this way, so he ordered the men to start using small rushes to move ahead. Men began running and hurtling themselves from shell hole to shell hole, gradually building up the line as they went. Haynes ordered two men to scout the situation ahead and determine what remained of the 47th's 3rd Battalion. They dashed forward and quickly returned to tell him that all they found were fourteen soldiers, five of them badly wounded, and no officers left. It was as though the battalion "had vanished into thin air."[32]

Meanwhile, A Company had been following on the heels of D Com-pany and taking the same terrible losses. Before they had gone fifty yards, all their officers were dead or wounded, leaving their company first ser-geant, John Wintrode, in command. Wintrode ably took charge and kept his line moving up the slope.[33]

To the left, C Company and B Company struggled to make progress. Eventually, they made it to the streambed, where they took what little cover it afforded. Haynes worked his way across the field to C Company and slowly reorganized the men into a line with B Company on the far left, C Company in the center, and D Company on the right. Just as Haynes finished getting the men set, the Germans spotted the position of the new line along the creek and rained shells down on them. With no artillery support of their own, there was nothing the 1st Battalion could do but hang on.[34]

During the 168th's assault, a combined unit made of the remainders of the 167th's 1st and 3rd Battalions and the 1st Battalion of the 47th In-fantry advanced on the Iowans' left. The men from the 47th also led the way here and met the same ferocious German machine gun fire. When they were brought to a halt, the Alabamians followed them up the slopes and secured a position atop the ridge. This allowed them to take posses-

Stretcher bearers carry a wounded doughboy to the aid station through the shattered streets of Sergy. (*National Archives*)

sion of at least part of the wheat field the Germans had been using to hold the Americans at bay.[35]

While Haynes and the rest of the 168th's 1st Battalion held on, the wounded were pouring back to the rear. The battalion PC, located in a small stone cellar in Sergy, was soon filled with the wounded. The battalion adjutant, Lieutenant Thomas Wood, gave them what help he could, assessed their wounds, and either sent them back to the aid station or sent for stretcher bearers, who were in short supply. One soldier from A Company stumbled in with a wound so horrible, Wood had a hard time looking at him. A German bullet had struck him in the face, and he could not talk because it had cut off part of his tongue. One ear hung from the side of his head, connected by only a thread of skin, and blood dripped down his shirt and covered his hands. Despite this, he listened carefully to the lieutenant as Wood gave him directions to the aid station. Then he and another soldier who had a slight hand wound joined forces and helped one another get to the rear.[36]

The aid stations were being heavily shelled like all the other positions around Sergy and Hill 212. At one forward aid station located in a farmhouse, Lawrence Stewart saw four stretcher bearers bringing in a wounded man. Just as they entered the farm's courtyard, a German artillery shell burst nearby, sending a shower of stones, shrapnel, and tiles across the yard. When the dust cleared, Stewart saw that two of the stretcher bearers and the wounded man they had been carrying had been killed and a third slightly wounded with a scratch on the head. He and the fourth stretcher bearer shook off the concussive effects of the blast, picked themselves up, grabbed their litter, and headed back up the hill to bring back more wounded men, as though nothing had happened.[37]

On the slopes north of Sergy, Captain Haynes met with Lieutenants Silver and Witherell and their sergeant to discuss their options. Going forward was impossible and staying put meant they would be steadily pounded until no one was left. Haynes sent a message back to Major Brewer, telling him that the battalion could not continue the advance without artillery support. Brewer replied with a message saying that he would have to go on foot personally to get the artillery support, which would take time. If Haynes felt his men could not wait that long, Brewer told him that he should fall back to Sergy. The captain already knew the only viable choice, so he sent a runner to the far left and up to the remnants of the 47th, telling them to pull out and head back down the hill. With that, the surviving men followed the stream's course back to Sergy, which gave them enough cover to avoid any more losses.[38]

When they reached the comparative safety of the village, Haynes discovered he had lost 119 men, and the 47th's battalion had lost almost 250. Major Stanley put together a detailed report that night on the status of the entire regiment. He found all they had left were 805 men and 32 officers, less than the typical strength of a battalion.[39]

When he got back to his PC, Major Brewer found orders waiting that directed him to report in person to General Brown at brigade headquarters without informing the regimental headquarters of the day's events. Unknown to Brewer, his regimental chain of command was effectively cut off by the brigade and was not allowed to take part in the operations. This was due to the command shakeup that had started that afternoon. Brown had relieved Colonel Bennett and Major Worthington of their commands and had replaced Bennett with Lieutenant Colonel Mathew Tinley, the regiment's executive officer.[40] Due to his constant unexplained absences and odd behavior, Worthington almost certainly deserved to be dismissed from command of his battalion. But Bennett had, for the most part, done an admirable job commanding the regiment under the most trying of circumstances, circumstances that were a direct result of poor

Men from the 167th Infantry Regiment killed in the fighting above Sergy. (*National Archives*)

leadership from further up the chain of command. However, in all likelihood, Brown replaced Bennet to save his own position, but it was already too late.

During the day on July 30, General Brown was visited by a delegation that included Major General Hunter Liggett, commander of the US I Corps, and his aide-de-camp, Lieutenant Colonel Pierpont Stackpole along with Major General Charles Menoher, commander of the Rainbow Division, and Colonel Douglas MacArthur, Menoher's chief of staff. The purpose of their visit was what they saw as the 84th Brigade's lackluster performance and General Brown's fitness for command.[41] Brown's reaction to the visit was to replace Bennett and Worthington. However, Menoher would recommend Brown be replaced, and Liggett approved the recommendation, forwarding his decision to AEF Headquarters that night. The next day, July 31, General James McAndrew, the AEF chief of staff, sent a telegram to General Liggett directing that Brown be relieved of duty as brigade commander. His replacement was Douglas MacArthur, who also received a brevet promotion to the rank of brigadier general along with Brown's job.[42]

A formal report by the AEF Inspector General would follow, and it supported Brown's sacking as brigade commander. The report was essentially a whitewash, designed from its inception to blame Brown and justify his removal. The fifty-nine-page report indicated that Menoher and Liggett's firing of Brown and replacing him with MacArthur was supported by six officers from 42nd Division Headquarters. However, those closest to Brown, including seven officers serving in the 167th and 168th Infantry, testified that they saw nothing in Brown's performance that justified his removal. They made their statements supporting Brown despite what some of them felt was pressure from the Inspector General to say otherwise.[43]

The report contained several interesting items. First, it was stated that Brown constantly complained about the fitness of his command. These complaints were said to be unjustified because no such similar grievances were received from the 83rd Brigade commander, General Lenihan, and "the two brigades had practically the same hardships, practically the same amount of fighting and practically the same officers. . . . They [the soldiers in the 84th Brigade] had been subjected to exactly the same conditions as the rest of the Division."[44] This, of course, was patently false. The 84th Brigade had suffered in two days of fighting at La Croix Rouge Farm while the 83rd Brigade was still moving into the theater of operations. Finally, the report stated bluntly that Brown was unfit for combat command. Interestingly, both allegations were directly attributed to Brown's replacement, Douglas MacArthur.

At best, Brown's removal was an effort by the staff at I Corps and the 42nd Division to assuage themselves of any guilt for their miserable and almost criminal mismanagement of the campaign. At worst, however, it may have resulted from a carefully executed plan by Menoher and MacArthur to move MacArthur into the brigade commander's position. MacArthur was a vain man and an ambitious officer who had strong support from General Menoher. He had been slated to return to the United States to take command of a new and untrained brigade, one that might not ever make it to combat in France. By removing Brown and replacing him in this way, Menoher would not lose someone he saw as an indispensable officer. Furthermore, MacArthur would not only get his wish for a brigade command, but he would also get a position leading one of the best combat brigades in the AEF. For anyone who has spent time at a major military headquarters and had to maneuver its inevitable political labyrinth, Brown's firing clearly seemed to have had someone's fingerprints all over it. Those fingerprints likely belonged to Douglas MacArthur.

The night of July 30–31 was a relatively quiet one for the men on the Rainbow Division's line. There had been a brief thirty-minute bombardment around 10:00 p.m. and a visit by German bombers, but nothing more than that, allowing the exhausted soldiers to get some sleep at last.[45] At 12:30 a.m., while the men were resting, I Corps issued a new field order that finally recognized the critical role played by the German positions in the three forests east of the 168th's sector of the front line. Therefore, they ordered the 84th Brigade to take Hill 177, which was over 300 yards east of the Meurcy Farm, and Hill 204, which was just west of the Bois de la Planchette. However, this attack was to be carried out in coordination with the advance of the 32nd Division, which had replaced the 28th Division in the sector to the right of the Rainbow Division. They were to take Cierges, attack up Hill 212, move over the positions formerly held there by the 168th Infantry, and take Hill 220 just south of the Bois de la Planchette. Once this was accomplished, they would be aligned with the 168th's right flank, and the entire American line could advance toward Nesles. The attack was to commence at 4:30 p.m.[46]

When 4:30 p.m. arrived, the 168th's men on Hill 212 could see the troops from the 125th Infantry of the 32nd Division moving forward from the area just beyond the La Motte Farm. They came on in perfect formation, and everyone watching awaited the dreadful German artillery barrage they knew would soon start. When the first German shells arrived and exploded in the middle of the 125th's formation, their men did the right thing by scattering and moving in small groups. When they finally reached the top of Hill 212 and were almost up to the right of the 168th's line, the Germans in the woods once again opened up with "an overwhelming blast of fire." Within seconds, more than half of the 125th's first line went down, and the rest struggled on as the Iowans watched in horror.[47]

As a crowd of newly wounded men fell back down the hill, the Germans added a barrage of high-explosive and gas shells to the mix. The 125th was expecting artillery support that might silence the German artillery and machine guns. Yet, once again, that support did not materialize. They fought on but could not secure a single yard forward. By 5:35 p.m., it was reported that M Company of the 125th had been almost completely wiped out. Their advance came to a halt, which meant the 42nd Division could not move forward. As night fell, there had been no substantive change in the lines north of the Ourcq, only another day of useless slaughter.[48]

To the west, things were mostly quiet for the 165th, but the New York-ers were finally able to take Meurcy Farm with the assistance of the 30th Engineering Regiment. The engineers arrived on the scene armed with thermite and smoke bombs, which they proceeded to launch into the farm complex. As these bombs exploded in their midst, the remaining Germans immediately fled the farm complex, retreating back to the Bois Brûle. A Company then moved in and secured the farm that the regiment had been seeking to take for the last three days.[49]

On the far left of the division's line, the shelling of Seringes-de-Nesles continued. Captain Geran, the 2nd Battalion commander, called for some organic artillery support from the regiment's 37mm one-pounders, which the Ohioans had not employed up to this point. Lieutenant Theodore Bundy had been given command of this small battery, and he had been rigorously training his men and the mule teams used to move the guns. Now, he had his first opportunity to take his battery into action.

Geran sent word back to the 166th's PC asking for Bundy's help using what everyone was calling his "Pound-Wonders." Their target would be a small group of German guns hidden in the woods northwest of Seringes-de-Nesles. Bundy's team hurried forward and set up their guns near La Fontaine sous Pierre. They rapidly got their one-pounders into action, and within minutes, the battery's fire had put the German guns out of action. However, the Germans responded to Bundy's barrage with coun-terbattery fire. In trying to find Bundy's battery, the enemy began drop-ping shells close to Captain Geran's position. He sent word for Bundy to get out and to do so quickly. Apparently, the captain's desire for Bundy to leave was now much more substantial than his desire for him to stay. While Bundy was happy that his battery had done its job, he was "discon-solate at the apparent ingratitude of the Captain."[50]

About 1:00 p.m. that day, as the German shells continued to fall on Seringes-et-Nesles, Corporal Dana Daniels took cover in a shell hole in the village with two of his buddies, Corporal Richard Thrall and Private Millard Heiberger. As the explosions occurred all around them, Daniels realized that Heiberger was in a bad way. The two days of intense German artillery had apparently been too much for the private, and he was clearly suffering from shell shock. Daniels went to Lieutenant Doellinger, who then came over to the shell hole to talk to Heiberger. The lieutenant agreed with Daniels and told him to take Heiberger back to the field hospital in the rear. Along the way, Daniels picked up two more wounded men from E Company and got them back to the hospital about 6:30 p.m. Later that night, when Daniels returned, he found the last two survivors from his squad had also been sent to the rear with shell shock, and he no longer had any men to command.[51]

As night fell all along the line, no one in the Rainbow Division or their higher headquarters knew that the Germans were already beginning their final withdrawal north of the Vesle River to what they called the Bluecher Position. The orders to execute what General Ludendorff referred to as the Bluecher Movement had been issued by his headquarters at 10:30 a.m. on the morning of July 30, and they directed that the movement take place on the night of August 1–2.[52]

So, despite the reverses of the day, the enemy was finally pulling back behind the Vesle. The only question was whether the men of the Rainbow Division had enough strength left to pursue them.

10

THE RAINBOW IS RELIEVED

August 1–2, 1918

"Certain indications (statements of prisoners, artillery movements to the rear) suggests that the enemy is preparing for a new withdrawal. . . . Consequently, previous orders will be complied with—the enemy will be pursued along the entire front and close contact maintained with him."

—French Sixth Army General Orders No. 3,663,
July 31, 1918, 8:20 p.m.

The Iowans of the 168th Infantry could not believe their luck, which continued to be all bad. Earlier in the day, on August 2, they had been told that the 117th Engineer Regiment of their division would take over for them to advance toward Nesles and beyond. At last, they could get some rest after eight days of fighting. However, the situation soon changed when it was discovered that the Germans had withdrawn and withdrawn so far that all contact with the enemy had been lost. Now, while the 117th would still take the lead, they were ordered to form up and follow the engineers as their support.

The 117th moved forward quickly since there was now no one to stop their advance, and the 168th struggled to keep up. Major Stanley's 2nd Battalion took the lead with the battered remnants of the 1st and 3rd Battalions right behind them. As they marched over the ridgeline north of Sergy that they had fought so desperately to capture on July 30, they found it filled with the "bloated bodies of grey-green soldiers, abandoned machine guns, strips of web belting, and heaps of cartridge cases," along with the rotting bodies of dead German artillery horses.[1]

By afternoon, the 117th had made it as far as a position five miles northeast of Nesles. About halfway down the hill toward Nesles, the 168th's 2nd Battalion was ordered to move up faster and fill a gap between the 167th and the 117th Engineers. They halted in Nesles while they awaited the 117th to continue their advance, and around 4:00 p.m., it began to rain. The 2nd Battalion continued to advance until they held a line along the northeast edge of the Forêt de Nesles to the rear of the 117th. As the dreary rain continued, the men could hear scattered machine gun fire ahead, indicating the Germans were at least making some signs of resistance.[2]

Around 7:00 p.m., Major Stanley got the men on their feet and prepared to advance to keep pace with the 117th. As they lined up to move out, the regimental adjutant, Captain Van Order, arrived with new orders. "Dig in where you are," he told Major Stanley. "You are to be relieved tonight." The men might have been expected to cheer when they heard this news, but they were too tired, wet, and hungry to do anything but dig foxholes and climb into them for the night.[3]

On the night of July 31–August 1, the French Sixth Army was concerned about the possibility of a major German counterattack and ordered efforts be made to establish a defensive security line south of the Ourcq. However, at the same time, information gathered from captured German soldiers and signs of movement of German heavy artillery to the rear caused them to anticipate Ludendorff's Bluecher Movement. As a result, they issued a new General Order that called for a continuation of the advance, with the I Corps moving in the direction of Hill 190, which was just east of Les Bonne Hommes Farm and about a mile and a half north of Nesles.[4]

In response, I Corps issued its attack orders for August 1, which finally seemed to fully recognize the situation on the 42nd Division's right. The staff at both the French Sixth Army and I Corps was now convinced that, unless the German positions in the Bois de la Planchette, Bois Pelger, and Les Jomblets could be subdued, no advance to the north of Sergy could be made by the 42nd Division. Therefore, the French Sixth Army ordered the 32nd Division to advance on those woods at 4:15 a.m. At the same time, the 42nd Division would keep the enemy forces on the western side of the woods from reinforcing those on the southern side, which faced what would be the attacking forces from the 125th and 126th Infantries of the Michigan National Guard.[5]

The men from the 168th and 167th who would support the attack of the 125th and 126th were an exhausted lot. Captain Gardner Greene, who had taken over command of the 167th's combined 1st and 3rd Battalions, reported the condition of his men to Colonel Screws on the night of July 31. He told Screws that his men had been gassed for two straight days and had been unable to move to higher ground to avoid the effects of the gas. Furthermore, the process of marching to the rear when the 47th's battalion had relieved them only to turn around and march back into the line had left his men "completely out and jaded." As a result, he was unsure he could count on them if ordered to advance once more.[6]

Over on the right where the Iowans of the 168th remained in position, the Germans had laid down a heavy barrage of shells that night, which "drenched the valley in gas." The shelling lasted for two hours and preceded an attempted counterattack by the Germans around 9:00 p.m. But for once, American artillery was on the job and unleashed a barrage that stopped the Germans and continued on into the night. "Soothed by this sweet music," wrote John Taber, "our men could lie down to rest, if not to sleep, with some sense of security." As the friendly artillery fire continued, a message arrived at the regimental PC for Colonel Bennett. While Bennett had been verbally relieved of his position, no official written orders had come for him. Therefore, he seems to have continued administrative duties while Lieutenant Colonel Tinley saw to operational matters. The message told him that the division's 117th Engineering Regiment would be called up as infantry and moved forward to support any gains made by the Michigan regiments while the 168th remained in place.[7] This was great news, but two questions remained: Would the Michigan regiments be successful and, if so, would the 117th Engineers arrive in time?

At 3:30 a.m. on August 1, the 51st Field Artillery began a furious bombardment of the German positions in the woods. About thirty minutes later, the 125th and 126th started forward. They came up the slopes of Hill 212, and by 5:15 a.m., they had managed to advance seventy-five yards. Seeing the Michiganders make progress, the 168th's 2nd Battalion prepared to advance in their support. The 117th had not yet arrived, so it would be left to the 168th to advance once again. Lieutenant Colonel Tinsley put H Company in the lead with the sparse remnants of E, F, and G Companies right behind them. A platoon of machine gun support came up as well, and Tinsley sent a small advance party of thirty-six men led by Lieutenant Douglas Green forward up a ravine just ahead of the 125th and 126th line, where they would wait for them to move abreast of their position.[8]

The Michiganders advanced cautiously over the top of Hill 212 and steadily moved toward the Les Jomblets and Bois de la Planchette. Soon, they were close enough to advance at the double-quick, overrunning the enemy machine gun nests and forcing the Germans out of both woods. They next attacked the Bois Pelger, so Lieutenant Green moved his men up the slope and parallel with the Michigan regiments.[9]

Suddenly, the enemy launched a furious counterattack, driving the 125th out of the Bois de la Planchette and into the Les Jomblets. This left H Company's flank uncovered, and the Germans quickly moved against them, as well. It looked like the company might get cut off, but Captain Yates quickly dispatched a platoon from E Company to shore up H Company's right. The two companies fought the Germans off and were able to fall back to the foot of the hill, where they dug in and held their ground. Meanwhile, the 127th Infantry from the Wisconsin National Guard came up on the 125th's right and succeeded in driving well into the main German positions.[10]

Once the men from the 32nd Division were out of the Bois de la Planchette and Bois Pelger, artillery support was requested. In response, the American guns "smothered the woods" with shells. As John Taber would write, "No one could complain of the support of the guns now." At 3:00 p.m., the guns ceased their barrage, and the 32nd Division's regiments advanced again. They drove the Germans out of the Bois de la Planchette and Bois Pelger but were forced to withdraw back to the Bois de la Planchette in the face of another German counterattack.[11]

During the fighting on the right, both the 167th and the 165th were able to remain in position and saw no combat. Except for some German fighters that flew overhead and tried to drop bombs on the artillerymen, all was comparatively quiet for the New Yorkers and Alabamians. The 167th's 2nd Battalion was able to relieve the combined 1st and 3rd Battalions, who returned to the Forêt-de-Fère for a night's rest.[12]

As night fell, the Americans firmly held a line from Seringes-et-Nesles to north of Sergy into the Bois de la Planchette, which meant they now held all the key strong points on the heights above the Ourcq. Given that Ludendorff had already ordered the final withdrawal north of the Vesle, the Germans began their preparations to fall back. Before midnight on

August 1, the enemy began another heavy barrage against the 166th's forward positions in Seringes-et-Nesles. Usually, a barrage this intense meant that they were about to make some sort of significant move, perhaps even another counterattack. Soon, however, the nature of the move became clear when the ground reverberated from massive explosions behind the German lines—the enemy was destroying any remaining ammunition dumps in preparation to hurry their withdrawal out of the Marne salient. The artillery fire was merely an attempt to hold back any American advance while the Germans evacuated the area.[13]

In the late afternoon of August 1, the 42nd Division issued orders telling their subordinate units that the division would be relieved by the US 4th Division on the night of August 2–3. Each brigade was told they could stand relieved as soon as the corresponding brigade from the 4th Division passed through their frontline battalions. However, before then, they would have to continue the advance.[14]

On the morning of August 2, with the realization that the Germans really were making their last withdrawal, one might have thought that, given the Rainbow Division's heavy losses, those in the higher command echelons might decide that there was no reason to make another hurried pursuit. But that was not to be the case. MacArthur, who was still functioning officially as the division chief of staff while also commanding the 84th Brigade, issued orders that reflected his unique brand of bombast, calling for the division to "advance with audacity."[15]

Luckily for the exhausted Iowans of the 168th, the 117th Engineers had arrived on the scene, and they began the new advance from Sergy toward Nesles as the 32nd Division advanced on their right. However, once it was realized that contact had been lost with the Germans, the 168th was ordered to follow the 117th in support. This was met with dismay by the men in the line. They were "hollow-eyed, sunken-cheeked, feverish; worn almost to the snapping point from nervous strain, lack of proper food, water, sleep, and cover; alternately chilled from night exposure and scorched by day; sick with dysentery, throat and lungs raw from gas."[16] But they gathered up their gear, fell in line, and moved out as ordered.

The 117th was ordered to advance along with the 32nd Division at 4:15 a.m. Their A and B Companies led the way from a jumping-off point just north of Sergey. They advanced rapidly, as there was absolutely no opposition between them and Nesles. Once they reached Nesles, the engineers found two Germans who had remained behind, took them prisoner, and questioned them. Continuing the advance, the 117th

Soldiers of the U.S. 4th Division march on their way to relieve the men of the 42nd Division. (*National Archives*)

approached the Bois de Dôle just northeast of Nesles, where they encountered relatively light German machine gun fire. As soon as they were prepared to move on the guns, the German gun crews came out of the woods and surrendered. The 117th then continued their advance until dark when they reached Chéry-Chartreuve, almost five miles northeast of Nesles.[17]

The Iowans followed with their 2nd Battalion again in the lead and the 3rd and 1st Battalions following wearily behind them. They stopped in Nesles while waiting for the 117th to continue their advance. Around 4:00 p.m., as it began to rain, they continued their advance until they held a line along the northeast edge of the Forêt de Nesles to the rear of the 117th. At 7:00 p.m., as they prepared to move forward again, orders finally came telling them they were to be relieved.[18]

That night, the relief of the 168th began as promised. The 1st Battalion was the first to fall back when the 47th Infantry relieved them around 11:15 p.m. The 3rd Battalion followed at midnight, and the 2nd Battalion pulled out not long after. The regiment's kitchens were finally able to come forward, and they prepared hot meals. However, most of the men marched right past them. They wanted to get back to the Forêt-de-Fère, where they could lie down, close their eyes, and sleep in peace for the first time since July 24. They trudged back through the rain and the mud like a "motley throng— grimy, mud-stained, hairy-faced."[19] It was only a little over five miles to the forest, but the rain and the mud made it an arduous march. Once they arrived, men fell to the ground, pulled their shelter tent halves over them, and some slept for more than twenty-four hours.

When John Taber arrived in the woods, he first "relieved the HQ kitchen of a generous helping of bread, butter, and molasses" before getting ready to sleep. But as he removed his trousers for the first time in two weeks, he discovered a wound on his right leg apparently made by a piece of German shrapnel. But it had since healed, leaving nothing but some clotted blood.[20]

The 165th had also moved up during the day and encountered resistance near Moreuil-en-Dôle, just north of the Forêt-de-Nesles. The New Yorkers sent the 3rd Battalion forward, and they engaged the enemy. However, before the fighting really got started, they were ordered to fall back and prepare to be relieved. That night, they marched back past the Meurcy Farm, where so many of their comrades were now buried beneath French soil. They soon arrived in the Forêt-de-Fère, which was described by Father Duffy as a "dirty, dank, unwholesome spot" made even worse by the rain. Within days, 60 percent of the regiment was sick with dysentery and battling the usual infestation of cooties. Duffy recorded in his diary that the men were "sleeping in shelter tents or in holes in the ground in the woods" and were "a sorry looking lot."[21]

On the division's far left, the 166th still held Seringes-et-Nesles on the morning of August 2. The village was quite a sad sight. Colonel George Leach of the 151st Field Artillery recorded that the town was "a smoking ruin and the fields covered with dead." He added that there were "dead Americans and Germans in every house," and he counted eighteen German machine guns with the crews still lying dead at their posts. There were so many dead, in fact, that Leach's men had to pull bodies from the road so their vehicles could navigate between the shell holes.[22]

As far as the Ohioans of the 166th went, they were in bad shape just like the division's other three regiments, and relief needed to come sooner rather than later. E Company alone had lost over 100 men. However, the regiment was slow in getting the news about the coming relief. Soon, they received the assignment to pursue the enemy. At 6:00 a.m. on August 2, the orders to do precisely that arrived. Raymond Cheseldine wrote, "Exhausted men, worn from days of toil and nights of tortured nerves and bodies, pushed themselves out of the woods and villages and, led by the 2nd Battalion, moved up the hill beyond Seringes-et-Nesles."[23]

As the rain began to fall as it would all day, G Company from the 2nd Battalion took the lead. They had sustained the fewest casualties in the previous four days of fighting as E and F Companies followed along with H and M Companies from 3rd Battalion. The first objective was the village of Moreuil-en-Dôle and to secure a line 300 yards to the west of it. The French and the 165th moved in parallel to the left and right, respectively, covering the regiment's flanks. As the men advanced up to the crest of the ridge, the German machine guns opened fire from the Forêt-de-Nesles, but soon they stopped firing as the Germans quickly retreated.[24]

The leading skirmish lines of G Company reached a point about 400 yards south of Moreuil-en-Dôle, where they could see the enemy evacuating the village. The rest of the attacking Americans picked up the pace of their advance. As G Company cleared the ridge, the Germans saw them and opened fire with a massive artillery barrage. Despite the carnage caused by the shelling, the regiment's four companies pressed the attack. Dana Daniels wrote that "this was the worst shelling" the men had been through thus far, which was saying something.[25]

The attack was proceeding so fast now that contact with the French on the left was lost. G and E Company halted and dug in until the flanks were secure again. Dana Daniels said that, as he came over the hill, he immediately took cover in a shell hole with another soldier. The two men took out their trenching shovels and began to make the hole a little deeper, just to be on the safe side. At that point, the advance on Moreuil-en-Dôle stopped as the men enjoyed the sight of the enemy running about the village, burning supplies, and preparing for a hasty departure.[26]

While the men waited in their trenches and shell holes, the steady rain made things pretty miserable. But for some soldiers, the rain proved to be an unexpected blessing. Sergeant Peter Weiss later recalled, "Their artillery was firing point-blank—we could see the flame belch from their 77's on the opposite hill." But as the shells came screaming in and struck the ground at a ninety-degree angle, the soft, soggy mud cushioned their impact with the ground, causing many of them to be duds.[27]

Late that afternoon, the regiment finally received the news that they would be relieved that night. When Colonel Hough heard this, he wisely ordered the forward assault elements to withdraw to the reverse side of the ridge so they could avoid any further artillery fire from the enemy. Around 9:30 that night, the first units of the 4th Division arrived, and all of the 166th was on their way out of the area by midnight. Along with everyone else, they camped that night back in the Forêt-de-Fère, where they would remain until August 11.[28]

Their men also recorded what a miserable place that forest was to rest and recover. "Flies and mosquitoes abounded, dirty pools of stagnant water gave forth terrible odors, and the stench from dead bodies of German and American alike" made the place almost unbearable. But, for the most part, the men seemed not to care. Like the other regiments, as these exhausted soldiers made their way into the dense woods, they sank to the ground and went to sleep.[29]

The Rainbow Division's nightmare in the Marne salient was over at last.

EPILOGUE

"These Endured All and Gave All That Honor and Justice Might Prevail and That the World Might Enjoy Freedom and Inherit Peace."

—Inscription above the chapel columns at the Oise-Aisne American Cemetery

As the rain fell on the men of the Rainbow Division camped in the Forêt-de-Fère, many of them hoped for an extended thirty-day rest period, one that had been promised so often but was never provided. The nine days the division spent in the "pest-hole" of those woods were as miserable as one might expect. After the men had gotten some initial rest, the conditions in the forest led to many weakened men developing dysentery. Raymond Cheseldine of the 166th would write that, when the regiment finally left, "It was a dirty looking regiment, a sick regiment in fact, that swung down the road toward Château-Thierry that morning of August 11th."[1] When they reached Château-Thierry, many men made straight for the Marne River and a chance at last to get another much-needed bath.[2]

The division had suffered severely in the fighting from La Croix Rouge Farm to the Ourcq. Since the fight had started at La Croix Rouge Farm on July 25, the division had suffered 903 killed in action, 262 dead from wounds, and 4,311 wounded, a total of 5,476 casualties in nine days of combat.[3] Those nine days would be the most violent and costly of the war for the Rainbow Division.

Of all the losses in killed, wounded, and missing, worst of all, perhaps, was the fact that most of the new draftees the division's infantry had received just before the Aisne-Marne Offensive, men who were untrained and had been in the army less than a month, were among the dead. As one member of the division would later state most emphatically, "They didn't have a chance."[4]

The ultimate tragedy was that so many of the losses suffered by the division were avoidable and had been precipitated by poor leadership and bad decision-making at the French Sixth Army, I Corps, and 42nd Division Headquarters. Those headquarters continued to order headlong pursuit of an enemy that they believed was in a panicked retreat, even long after the evidence from their own front lines proved that was not the case. Further, it is obvious that the I Corps and 42nd Division staff simply did not have the experience or sophistication to provide adequate command and control of their infantry and artillery during the fluid, dynamic combat of open offensive warfare.

It is indeed ironic that even the man who was the most prominent advocate of that type of warfare, General John Pershing, began to question the soundness of his own thinking. Five days after the 42nd Division had been relieved, he tasked his chief of staff, General James McAndrew, "to make a study of the whole question of attack against machine guns and artillery," adding that "perhaps, we are losing too many men."[5] The soldiers of the Rainbow Division would almost certainly have agreed that they were.

After a brief rest at Château-Thierry, the division moved to a new training area on August 18, where they began a daily grind of close-order drill, athletic games, range practice, bayonet and gas drill, practice marches, and open warfare tactics. They also started to receive replacements for the men they had lost in the fighting of July and August. Naturally, these men would be new untrained draftees. On August 27, one regiment, the 166th, received more than 500 such men. Everyone hoped that the stay in the training area would provide sufficient time to get this large new group of men into some sort of fighting condition, unlike their predecessors. Unfortunately, on the same night that the replacements arrived, the division was ordered to break camp toward the Toul area and to do so only at night in order to maintain secrecy.

Once they arrived, they became part of a large force of American units gathering for the first American-led offensive of the war, one designed to again force the enemy out of a salient, this time in the area around Saint

Mihiel. The initial attack took place early on the morning of September 12. To everyone's surprise, the 42nd Division and all the other allied units moved much faster than planned. In fact, the Germans were withdrawing from the salient when the offensive was launched, catching the Germans by surprise. In only twenty-nine hours, the division advanced twelve miles, taking all their objectives thirty-six hours ahead of schedule.[6]

The division quickly settled in along the new front line opposite the Germans, but on September 30, they were ordered to move out once again. This time, they would be headed for the final great offensive of the war in the Meuse-Argonne. The offensive was well underway when the Rainbow Division arrived, and it had not gone according to plan. The Germans fought from fortified positions that they had been building for over four years, and many of the American divisions that made the initial attacks were new to France and very inexperienced. So the 42nd Division was sent forward on October 10 in an attempt to make the desired break-through. By now, even the Germans saw the division as an elite unit. Just a day before the division began to move up to the front, the Headquarters of the German Group of Armies in the Meuse-Argonne issued an analysis that said, "The engagement of the 42nd Division is to be expected soon. It is in splendid fighting condition and is counted among the best American divisions."[7]

Unfortunately, much of the fighting in the Meuse-Argonne would look more like that around the Ourcq River than at Saint Mihiel. The division spent days stuck in muddy, rain-filled foxholes eating reserve rations while the enemy poured shells down on them. Once they were finally able to move to the attack, their artillery support was insufficient to drive the enemy back from their entrenchments. It was the same old story as at the Ourcq—artillery fire was promised but was never up to the task. The result was also the same—gains measured in mere yards at a high cost in killed and wounded. After two days of unsuccessful attacks on October 14–15, the division remained in its foxholes, enduring a week of rain and artillery bombardment.

On October 26, the Rainbow Division fell back and was relieved. But by early November, they were on the move again, joining Allied forces that had finally broken through the Hindenburg Line and were advancing toward the key city of Sedan. As units raced to be the first to reach Sedan, the 42nd Division took village after village as they pursued retreating German rear-guard units. On November 7, they and all the other American units were told to stop their advance so that the privilege of taking Sedan

could be given to the 40th French Division. However, the French requested that one American unit be assigned to go with them. They asked
for that unit to come from the Rainbow Division. The division was rightfully proud of this honor, and a company from the 166th was selected to
move up with the French. [8]

As the Allies approached Sedan, however, a German delegation crossed
the lines to negotiate an armistice that would end the war. Not long after
the meetings began, the Kaiser abdicated, and a revolution broke out in
Germany. Marshal Foch gave the German representatives until 11:00 a.m.
on November 11 to sign the agreement. At 5:10 a.m. on November 11,
the Germans signed the armistice agreement, which would take effect at
11:00 a.m. that same day.[9]

The Great War was over at last.

When the armistice took effect, many of the division's men assumed they
would be headed home soon. However, the division was instead given the
somewhat dubious honor of being assigned to occupy the west bank of
the Rhine in Germany. As a result, the division's units would not start the
journey back to the United States until the spring of 1919. But by the end
of May 1919, the entire division had been demobilized and its men finally
sent home.[10]

The division earned its reputation as the finest of the National Guard
divisions that went to France. But nowhere were they tested as severely as
they were in the Aisne-Marne Offensive. Those nine days of combat
would be seared into the memories of the division's veterans, and they
would leave more than 1,200 friends and comrades behind forever at La
Croix Rouge Farm and the Ourcq River.

On August 2, 1918, as the offensive continued and the 42nd Division
moved to the rear, the burial details began their work in earnest to locate,
identify, and inter those men the division left behind. On that day, they
started establishing a temporary cemetery about 600 yards north of the
Meurcy Farm along the road from Fère-en-Tardenois. All of the men who
fell nearby during the offensive were eventually moved from their initial
burial sites to the cemetery. In 1921, the US Congress made the cemetery
a permanent site to be maintained by the War Department until the establishment of the American Battle Monuments Commission in 1937. In
1922, the remains of all the American dead in the area, including those
killed in the region west of Tours, Romorantin, Paris, and Le Havre, were

The 1937 dedication of the Oise-Aisne American Cemetery, where more than 1,000 men of the Rainbow Division who were killed in the Aisne-Marne Offensive are buried. (*American Battle Monument Commission*)

also moved to what was now designated as the Oise-Aisne American Cemetery. When the cemetery was formally dedicated on May 30, 1937, there were 6,012 graves along with a list of 241 men missing in action.[11]

Today, this final resting place for the men of the Rainbow Division is quiet, pastoral, and beautiful. The area surrounding it looks much as it did in July and August of 1918. The roads may now be paved and well-marked, but the fields still are filled with wheat in the summer, and the Ourcq still meanders through the valley. If one did not know better, it would be impossible to imagine the horrors that occurred there and the price the men of the Rainbow Division paid to gain so little. However, while we can be appalled by the many miscalculations and mistakes made at the headquarters level during the offensive here, one must still marvel at the courage, tenacity, and stubborn perseverance shown by those men who filled the ranks of the four National Guard infantry regiments and three machine gun battalions that bore the overwhelming weight of the battle. Any success achieved during the campaign was purely the result of raw "guts" and remarkable valor.

The soldiers of the Rainbow Division deserve to be remembered and, perhaps, they are honored best by the words of Joyce Kilmer, the soldier-poet of the 165th Infantry who was killed along the Ourcq River:

Comrades true,
Born anew,
Peace to you.
Your souls
Will be
Where heroes are
And your memory shine
Like the morning star.
Brave and dear,
Shield us here,
Farewell.[12]

NOTES

CHAPTER 1: THE RAINBOW APPEARS

1. Henry J. Reilly, *Americans All: The Rainbow at War; Official History of the 42nd Rainbow Division in the World War* (Columbus, OH: F. J. Heer Printing Co., 1936), 27.
2. Douglas MacArthur quoted in Reilly, *Americans All*, 19.
3. Edward M. Coffman, *The War to End All Wars: The American Military Experience in World War I* (Lexington: University Press of Kentucky, 1998), 19.
4. Newton Baker in Introduction to Reilly, *Americans All*, 5.
5. Newton Baker in Introduction to Reilly, *Americans All*, 5–6.
6. Douglas MacArthur quoted in Reilly, *Americans All*, 27.
7. Walter B. Wolf, *A Brief Story of the Rainbow* Division (New York: Rand McNally, 1919), 12; Douglas MacArthur quoted in Reilly, *Americans All*, 27.
8. Thompson, David G. "Ohio's Best: The Mobilization of the Fourth Infantry, Ohio National Guard, in 1917," *Ohio History Journal*, Volume 101, Winter-Spring 1992 (Columbus, OH: Ohio Historical Society, 1992), 43.
9. James J. Cooke, *The Rainbow Division in the Great War, 1917-1919* (Westport, CT: Praeger, 1994), 8.
10. Wolf, *Brief Story of the Rainbow Division*, 6–7.
11. Wolf, *Brief Story of the Rainbow Division*, 6–7.
12. George W. Cullum, *Biographical Register of the Officers and Graduates of the U.S. Military Academy at West Point, N.Y Since its Establishment in 1802, Volume III* (Boston: Houghton, Mifflin, and Company, 1891), 415; George W. Cullum, *Biographical Register of the Officers and Graduates of the U.S. Military Academy at West Point, N.Y Since its Establishment in 1802*, Supplement *Volume IV* (Cambridge, MA: Riverside Press, 1901), 457; George W. Cullum, ed. Lieutenant Charles Braden, *Biographical Register of the Officers and Graduates of the U.S. Military Academy at West Point, N.Y Since its Establishment in 1802*, Supplement *Volume V* (Saginaw, MI: Seemann & Peters, Printers, 1919), 414; George

W. Cullum, ed. Lieutenant Charles Braden, *Biographical Register of the Officers and Graduates of the U.S. Military Academy at West Point, N.Y Since its Establishment in 1802*, Supplement *Volume VI* (Saginaw, MI: Seemann & Peters, Printers, 1920), 482.

13. Wolf, *Brief Story of the Rainbow Division*, 6–7.

14. John Mahon, *New York's Fighting 69th: A Regimental History of Service in the Civil War's Irish Brigade and the Great War's Rainbow Division* (Jefferson, NC: McFarland & Company, 2004), 1.

15. Mahon, *New York's Fighting 69th*, 9, 107.

16. Joyce Kilmer quoted in Francis P. Duffy, *Father Duffy's Story: A Tale of Humor and Heroism, of Life and Death with the Fighting Sixty-Ninth* (New York: George B. Doran Company, 1919), 332.

17. Duffy, *Father Duffy's Story*, 13.

18. Duffy, *Father Duffy's Story*, 13.

19. Martin J. Hogan, *The Shamrock Battalion of the Rainbow* (New York: D. Appleton and Company, 1919), 6.

20. Hogan, *The Shamrock Battalion*, 7–8.

21. Mahon, *New York's Fighting 69th*, 110.

22. *New York Times*, October 7, 1946.

23. Duffy, *Father Duffy's Story*, 23.

24. Hogan, *The Shamrock Battalion*, 8–9.

25. R.M Cheseldine, *Ohio in the Rainbow: Official Story of the 166th Infantry, 42nd Division, in the World War* (Columbus, OH: F.J. Heer Printing Company, 1924), 46.

26. Mahon, *New York's Fighting 69th*, 110.

27. Albert M. Ettinger and A. Churchill Ettinger, *A Doughboy with the Fighting 69th* (New York: Pocket Books, 1992), 6.

28. George W. Cullum, ed. Colonel Wirt Robinson, *Biographical Register of the Officers and Graduates of the U.S. Military Academy at West Point, N.Y Since its Establishment in 1802*, Supplement *Volume VI-A* (Saginaw, MI: Seemann & Peters, Printers, 1920), 592.

29. Duffy, *Father Duffy's Story*, 22–23.

30. Hogan, *The Shamrock Battalion*, 9–11.

31. *Official Roster of the Soldiers of the State of Ohio In the War with Mexico, 1846 -1848* (Reprint Edition) (Mansfield: Ohio Genealogical Society, 1991), 453.

32. *The Army Lineage Book, Volume II: Infantry* (Washington, DC: US Government Printing Office, 1953), 477–90.

33. Cheseldine, *Ohio in the Rainbow*, 37–41.

34. Cheseldine, *Ohio in the Rainbow*, 43.

35. *Marysville Journal-Tribune*, Marysville, Ohio, April 4, 1917, 3.

36. Thompson, "Ohio's Best," 43.

37. Cheseldine, *Ohio in the Rainbow*, 44.

38. Alison Reppy, *Rainbow Memories: Character Sketches and History of the First Battalion, 166th Infantry, 42nd Division, American Expeditionary Force* (Columbus, OH: Executive Committee, First Battalion, 166th Infantry, 1919), 7–8.

39. Reppy, *Rainbow Memories*, 8.

40. Ibid.

41. Thompson, "Ohio's Best," 46.

42. Enoch Williams to his mother, August 22, 1917. Enoch Williams, *Letters Home from Somewhere in France (P.S. Send cigarettes & chocolate)*, Gary Williams, ed. Unpublished. Accessed at https://archive.org/details/EnochWilliamsWwiLettersHome1917-1919, 10.

43. Cheseldine, *Ohio in the Rainbow*, 48.

44. Enoch Williams to his mother, September 2, 1917. Enoch Williams, *Letters Home*, 12.

45. Cheseldine, *Ohio in the Rainbow*, 53.

46. Ruth Smith Truss, "The Alabama National Guard's 167th Infantry Regiment in World War I." Alabama Review 56 (January 2003), 3–34.

47. William H. Amerine, *Alabama's Own in France* (New York: Eaton & Gettinger, 1919), 30, 40.

48. Nimrod Thompson Frazer, *Send the Alabamians* (Tuscaloosa: University of Alabama Press, 2014), Kindle Edition, 21.

49. Frazer, *Send the Alabamians*, Kindle Edition, 35.

50. Amerine, *Alabama's Own*, 47.

51. Amerine, *Alabama's Own*, 49–50.

52. Frazer, *Send the Alabamians*, Kindle Edition, 66.

53. Frazer, *Send the Alabamians*, Kindle Edition, 67.

54. One must wonder how these grandsons of Confederate veterans must have felt about their camp being named after Union General Phillip Sheridan.

55. Frazer, *Send the Alabamians*, Kindle Edition, 70–71.

56. Winfred E. Robb, *The Price of Our Heritage: In Memory of the Heroic Dead of the 168 Infantry* (Des Moines, IA: American Lithographing and Printing Co., 1919), 13.

57. Robb, *The Price of Our Heritage*, 15.

58. John H. Taber, *The Story of the 168th Infantry Regiment, Volume I* (Iowa City: State Historical Society of Iowa, 1925), 3.

59. Taber, *168th Infantry Regiment, Volume 1*, 3.

60. Taber, *168th Infantry Regiment, Volume 1*, 4.

61. Robb, *The Price of Our Heritage*, 23.

62. Taber, *168th Infantry Regiment, Volume 1*, 6.

63. Taber, *168th Infantry Regiment, Volume 1*, 6–7.

64. Ettinger and Ettinger, *A Doughboy with the Fighting 69th*, 7.

65. Enoch Williams to his mother, September 10, 1917. Enoch Williams, *Letters Home*, 24.

66. Enoch Williams to his mother, October 8, 1917. Enoch Williams, *Letters Home*, 48.

67. Taber, *168th Infantry Regiment, Volume 1*, 9–10.

68. Frazer, *Send the Alabamians*, Kindle Edition, 71.

69. Leon Miesse to his wife, September 12, 1917. Leon Miesse, *100 Years On: WW I – Leon Miesse, Captain, 166th*, Ed. Robert Laird (Location Unknown: Zerone Publishing, 2017), Kindle Edition, 11.

70. Enoch Williams to his mother, October 2, 1917. Enoch Williams, *Letters Home*, 44.

71. Enoch Williams to his mother, September 20, 1917. Enoch Williams, *Letters Home*, 28.

72. Frazer, *Send the Alabamians*, Kindle Edition, 71.

73. Taber, *168th Infantry, Volume I*, 11.

74. Cheseldine, *Ohio in the Rainbow*, 57.

75. Leon Miesse to his wife, September 12, 1917. Leon Miesse, *100 Years On*, 11.

76. Leon Miesse to his wife, October 9, 1917. Leon Miesse, *100 Years On*, 26.

77. Frazer, *Send the Alabamians*, Kindle Edition, 72.

78. Cheseldine, *Ohio in the Rainbow*, 56.

79. Taber, *168th Infantry, Volume I*, 12.

80. Cheseldine, *Ohio in the Rainbow*, 59–60.

81. Enoch Williams to his mother, October 2, 1917. Enoch Williams, *Letters Home*, 45.

82. Cooke, *The Rainbow Division*, 18.

83. Taber, *168th Infantry, Volume I*, 12.

84. Cooke, *The Rainbow Division*, 13.

85. Hogan, *The Shamrock Battalion*, 12.

86. Raymond S. Tompkins, *The Story of the Rainbow Division* (New York: Boni and Liveright, 1919), 18.

87. Taber, *168th Infantry, Volume I*, 11–12.

88. Taber, *168th Infantry, Volume I*, 11–12.

89. Cooke, *The Rainbow Division*, 17.

90. Ibid., 60.

91. Leon Miesse to his wife, September 12, 1917. Leon Miesse, *100 Years On*, 12.

92. Enoch Williams to his mother, September 24, 1917. Enoch Williams, *Letters Home*, 31.

93. Cheseldine, *Ohio in the Rainbow*, 64.

CHAPTER 2: THE RAINBOW ARRIVES IN FRANCE

1. Cheseldine, *Ohio in the Rainbow*, 102.

2. Tompkins, *The Story of the Rainbow Division*, 10–11.

3. Benedict Crowell and Robert Forrest Wilson, *The Road to France: The Transportation of Troops and Military Supplies, 1917–1918-How America Went to War: An Account from Official Sources of the Nation's War Activities, 1917–1920* (New Haven, CT: Yale University Press, 1921), 314–315.

4. Cooke, *The Rainbow Division*, 18–19.

5. Wolf, *Brief Story of the Rainbow Division*, 7.

6. John B. Hayes, *Heroes Among the Brave* (Loachapoka, AL: Lee County Historical Society, 1973), 9–10.

7. Carl F. Ebert, *A Brief History of Co. D, 166th Infantry* (Marion, OH: Unknown Publisher, 1939), 10.

8. Dana Daniels, *Dana Daniels Diary, 1917-1919* (Columbus, OH: Dana Daniels Collection, Ohio Historical Society, MS 5; Box 1, Folder 6), 2.

9. Ebert, *A Brief History of Co. D*, 10.

10. Cheseldine, *Ohio in the Rainbow*, 73.

11. Wolf, *Brief Story of the Rainbow Division*, 8.

12. *United States Army in the World War, 1917-1919, Volume 3: Training and Use of American Units with the British and French* (Washington, DC: Center of Military History, United States Army, 1989), 666–667.

13. Douglas MacArthur, *Reminiscences* (New York: McGraw-Hill, 1964), 53.

14. *United States Army in the World War, Volume 3*, 667–668.

15. Cooke, *The Rainbow Division*, 22–23.

16. *United States Army in the World War, Volume 3*, 669–670.

17. Reilly, *Americans All*, 111.

18. Tompkins, *The Story of the Rainbow Division*, 21.

19. *History of Machine Guns and Automatic Rifles*, (Washington DC: US Government Printing Office, Small Arms Division, Office of the Chief of Ordnance, 13–14.

20. Virgil Ney, *Evolution of the US Army Infantry Mortar Squad: The Argonne To Pleiku* (Fort Belvoir, VA: Technical Operations, Incorporated, Combat Operations Research Group, 1966), 20–30.

21. George M. Chinn, *The Machine Gun: History, Evolution and Development of Manual, Automatic, and Airborne Repeating Weapons, Volume I* (Washington DC: US Government Printing Office, 1951), 200.

22. *History of Machine Guns and Automatic Rifles*, 1922), 12; *Handbook of the Hotchkiss Machine Gun, Model of 1914* (Washington DC: US War Department, Office of the Chief of Ordnance, 1917), 25.

23. *History of Machine Guns and Automatic Rifles*, 12.

24. *Handbook of the Hotchkiss Machine Gun, Model of 1914*, 26.

25. Tompkins, *The Story of the Rainbow Division*, 23.

26. Cheseldine, *Ohio in the Rainbow*, 87.

27. Cheseldine, *Ohio in the Rainbow*, 88.

28. Cheseldine, *Ohio in the Rainbow*, 88.

29. Wolf, *Brief Story of the Rainbow Division*, 10.

30. Wolf, *Brief Story of the Rainbow Division*, 10–11.

31. Edward M. Coffman, *The War to End All Wars: The American Military Experience in World War I* (Lexington: University Press of Kentucky, 1998), 145.

32. Sanitary Report, 26th Division, October 1918, Box 22, Clarence R. Edwards Papers, 1879-1937, Massachusetts Historical Society (MHS), Boston, cited in Mark Ethan Grotelueschen, "The AEF Way of War: The American Army and Combat in the First World War," PhD dissertation, Texas A&M University, 2003, 134.

33. Leon Miesse to his wife, February 9, 1918. Miesse, *100 Years On*, 71.

34. Robb, *The Price of Our Heritage*, 41; Cheseldine, *Ohio in the Rainbow*, 105.

35. Coffman, *The American Experience in World War I*, 150.

36. Allan R. Millett, *Well Planned, Splendidly Executed: The Battle of Cantigny May 28-31, 1918* (Chicago: Cantigny First Division Foundation, 2010), 154.

37. John J. Pershing, *My Experiences in the World War, Volume I* (New York: Frederick Stokes, 1931), 349.

38. Peter H. Ottosen, *Trench Artillery AEF* (Boston: Lothrop, Lee, and Shepard, 1931), 97–100.

39. Tompkins, *The Story of the Rainbow Division*, 31–32.

40. Wolf, *Brief Story of the Rainbow Division*, 11.

41. Robb, *Price of Our Heritage*, 41.

42. Taber, *168th Infantry, Volume I*, 63.

43. Lawrence O. Stewart, *Rainbow Bright* (Philadelphia: Dorrence, 1923), 45.

44. Tomkins, *The Story of the Rainbow Division*, 29.

45. Cheseldine, *Ohio in the Rainbow*, 113.

46. Amerine, *Alabama's Own*. 94.

47. Taber, *168th Infantry, Volume I*, 76.

48. Louis L. Collins, *History of the 151st Field Artillery Rainbow Division*, ed. Wayne E. Stevens, vol. 1 (St. Paul: Minnesota War Records Commission, 1924), 36.

49. Leon Miesse to his wife, March 15, 1918. Miesse, *100 Years On*, 84–85.

50. Hogan, *The Shamrock Battalion*, 89.

51. *Richwood Gazette*, Richmond, Ohio, March 14, 1918, 1; *Marysville Journal-Tribune*, Marysville, Ohio, March 7, 1918, 2.

52. Notes on Photo from U.S. Army Signal Corps. Subject 7659, March 3, 1918, National Archives and Records Administration (NARA).

53. Cheseldine, *Ohio in the Rainbow*, 113.

54. Taber, *168th Infantry, Volume I*, 91.

55. Taber, *168th Infantry, Volume I*, 88.

56. Robb, *Price of Our Heritage*, 41.

57. Taber, *168th Infantry, Volume I*, 89.

58. Taber, *168th Infantry, Volume I*, 89–90.

59. Stewart, *Rainbow Bright*, 46–47.

60. Stewart, *Rainbow Bright*, 49.

61. Wolf, *Brief Story of the Rainbow Division*, 13.

62. Taber, *168th Infantry, Volume I*, 91.

63. Hogan, *The Shamrock Battalion*, 82.

64. Wolf, *Brief Story of the Rainbow Division*, 14–15.

65. Cheseldine, *Ohio in the Rainbow*, 171–174.

66. Robb, *Price of Our Heritage*, 45.

67. Hogan, *The Shamrock Battalion*, 87.

68. Duffy, *Father Duffy's Story*, 92–93.

69. Cheseldine, *Ohio in the Rainbow*, 148–149.

CHAPTER 3: THE RAINBOW MEETS THE GERMANS IN CHAMPAGNE

1. Taber, *168th Infantry, Volume I*, 282.

2. William Manchester, *American Caesar: Douglas MacArthur, 1880–1964* (1978; reprint, New York: Back Bay Books, 2008), 92.

3. Leon Miesse journal entry for June 28, 1918. Miesse, *100 Years On*, 125.

4. Neiberg, *The Second Battle of the Marne*, Kindle Location 160.

5. Ibid., Kindle Location 171–172.

6. John J. Pershing, *My Experiences in the World War, Volume 2* (New York: Frederick Stokes, 1931), 159.

7. Patrick Takle, *Nine Divisions in Champagne: The Second Battle of Marne* (Barnsley, UK: Pen & Sword Books, 2015), Kindle Edition, Kindle Location 171–174.

8. Takle, *Nine Divisions in Champagne*, Kindle Location 175–180.

9. Takle, *Nine Divisions in Champagne*, Kindle Location 180–182.

10. Takle, *Nine Divisions in Champagne*, Kindle Location 622–645.

11. Takle, *Nine Divisions in Champagne*, Kindle Location 622–645.

12. Wolf, *Brief Story of the Rainbow Division*, 24–25.

13. Wolf, *Brief Story of the Rainbow Division*, 24–25.

14. Reilly, *Americans All*, 246.

15. Cheseldine, *Ohio in the* Rainbow, 153–154.

16. Duffy, *Father Duffy's Story*, 120.

17. Stewart, *Rainbow Bright*, 60–61.

18. Douglas MacArthur quoted in Reilly, *Americans All*, 247.

19. Reilly, *Americans All*, 248.

20. Reilly, *Americans All*, 249; Cooke, *The Rainbow Division*, 104.

21. Reilly, *Americans All*, 249; Cooke, *The Rainbow Division*, 104.

22. Reilly, *Americans All*, 249.

23. Reilly, *Americans All*, 249.

24. Reilly, *Americans All*, 250.

25. Cheseldine, *Ohio in the Rainbow*, 152.

26. Henry J. Reilly, *America's Part* (New York: Cosmopolitan Book Corporation, 1928), 241.

27. Neiberg, *The Second Battle of the Marne*, Kindle Location 1166–1171.

28. Cooke, *The Rainbow Division*, 109.

29. Cheseldine, *Ohio in the Rainbow*, 162.

30. Cheseldine, *Ohio in the Rainbow*, 162.

31. Wolf, *Brief Story of the Rainbow Division*, 25.

32. Wolf, *Brief Story of the Rainbow Division*, 25.

33. Michael S. Neiberg, *The Second Battle of the Marne* (Bloomington, Indiana: University of Indiana Press, 2008), Kindle Edition, Kindle Location 1221–1227.

34. Reilly, *Americans All*, 254.

35. Neiberg, *The Second Battle of the Marne*, Kindle Edition, Kindle Locations 1260–1265.

36. Amerine, *Alabama's Own*, 123.

37. Cheseldine, *Ohio in the Rainbow*, 164.

38. Wolf, *Brief Story of the Rainbow Division*, 27.

39. Tompkins, *The Story of the Rainbow Division*, 56.

40. Clyde Vaughn quoted in Reilly, *Americans All*, 281–282.

41. *American Armies and Battlefields in Europe: A History, Guide, and Reference Book* (Washington, DC: US Government Printing Office, 1938), 344; Reilly, *America's Part*, 241; Report of Captain Henry Grave, Commanding Officer, I Company, cited in Cheseldine, *Ohio in the Rainbow*, 167.

42. Duffy, *Father Duffy's Story*, 132–133.

43. Hogan, *The Shamrock Battalion*, 125.

44. Hogan, *The Shamrock Battalion*, 126–128.

45. Cheseldine, *Ohio in the Rainbow*, 173.

46. Stewart, *Rainbow Bright*, 69.

47. Leon Miesse to his wife, July 20, 1918. Miesse, *100 Years On*, 140.

48. Reilly, *Americans All*, 421.

49. Lawrence Sondhaus, *World War I: The Global Revolution* (New York: Cambridge University Press, 2011), 414.

CHAPTER 4: THE RAINBOW ADVANCES

1. Hogan, *The Shamrock Battalion*, 142.

2. Charles MacArthur, *War Bugs* (New York: Doubleday, Doran & Company, 1929), 97.

3. MacArthur, *War Bugs*, 97.

4. Hogan, *The Shamrock Battalion*, 143.

5. Pershing, *My Experiences in the World War*, 159.

6. Stephen C. McGeorge and Mason W. Watson, *The Marne, 15 July-6 August 1918* (Washington, DC: Center of Military History, United States Army, 2018), 36.

7. Cooke, *The Rainbow Division*, 117.

8. Cooke, *The Rainbow Division*, 120.

9. *United States Army in the World War, 1917-1919: Military Operations of the American Expeditionary Forces, Volume 5* (Washington, DC: Center of Military History, United States Army, 1989), 448.

10. General Staff, No. 2109, from General Foch, Commander-in-Chief of the Allied Armies, to the General, Commander-in-Chief of the Armies of the North and Northeast, July 16, 1918, *United States Army in the World War, Volume 5*, 244.

11. French Sixth Army, Special Orders No. 3,543, Trilport, Seine-et-Marne. July 21, 1918—11:15 a.m., *United States Army in the World War, Volume 5*, 357.

12. Cooke, *The Rainbow Division*, 118–119.

13. 3d Section, General Staff French Sixth Army, No. 2,184/3 Trilport, Seine-et-Marne, July 21, 1918—-6:30 p. m., General Orders No. 3,563 for July 22, *United States Army in the World War, Volume 5*, 358.

14. Reilly, *The Rainbow Division*, 312.

15. Stewart, *Rainbow Bright*, 73–74.

16. Duffy, *Father Duffy's Story*, 145.

17. Stewart, *Rainbow Bright*, 74.

18. Amerine, *Alabama's Own*, 140–141.

19. Duffy, *Father Duffy's Story*, 152.

20. John H. Taber, ed. Stephen H. Taber, *A Rainbow Division Lieutenant in France: The World War I Diary of John H. Taber* (Jefferson, NC: McFarland & Co., 2015), 98.

21. Daniels, *Dana Daniels Diary, 1917-1919*, 23; Cheseldine, *Ohio in the Rainbow*, 194.

22. Duffy, *Father Duffy's Story*, 153.

23. Stewart, *Rainbow Bright*, 74–75.

24. Amerine, *Alabama's Own*, 141–142.

25. Taber, *Diary*, 98.

26. Stewart, *Rainbow Bright*, 74–75.

27. Duffy, *Father Duffy's Story*, 153.

28. McGeorge and Watson, *Battle of the Marne*, 58.

29. McGeorge and Watson, *Battle of the Marne*, 58–59.

30. Emerson Gifford Taylor, *New England in France, 1917-1919: A History of the Twenty-Sixth Division U.S.A.* (Boston: Houghton Mifflin Company, 1920), 191–193.

31. Taylor, *New England in France*, 195.

32. McGeorge and Watson, *Battle of the Marne*, 61.

33. 3d Section, General Staff French Sixth Army, No. 2.231/3, Marigny-en-Orxois. Aisne, July 23, 1918, Memorandum for the American I Army Corps, *United States Army in the World War, Volume 5*, 365.

34. Amerine, *Alabama's Own*, 142.

35. Amerine, *Alabama's Own*, 142–143.

36. Taber, *Diary*, 98–99.

37. Hogan, *The Shamrock Battalion*, 140.

38. Duffy, *Father Duffy's Story*, 152.

39. Daniels, *Dana Daniels Diary, 1917-1919*, 23; Cheseldine, *Ohio in the Rainbow*, 194.

40. 3d Section, General Staff, No. 2.220/3, Trilport, Seine-et-Marne, July 23. 1918. Memorandum for the American I Army Corps, *United States Army in the World War, Volume 5*, 364.

41. 3d Section, General Staff French Sixth Army, No. 2.231/3, Marigny-en-Orxois. Aisne, July 23, 1918, Memorandum for the American I Army Corps, *United States Army in the World War, Volume 5*, 365.

42. Taber, *168th Infantry, Volume I*, 314.

43. Taber, *168th Infantry, Volume I*, 315.

44. Taber, *168th Infantry, Volume I*, 315.

45. Amerine, *Alabama's Own*, 143.

46. Amerine, *Alabama's Own*, 143; Frazer, *Send the Alabamians*, Kindle Edition, 163

47. Hogan, *The Shamrock Battalion*, 139.

48. Taber, *Diary*, 99.

49. Hayes, *Heroes Among the Brave*, 20–22.

50. Frazer, *Send the Alabamians*, 166.

51. Frazer, *Send the Alabamians*, 167.

52. Taber, *168th Infantry, Volume I*, 317.

53. Taber, *168th Infantry, Volume I*, 317–318.

54. Taber, *168th Infantry, Volume I*, 318.

55. Taber, *168th Infantry, Volume I*, 318–319.

56. Frazer, *Send the Alabamians*, 167.

57. Taber, *168th Infantry, Volume I*, 319–320.

58. Frazer, *Send the Alabamians*, 167.

59. Lawrence Stewart, *Rainbow Bright*, 77–78.

60. Taber, *168th Infantry, Volume I*, 320.

61. Frazer, *Send the Alabamians*, 167.

CHAPTER 5: THE BATTLE FOR LA CROIX ROUGE FARM

1. 2d Section. General Staff, No. 22, July 24 to July 25, 1918 (20 h. to 20 h), I Army Corps, AEF, Buire, Aisne. July 26. 1918, *United States Army in the World War, Volume 5*, 447.

2. Hayes, *Heroes Among the Brave*, 22–23.

3. Hayes, *Heroes Among the Brave*, 23.

4. Hayes, *Heroes Among the Brave*, 23.

5. Taber, *168th Infantry, Volume I*, 324.

6. Reilly, *Americans All*, 347.

7. 2d Section. General Staff, No. 22, July 24 to July 25, 1918 (20 h. to 20 h), I Army Corps, AEF, Buire, Aisne. July 26. 1918, *United States Army in the World War, Volume 5*, 447.

8. 3d Section. General Staff, No. 2.244/3, Plan of Attack, French Sixth Army, Marigny-en-Orxois, Aisne, July 24, 1918—-7 p.m., General Orders No. 3,592, *United States Army in the World War, Volume 5*, 365.

9. Reilly, *Americans All*, 322.

10. Frazer, *Send the Alabamians*, 169–170.

11. Hayes, *Heroes Among the Brave*, 22; Frazer, *Send the Alabamians*, 169–170.

12. Frazer, *Send the Alabamians*, 169–170.

13. Hayes, *Heroes Among the Brave*, 22.

14. Reilly, *Americans All*, 351; Hayes, *Heroes Among the Brave*, 22.

15. Walter Bare quoted in Reilly, *Americans All*, 348.

16. Hayes, *Heroes Among the Brave*, 22.

17. Frazer, *Send the Alabamians*, 171.

18. Reilly, *Americans All*, 322.

19. Taber, *168th Infantry, Volume I*, 334.

20. Frazer, *Send the Alabamians*, 169.

21. Reilly, *Americans All*, 351–352.

22. Frazer, *Send the Alabamians*, 171–172.

23. Taber, *168th Infantry, Volume I*, 322.

24. Taber, *168th Infantry, Volume I*, 322.

25. Claude Stanley quoted in Reilly, *Americans All*, 358.

26. Cooke, *The Rainbow Division*, 122.

27. Reilly, *Americans All*, 345.

28. Dallas Smith quoted in Reilly, *Americans All*, 352.

29. Reilly, *Americans All*, 347–348.

30. Frazer, *Send the Alabamians*, 174; Taber, *168th Infantry, Volume I*, 326.

31. Claude Stanley quoted in Reilly, *Americans All*, 358.

32. Claude Stanley quoted in Reilly, *Americans All*, 358; Taber, *168th Infantry*, 324–325.

33. Taber, *168th Infantry, Volume I*, 325.

34. Taber, *168th Infantry, Volume I*, 325.

35. Taber, *168th Infantry, Volume I*, 325–326.

36. Taber, *168th Infantry, Volume I*, 326.
37. Claude Stanley quoted in Reilly, *Americans All*, 359.
38. Taber, *168th Infantry, Volume I*, 326–327.
39. Taber, *168th Infantry, Volume I*, 327.
40. Frazer, *Send the Alabamians*, 174–175.
41. Frazer, *Send the Alabamians*, 174–175; Reilly, *Americans All*, 348.
42. Hayes, *Heroes Among the Brave*, 22.
43. The 37mm was a French-manufactured gun intended to provide fire support at ranges from 1,300 to 4,900 feet, and it was the smallest field gun used by the US Army. It was designed for mobility and could fire up to 35 rounds per minute. *Handbook of Artillery Including Mobile, Anti-Aircraft and Trench Materiel* (Washington, DC: Office of the Chief of Ordnance, US Government Printing Office, 1920), 51–53.
44. Hayes, *Heroes Among the Brave*, 22.
45. Taber, *168th Infantry, Volume I*, 328–329.
46. Taber, *168th Infantry, Volume I*, 329.
47. Taber, *168th Infantry, Volume I*, 330.
48. Taber, *168th Infantry, Volume I*, 330.
49. Frazer, *Send the Alabamians*, 177; Walter Bare quoted in Reilly, *Americans All*, 349.
50. Frazer, *Send the Alabamians*, 176.
51. Frazer, *Send the Alabamians*, 177.
52. Frazer, *Send the Alabamians*, 178.
53. Taber, *168th Infantry, Volume I*, 334–335.
54. Taber, *168th Infantry, Volume I*, 336.
55. Claude Stanley quoted in Reilly, *Americans All*, 360.
56. Taber, *168th Infantry, Volume I*, 335.
57. Taber, *168th Infantry, Volume I*, 336.
58. Taber, *168th Infantry, Volume I*, 332.
59. Taber, *168th Infantry, Volume I*, 333.
60. Taber, *168th Infantry, Volume I*, 333.
61. Taber, *168th Infantry, Volume I*, 333–334.
62. Taber, *168th Infantry, Volume I*, 334.
63. Walter Bare quoted in Reilly, *Americans All*, 349–350.
64. Taber, *168th Infantry, Volume I*, 338.
65. Walter Bare quoted in Reilly, *Americans All*, 350–351.
66. Walter Bare quoted in Reilly, *Americans All*, 350–351.
67. Claude Stanley quoted in Reilly, *Americans All*, 361.
68. Claude Stanley quoted in Reilly, *Americans All*, 361.
69. Taber, *168th Infantry, Volume I*, 339.
70. Taber, *168th Infantry, Volume I*, 341.
71. Taber, *168th Infantry, Volume I*, 340.
72. Walter Bare quoted in Reilly, *Americans All*, 350.
73. Taber, *168th Infantry, Volume I*, 340.
74. Frazer, *Send in the Alabamians*, 181–182.
75. Frazer, *Send the Alabamians*, 180–181.
76. From: Commanding General, I Army Corps. AEF, La Ferte-sous-Jouarre, August 13. 1918. To: Adjutant General. GHQ, AEF, 181-33.6: Report, 3d Section, General Staff I Army Corps, AEF, "Report of Operations of the I Army corps, while serving under the French Sixth Army, July 4 to Aug. 14, 1918," *United States Army in the World War, Volume 5*, 483

77. Dallas Smith quoted in Reilly, *Americans All*, 353.

78. Taber, *168th Infantry, Volume I*, 337–338.

79. Taber, *168th Infantry, Volume I*, 337–338.

80. Walter Bare quoted in Reilly, *Americans All*, 348–349.

81. Walter Bare quoted in Reilly, *Americans All*, 351.

82. Dallas Smith quoted in Reilly, *Americans All*, 351.

CHAPTER 6: THE ADVANCE TO THE OURCQ

1. Field Orders, No. 26, I Army Corps, AEF, Buire, Aisne, July 27, 1918, 1:10 a.m., *United States Army in the World War, Volume 5*, 668.

2. General Orders, No. 51, Plan of Attack, 42nd Division AEF, Trugny, Aisne, July 27. 1918, 9:30 a.m., *United States Army in the World War, Volume 5*, 551.

3. General Orders, No. 51, Plan of Attack, 42nd Division AEF, Trugny, Aisne, July 27. 1918, 9:30 a.m., *United States Army in the World War, Volume 5*, 551.

4. Reilly, *Americans All*, 326-327.

5. Relief of French Divisions, 42nd Division, AEF, Trugny, Aisne, July 27. 1918, 10:45 a.m., *United States Army in the World War, Volume 5*, 523.

6. Reilly, *Americans All*, 327.

7. Supreme Headquarters, Operations Section to Group of Armies German Crown Prince, No.: 9536, July 27, 1918, 11:00 p.m., *United States Army in the World War, Volume 5*, 669.

8. Neiberg, *The Second Battle of the Marne*, Kindle Edition, Kindle Locations 2097–2100.

9. Reilly, *Americans All*, 328.

10. Reilly, *Americans All*, 328–329.

11. Leon Miesse journal entry for July 25, 1918. Miesse, *100 Years On*, 141–142.

12. Cheseldine, *Ohio in the Rainbow*, 192.

13. Daniels, *Dana Daniels Diary, 1917-1919*, 23–24.

14. Cheseldine, *Ohio in the Rainbow*, 190–191.

15. Cheseldine, *Ohio in the Rainbow*, 192.

16. Reilly, *Americans All*, 405–406; Cheseldine, *Ohio in the Rainbow*, 193.

17. Cheseldine, *Ohio in the Rainbow*, 193.

18. Reilly, *Americans All*, 406.

19. Reilly, *Americans All*, 406.

20. Benson Hough quoted in Reilly, *Americans All*, 406.

21. Benson Hough quoted in Reilly, *Americans All*, 406.

22. Cheseldine, *Ohio in the Rainbow*, 194.

23. Cheseldine, *Ohio in the Rainbow*, 194.

24. Reilly, *America's Part*, 282–283.

25. Hogan, *The Shamrock Battalion*, 151.

26. Hogan, *The Shamrock Battalion*, 151–152.

27. Reilly, *Americans All*, 330; Duffy, *Father Duffy's Story*, 161.

28. Duffy, *Father Duffy's Story*, 160.

29. Taber, *168th Infantry, Volume I*, 342.

30. Taber, *168th Infantry, Volume I*, 342–343.

31. Claude Stanley quoted in Reilly, *Americans All*, 362.

32. Taber, *168th Infantry, Volume I*, 343–344.

33. Taber, *168th Infantry, Volume I*, 344.

34. Taber, *Diary*, 101; Taber, *168th Infantry, Volume I*, 344–345.

35. Taber, *168th Infantry, Volume I*, 345.

36. Taber, *Diary*, 103.
37. Taber, *168th Infantry, Volume I*, 345.
38. Taber, *168th Infantry, Volume I*, 345–346.
39. Taber, *168th Infantry, Volume I*, 346.
40. Taber, *168th Infantry, Volume I*, 346–347.
41. Taber, *168th Infantry, Volume I*, 347.
42. Taber, *168th Infantry, Volume I*, 347–348.
43. Taber, *168th Infantry, Volume I*, 348.
44. Taber, *168th Infantry, Volume I*, 348.
45. Taber, *168th Infantry, Volume I*, 348–349.
46. Taber, *Diary*, 104.
47. Taber, *168th Infantry, Volume I*, 349.
48. Taber, *168th Infantry, Volume I*, 349–350.
49. Amerine, *Alabama's Own*, 155.
50. Frazer, *Send the Alabamians*, 188.
51. Amerine, *Alabama's Own*, 156.
52. Amerine, *Alabama's Own*, 156–157.
53. Reilly, *Americans All*, 369.
54. Hayes, *Heroes Among the Brave*, 26.
55. Reilly, *Americans All*, 378–379.

CHAPTER 7: CROSSING THE OURCQ

1. Taber, *168th Infantry, Volume I*, 352
2. Stewart, *Rainbow Bright*, 81.
3. Taber, *168th Infantry, Volume I*, 355.
4. Taber, *168th Infantry, Volume I*, 355.
5. Taber, *168th Infantry, Volume I*, 356.
6. Duffy, *Father Duffy's Story*, 163; Taber, *168th Infantry, Volume I*, 351.
7. Reilly, *Americans All*, 380–381.
8. Reilly, *Americans All*, 380–381.
9. Reilly, *Americans All*, 380–381.
10. Reilly, *Americans All*, 381.
11. Adam Hochschild, *To End All Wars: A Story of Loyalty and Rebellion, 1914-1918* (New York: Houghton Mifflin Harcourt, 2011), Kindle Edition, 231.
12. Reilly, *Americans All*, 381–382.
13. Duffy, *Father Duffy's Story*, 158–159.
14. Duffy, *Father Duffy's Story*, 158–159.
15. Duffy, *Father Duffy's Story*, 158–159.
16. Duffy, *Father Duffy's Story*, 158–159.
17. Neiberg, *The Second Battle of the Marne*, Kindle Location 2226–2230.
18. Tompkins, *The Story of the Rainbow Division*, 86.
19. Tompkins, *The Story of the Rainbow Division*, 86–87.
20. Tompkins, *The Story of the Rainbow Division*, 86–87.
21. MacArthur, *Reminiscences*, 68.
22. Reilly, *Americans All*, 384–386; Hogan, *The Shamrock Battalion*, 153–154.
23. Duffy, *Father Duffy's Story*, 166.
24. Hogan, *The Shamrock Battalion*, 154.
25. Hogan, *The Shamrock Battalion*, 155–156, 160.

26. Reilly, *Americans All*, 385–386.

27. Hogan, *The Shamrock Battalion*, 162–163.

28. Reilly, *Americans All*, 385–386.

29. Hogan, *The Shamrock Battalion*, 159–160.

30. Reilly, *Americans All*, 385–386.

31. Duffy, *Father Duffy's Story*, 165.

32. Hogan, *The Shamrock Battalion*, 163–164; Duffy, *Father Duffy's Story*, 165–166.

33. Reilly, *Americans All*, 386.

34. Reilly, *Americans All*, 386–387.

35. Reilly, *Americans All*, 386–387.

36. Reilly, *Americans All*, 386–387.

37. Reilly, *Americans All*, 386–387.

38. Duffy, *Father Duffy's Story*, 166.

39. Hogan, *The Shamrock Battalion*, 164.

40. Hogan, *The Shamrock Battalion*, 164–165.

41. Hogan, *The Shamrock Battalion*, 165.

42. Hogan, *The Shamrock Battalion*, 167–169.

43. Hogan, *The Shamrock Battalion*, 169.

44. Duffy, *Father Duffy's Story*, 166–167.

45. Duffy, *Father Duffy's Story*, 171.

46. Duffy, *Father Duffy's Story*, 171.

47. Duffy, *Father Duffy's Story*, 172.

48. Duffy, *Father Duffy's Story*, 175.

49. Duffy, *Father Duffy's Story*, 173–174.

50. Duffy, *Father Duffy's Story*, 176–177.

51. Duffy, *Father Duffy's Story*, 177.

52. Duffy, *Father Duffy's Story*, 178.

53. Duffy, *Father Duffy's Story*, 178–180.

54. Duffy, *Father Duffy's Story*, 180.

55. Duffy, *Father Duffy's Story*, 180–182.

56. Taber, *168th Infantry, Volume I*, 351–352.

57. Taber, *168th Infantry, Volume I*, 352; Stewart, *Rainbow Bright*, 81.

58. Taber, *168th Infantry, Volume I*, 352.

59. Taber, *168th Infantry, Volume I*, 352.

60. Taber, *168th Infantry, Volume I*, 353.

61. Reilly, *Americans All*, 363; Taber, *168th Infantry, Volume I*, 353.

62. Taber, *168th Infantry, Volume I*, 353–354.

63. Taber, *168th Infantry, Volume I*, 354.

64. Percy Lanison quoted in Reilly, *Americans All*, 363; Taber, *168th Infantry, Volume I*, 354.

65. Taber, *168th Infantry, Volume I*, 355.

66. Percy Lanison quoted in Reilly, *Americans All*, 363-364.

67. Taber, *168th Infantry, Volume I*, 356.

68. Taber, *168th Infantry, Volume I*, 357.

69. Taber, *168th Infantry, Volume I*, 358.

70. Percy Lanison quoted in Reilly, *Americans All*, 363–364.

71. Reilly, *Americans All*, 364.

72. Taber, *168th Infantry, Volume I*, 361.

73. Taber, *168th Infantry, Volume I*, 359–360.

74. Taber, *168th Infantry, Volume I*, 360–361.

75. Taber, *168th Infantry, Volume I*, 362.

76. Taber, *168th Infantry, Volume I*, 362–363.

77. Taber, *168th Infantry, Volume I*, 363–364.

78. Taber, *168th Infantry, Volume I*, 364–365.

79. Taber, *168th Infantry, Volume I*, 365.

80. Taber, *168th Infantry, Volume I*, 367.

81. Taber, *168th Infantry, Volume I*, 366.

82. Taber, *168th Infantry, Volume I*, 367.

83. Taber, *168th Infantry, Volume I*, 367–368; Percy Lanison quoted in Reilly, *Americans All*, 364.

84. Taber, *168th Infantry, Volume I*, 368–369.

85. Taber, *168th Infantry, Volume I*, 368–369.

86. Taber, *168th Infantry, Volume I*, 370–371.

87. Taber, *168th Infantry, Volume I*, 376.

88. Taber, *168th Infantry, Volume I*, 379–380.

89. Walter Bare quoted in Reilly, *Americans All*, 371–372.

90. William P. Screws quoted in Reilly, *Americans All*, 369.

91. Reilly, *Americans All*, 330–331.

92. Hayes, *Heroes Among the Brave*, 26–27.

93. Amerine, *Alabama's Own*, 158–159.

94. Reilly, *Americans All*, 373–374.

95. William P. Screws quoted in Reilly, *Americans All*, 370.

96. Benson W. Hough quoted in Reilly, *Americans All*, 438.

97. Cheseldine, *Ohio in the Rainbow*, 193.

98. Cheseldine, *Ohio in the Rainbow*, 196.

99. Cheseldine, *Ohio in the Rainbow*, 197–198.

100. Cheseldine, *Ohio in the Rainbow*, 197–198.

101. Cheseldine, *Ohio in the Rainbow*, 198.

102. Cheseldine, *Ohio in the* Rainbow, 198.

103. George Geran quoted in Reilly, *Americans All*, 412.

104. George Geran quoted in Reilly, *Americans All*, 412–413.

105. George Geran quoted in Reilly, *Americans All*, 413.

106. Leon Miesse journal entry for July 28, 1918. Miesse, *100 Years On*, 142.

107. Taber, *168th Infantry, Volume I*, 373-374.

CHAPTER 8: THROUGH THE WHEAT FIELDS

1. Taber, *168th Infantry, Volume I*, 385.

2. Taber, *168th Infantry, Volume I*, 385–386.

3. Taber, *168th Infantry, Volume I*, 388.

4. Taber, *168th Infantry, Volume I*, 386.

5. 3d Section. General Staff, No. 2.329/3, French Sixth Army, Marigny-en-Orxois. Aisne. July 28, 1918—-7 p. m., General Orders No. 3,627, *United States Army in the World War, Volume 5*, 379; Field Orders, No. 29, 159/G3, Corps Mission, I Army Corps, AEF, Moucheton-Chateau, Aisne, July 28, 1918—-10:55 p.m., *United States Army in the World War, Volume 5*, 455.

6. Taber, *168th Infantry Regiment, Volume I*, 382.

7. Field Orders, No. 29, 159/G3, Corps Mission, I Army Corps, AEF, Moucheton-Chateau,

Aisne, July 28, 1918—-10:55 p.m., *United States Army in the World War, Volume 5*, 455.

8. From Commanding General. I Army Corps, AEF, to Commanding General. Sixth Army, I Army Corps, AEF, 158/G3 Moucheton-Chateau, Aisne, July 28, 1918, *United States Army in the World War, Volume 5*, 456.

9. Taber, *168th Infantry Regiment, Volume I*, 381.

10. Taber, *Diary*, 104.

11. Taber, *168th Infantry Regiment, Volume I*, 381; Claude Stanley quoted in Reilly, *Americans All*, 366.

12. Taber, *168th Infantry Regiment, Volume I*, 382.

13. Taber, *168th Infantry Regiment, Volume I*, 382–383.

14. Taber, *168th Infantry Regiment, Volume I*, 383.

15. Taber, *168th Infantry Regiment, Volume I*, 383.

16. Taber, *168th Infantry Regiment, Volume I*, 383–384.

17. Taber, *168th Infantry Regiment, Volume I*, 385.

18. Taber, *168th Infantry Regiment, Volume I*, 387.

19. Taber, *168th Infantry Regiment, Volume I*, 387–388.

20. Taber, *168th Infantry Regiment, Volume I*, 388.

21. Taber, *168th Infantry Regiment, Volume I*, 388.

22. Taber, *168th Infantry Regiment, Volume I*, 389.

23. Taber, *168th Infantry Regiment, Volume I*, 389–391.

24. Taber, *168th Infantry Regiment, Volume I*, 390–391.

25. Taber, *168th Infantry Regiment, Volume I*, 390–391.

26. Claude Stanley quoted in Reilly, *Americans All*, 366; Taber, *168th Infantry Regiment, Volume I*, 391.

27. Taber, *168th Infantry Regiment, Volume I*, 391.

28. Claude Stanley quoted in Reilly, *Americans All*, 366–367; Taber, *168th Infantry Regiment, Volume I*, 391–392.

29. Claude Stanley quoted in Reilly, *Americans All*, 366–367; Taber, *168th Infantry Regiment, Volume I*, 392–393.

30. Taber, *168th Infantry Regiment, Volume I*, 393.

31. Claude Stanley quoted in Reilly, *Americans All*, 366–367; Taber, *168th Infantry Regiment, Volume I*, 392–393.

32. Taber, *168th Infantry Regiment, Volume I*, 393–394.

33. Taber, *168th Infantry Regiment, Volume I*, 394.

34. Taber, *168th Infantry Regiment, Volume I*, 395.

35. Taber, *168th Infantry Regiment, Volume I*, 396.

36. Walter Bare quoted in Reilly, *Americans All*, 372–373; Hayes, *Heroes Among the Brave*, 28.

37. Reilly, *Americans All*, 335; Amerine, *Alabama's Own*, 159–160.

38. Hogan, *The Shamrock Battalion*, 174–175.

39. Hogan, *The Shamrock Battalion*, 175–177.

40. William Donovan quoted in Reilly, *Americans All*, 390; Duffy, *Father Duffy's Story*, 183.

41. William Donovan quoted in Reilly, *Americans All*, 390.

42. William Donovan quoted in Reilly, *Americans All*, 390–391.

43. William Donovan quoted in Reilly, *Americans All*, 391; Duffy, *Father Duffy's Story*, 183–184.

44. William Donovan quoted in Reilly, *Americans All*, 390–391.

45. William Donovan quoted in Reilly, *Americans All*, 390–391.

46. Duffy, *Father Duffy's Story*, 185.
47. William Donovan quoted in Reilly, *Americans All*, 390–391; Duffy, *Father Duffy's Story*, 187–188.
48. Duffy, *Father Duffy's Story*, 186.
49. Duffy, *Father Duffy's Story*, 187.
50. Duffy, *Father Duffy's Story*, 188.
51. William Donovan quoted in Reilly, *Americans All*, 390–391.
52. Cheseldine, *Ohio in the Rainbow*, 199; 214.
53. Cheseldine, *Ohio in the Rainbow*, 200.
54. Cheseldine, *Ohio in the Rainbow*, 201.
55. Daniels, *Dana Daniels Diary, 1917-1919*, 27–28.
56. Daniels, *Dana Daniels Diary, 1917-1919*, 25–27.
57. Daniels, *Dana Daniels Diary, 1917-1919*, 27–28.
58. Daniels, *Dana Daniels Diary, 1917-1919*, 29–30.
59. Daniels, *Dana Daniels Diary, 1917-1919*, 30–31.
60. Cheseldine, *Ohio in the Rainbow*, 202.
61. Cheseldine, *Ohio in the Rainbow*, 202.
62. Cheseldine, *Ohio in the Rainbow*, 202.
63. Cheseldine, *Ohio in the Rainbow*, 205.
64. Cheseldine, *Ohio in the Rainbow*, 205-207. Interestingly, in *Reminiscences*, General Douglas MacArthur claims credit for the advance of the 166th's 2nd Battalion on Seringes-et-Nesles. On pages 68–69, he wrote, "I formed our infantry on the south bank of the stream and rushed the town." However, it seems no one else recalls seeing MacArthur anywhere in the vicinity on July 29. In fact, Colonel Hough stated in Reilly's *Americans All* (page 410) that the only time he saw MacArthur was on August 2, the day the 42nd Division was finally relieved.
65. Cheseldine, *Ohio in the Rainbow*, 203.
66. Cheseldine, *Ohio in the Rainbow*, 203.
67. 3d Section, General Staff, No. 2,351/3, French Sixth Army, Marigny-en-Orxois, Aisne, July 29, 1918—8:20 p.m., General Orders No. 3,635, *United States Army in the World War, Volume 5*, 380.

CHAPTER 9: SENSELESS SACRIFICE

1. Taber, *168th Infantry, Volume 2*, 2–3.
2. Daniels, *Dana Daniels Diary, 1917-1919*, 32.
3. Daniels, *Dana Daniels Diary, 1917-1919*, 33–34.
4. Cheseldine, *Ohio in the Rainbow*, 203–204.
5. Cheseldine, *Ohio in the Rainbow*, 204.
6. Duffy, *Father Duffy's Story*, 192; William Donovan quoted in Reilly, *Americans All*, 393.
7. Duffy, *Father Duffy's Story*, 192–193.
8. William Donovan quoted in Reilly, *Americans All*, 393.
9. Duffy, *Father Duffy's Story*, 192–193; William Donovan quoted in Reilly, *Americans All*, 393.
10. Duffy, *Father Duffy's Story*, 193–195; Reilly, *Americans All*, 397.
11. Duffy, *Father Duffy's Story*, 195; William Donovan quoted in Reilly, *Americans All*, 393.
12. William Donovan quoted in Reilly, *Americans All*, 393; Edwin Stubbs quoted in Reilly, *Americans All*, 399–400.
13. Edwin Stubbs quoted in Reilly, *Americans All*, 400–401.

14. Taber, *168th Infantry, Volume 2*, 1.

15. Taber, *168th Infantry, Volume 2*, 1.

16. Reilly, *Americans* All, 338; Taber, *168th Infantry, Volume 2*, 1–2.

17. Taber, *168th Infantry, Volume 2*, 2.

18. Taber, *168th Infantry, Volume 2*, 2–3.

19. Taber, *168th Infantry, Volume 2*, 3.

20. Taber, *168th Infantry, Volume 2*, 3–4.

21. Taber, *168th Infantry, Volume 2*, 4.

22. Taber, *168th Infantry, Volume 2*, 4.

23. Taber, *168th Infantry, Volume 2*, 4.

24. Taber, *168th Infantry, Volume 2*, 4–5.

25. Taber, *168th Infantry, Volume 2*, 5.

26. Taber, *168th Infantry, Volume 2*, 19–20.

27. Taber, *168th Infantry, Volume 2*, 5–6.

28. Taber, *168th Infantry, Volume 2*, 6.

29. Taber, *168th Infantry, Volume 2*, 6–7.

30. Taber, *168th Infantry, Volume 2*, 7.

31. Taber, *168th Infantry, Volume 2*, 8–9.

32. Taber, *168th Infantry, Volume 2*, 10.

33. Taber, *168th Infantry, Volume 2*, 10.

34. Taber, *168th Infantry, Volume 2*, 11–12.

35. Amerine, *Alabama's Own*, 161.

36. Taber, *168th Infantry, Volume 2*, 12–13.

37. Stewart, *Rainbow Bright*, 83–84.

38. Taber, *168th Infantry*, 13–14.

39. Taber, *168th Infantry*, 16–17.

40. Taber, *168th Infantry*, 21; Frazer, *Send in the Alabamians*, 201–203.

41. Pierpont J. Stackpole, Ferrell, Robert H., ed., *In the Company of Generals: The World War I Diary of Pierpont L. Stackpole* (Columbia, MO: University of Missouri Press, 2009), 116.

42. National Archives and records Administration (NARA), Record Group (RG) 200, Index and Case Files relating to Reclassification and Reassignment of Officers, Reclassification of Regular Army Brigadier Generals and Major Generals, Entry NM 1022, Relief History of Brigadier General R. A. Brown, 130-84-2-5, August 21, 1918, 24, cited in Frazer, *Send the Alabamians*, 202–203.

43. Frazer, *Send the Alabamians*, 202–203.

44. Frazer, *Send the Alabamians*, 202–203.

45. Taber, *168th Infantry, Volume 2*, 22.

46. Field Orders No. 31, I Army Corps, AEF, Moucheton-Chateau, Aisne, July 31, 1918, 12:30 a. m., *United States Army in the World War, Volume 5*, 465; Reilly, *Americans All*, 340.

47. Taber, *168th Infantry*, 24–26.

48. Taber, *168th Infantry*, 26-27.

49. Duffy, *Father Duffy's Story*, 196.

50. Cheseldine, *Ohio in the Rainbow*, 213.

51. Daniels, *Dana Daniels Diary, 1917-1919*, 34–37.

52. From: Operations Section, Supreme Headquarters, July 30, 1918, 10:30 a.m. To: Group of Armies German Crown Prince, *United States Army in the World War, Volume 5*, 670.

CHAPTER 10: THE RAINBOW IS RELIEVED

1. Taber, *168th Infantry, Volume 2*, 34–36.
2. Taber, *168th Infantry, Volume 2*, 34–36.
3. Taber, *168th Infantry, Volume 2*, 34–36.
4. 3d Section, General Staff, No. 2,411/3, French Sixth Army, Marigny-en-Orxois, Aisne, July 31, 1918—-8:20 p.m., General Orders No. 3,663, *United States Army in the World War, Volume 5*, 386.
5. Reilly, *Americans All*, 341.
6. Frazer, *Send the Alabamians*, 200.
7. Taber, *168th Infantry, Volume 2*, 31.
8. Taber, *168th Infantry, Volume 2*, 29–30.
9. Reilly, *Americans All*, 342; Taber, *168th Infantry, Volume 2*, 29–30.
10. Taber, *168th Infantry, Volume 2*, 31; Reilly, *Americans All*, 342.
11. Taber, *168th Infantry, Volume 2*, 31; Reilly, *Americans All*, 342.
12. Duffy, *Father Duffy's Story*, 205; Amerine, *Alabama's Own*, 161–162.
13. Cheseldine, *Ohio in the Rainbow*, 209.
14. General Orders, No. 53, 42nd Division AEF, Beuvardes, Aisne, August 1, 1918—3:30 p. m., *United States Army in the World War, Volume 5*, 526–527.
15. Frazer, *Send the Alabamians*, 204.
16. Taber, *168th Infantry, Volume 2*, 33.
17. Major W.F.R. Johnson quoted in Reilly, *Americans All*, 479–480.
18. Taber, *168th Infantry, Volume 2*, 34–36.
19. Taber, *168th Infantry, Volume 2*, 37–38.
20. Taber, *Diary*, 105–106.
21. Duffy, *Father Duffy's Story*, 205–207.
22. Frazer, *Send the Alabamians*, 204–205.
23. Cheseldine, *Ohio in the Rainbow*, 209; Daniels, *Dana Daniels Diary, 1917-1919*, 36.
24. Cheseldine, *Ohio in the Rainbow*, 210.
25. Cheseldine, *Ohio in the Rainbow*, 210; Daniels, *Dana Daniels Diary, 1917-1919*, 37.
26. Daniels, *Dana Daniels Diary, 1917-1919*, 37–38.
27. Cheseldine, *Ohio in the Rainbow*, 212.
28. Cheseldine, *Ohio in the Rainbow*, 210–211.
29. Cheseldine, *Ohio in the Rainbow*, 211.

EPILOGUE

1. Cheseldine, *Ohio in the Rainbow*, 217.
2. Daniels, *Dana Daniels Diary, 1917-1919*, 39.
3. American Battle Monuments Commission, *42nd Division Summary of Operations in the World War* (Washington, DC: US Government Printing Office, 1944), 32.
4. Cheseldine, *Ohio in the Rainbow*, 216, 212.
5. Frazer, *Send the Alabamians*, 206.
6. Cheseldine, *Ohio in the Rainbow*, 232–234; Leon Miesse journal entry for September 13, 1918. Miesse, *100 Years On*, 155–156.
7. Cheseldine, *Ohio in the Rainbow*, 248.
8. Cheseldine, *Ohio in the Rainbow*, 275–276.
9. Coffman, *The American Experience in World War I*, 355.
10. Cooke, *The Rainbow Division*, 239.

11. American Battle Monuments Commission, *Oise-Aisne American Cemetery and Memorial Brochure* (Arlington, VA: American Battle Monuments Commission, 2008), 1–2; American Battle Monuments Commission, *American Armies and Battlefields in Europe* (Washington, DC: US Government Printing Office, 1938), 75.
12. Reilly, *Americans All*, 401.

BIBLIOGRAPHY

American Armies and Battlefields in Europe: A History, Guide, and Reference Book. US Government Printing Office, Washington, DC, 1938.

American Battle Monuments Commission. *42nd Division Summary of Operations in the World War*. US Government Printing Office, Washington, DC, 1944.

_____. *Oise-Aisne American Cemetery and Memorial Brochure*. American Battle Monuments Commission, Arlington, Virginia, 2008.

Amerine, William H. *Alabama's Own in France*. Eaton & Gettinger, New York, New York, 1919.

Armstrong, David A. *Bullets and Bureaucrats: The Machine Gun and the United States Army, 1861-1916*. Greenwood Press, Westport, Connecticut, 1982.

The Army Lineage Book, Volume II: Infantry. Washington, DC, US Government Printing Office, 1953.

Asprey, Robert B. *The German High Command at War: Hindenburg and Ludendorff Conduct World War I*. Quill House, Fort Mill, South Carolina, 1993.

Baily, Roy. *Roy Baily Diary, 1917-1918*. Unpublished. Accessed at www.markboyd.info/MarionsOwn/Sgt_Bailey/pages_62-70.html.

Boyd, Austin Dewitt. *Austin Dewitt "Dusty" Boyd in WWI: Service in France and Germany*, Mark Boyd, ed. Unpublished. Accessed at www.markboyd.info/adboyd/war.html#mar-15-1919.

Braden, Lieutenant Charles, ed. *Biographical Register of the Officers and Graduates of the U.S. Military Academy at West Point, N.Y Since its Establishment in 1802*, Supplement *Volume V*. Seeman & Peters, Printers, Saginaw, Michigan, 1919.

_____. *Biographical Register of the Officers and Graduates of the U.S. Military Academy at West Point, N.Y Since its Establishment in 1802*, Supplement *Volume VI*. Seeman & Peters, Printers, Saginaw, Michigan, 1920.

Cheseldine, R.M. *Ohio in the Rainbow: Official Story of the 166th Infantry, 42nd Division, in the World War*. F.J. Heer Printing Company, Columbus, Ohio, 1924.

Chillicothe Gazette, Chillicothe, Ohio.

Chinn, George M. *The Machine Gun: History, Evolution and Development of Manual, Automatic, and Airborne Repeating Weapons, Volume I*. US Government Printing Office, Washington, DC, 1951.

Coffman, Edward M. *The War to End All Wars: The American Military Experience in World War I*. The University Press of Kentucky, Lexington, Kentucky, 1998.

Collins, Louis L. *History of the 151st Field Artillery Rainbow Division*, ed. Wayne E. Stevens, vol. 1. Minnesota War Records Commission, St. Paul, Minnesota, 1924.

Cooke, James J. *The Rainbow Division in the Great War, 1917-1919*. Praeger, Westport, Connecticut, 1994.

Crowell, Benedict and Robert Forrest Wilson. *The Road to France: The Transportation of Troops and Military Supplies, 1917–1918-How America Went to War: An Account from Official Sources of the Nation's War Activities, 1917–1920*. Yale University Press, New Haven, Connecticut, 1921.

Cullum, George W. *Biographical Register of the Officers and Graduates of the U.S. Military Academy at West Point, N.Y Since its Establishment in 1802, Volume III*. Houghton, Mifflin, and Company, Boston, Massachusetts, 1891.

_____. *Biographical Register of the Officers and Graduates of the U.S. Military Academy at West Point, N.Y Since its Establishment in 1802, Volume IV*. Riverside Press, Cambridge, Massachusetts, 1901.

Daniels, Dana. *Dana Daniels Diary, 1917-1919*. Dana Daniels Collection, Ohio Historical Society (MS 5; Box 1, Folder 6), Columbus, Ohio.

Duffy, Francis P. *Father Duffy's Story: A Tale of Humor and Heroism, of Life and Death with the Fighting Sixty-Ninth*. George B. Doran Company, New York, 1919.

Ebert, Carl F. *A Brief History of Co. D, 166th Infantry*. Unknown Publisher, Marion. Ohio, 1939.

Eisenhower, John S.D. *Yanks: The Epic Story of the American Army in World War I*. Simon and Schuster, New York, Kindle Edition, 2001.

Ettinger, Albert M. and A. Churchill. *A Doughboy with the Fighting 69th*. Pocket Books, New York, 1992.

Frazer, Nimrod Thompson. *Send the Alabamians*. University of Alabama Press, Tuscaloosa, Alabama, Kindle Edition, 2014.

Grotelueschen, Mark Ethan. "The AEF Way of War: The American Army and Combat in the First World War." PhD dissertation, Texas A&M University, 2003.

_____. *Into the Fight, April–June 1918*. Center of Military History, US Army, Washington, DC, 2018.

Guild, George R. and Frederick C. Test. *Pocket Field Manual: A Manual Designed for Use of Troops in the Field*. George Banta Publishing Company, Menasha, Wisconsin, 1917.

Haig, Douglas, eds. Gary Sheffield and John Bourne. *War Diaries and Letters, 1914–1918*. Weidenfeld & Nicolson, London, 2005.

Handbook of Artillery Including Mobile, Anti-Aircraft and Trench Materiel. Office of the Chief of Ordnance, US Government Printing Office, Washington, DC, 1920.

Handbook of the Hotchkiss Machine Gun, Model of 1914. US War Department, Office of the Chief of Ordnance, Washington, DC, 1917.

Hayes, John B. *Heroes Among the Brave*. Lee County Historical Society, Loachapoka, Alabama, 1973.

History of Machine Guns and Automatic Rifles. Small Arms Division, Office of the Chief of Ordnance, US Government Printing Office, Washington, DC, 1922.

Hochschild, Adam. *To End All Wars: A Story of Loyalty and Rebellion, 1914-1918*. Houghton Mifflin Harcourt, New York, 2011.

Hogan, Martin. *The Shamrock Battalion of the Rainbow*. D. Appleton and Company, New York, New York, 1919.

Joffre, Joseph Jacques Césaire. *The Personal Memoirs of Joffre: Field Marshal of the French Army, Volume II*. Harper and Brothers, New York, 1932.

Lanza, Conrad H. "The Artillery Support of Infantry in the A.E.F.," *Field Artillery Journal 26*, January-March 1936, The United States Field Artillery Association, Washington, DC, 1936.

MacArthur, Charles. *War Bugs*. Doubleday, Doran & Company, New York, New York, 1929.

MacArthur, Douglas. *Reminiscences*. McGraw-Hill, New York, New York, 1964.

Mahon, John. *New York's Fighting 69th: A Regimental History of Service in the Civil War's Irish Brigade and the Great War's Rainbow Division*. McFarland & Company, Inc., Jefferson, North Carolina, 2004.

Manchester, William. *American Caesar: Douglas MacArthur, 1880–1964*. 1978; reprint, Back Bay Books, New York, New York, 2008.

Marysville Journal-Tribune, Marysville, Ohio.

McGeorge, Stephen C. and Mason W. Watson. *The Marne, 15 July-6 August 1918*. Center of Military History, United States Army, Washington, DC, 2018.

Miesse, Leon, *100 Years On: WW I – Leon Miesse, Captain, 166th*, Robert Laird, ed. Zerone Publishing, Location Unknown, Kindle Edition, 2017.

Millett, Allan R. *Well Planned, Splendidly Executed: The Battle of Cantigny May 28-31, 1918*. Cantigny First Division Foundation, Chicago, 2010.

Moffett, Burt. *Burt Moffett Diary, January 1, 1918 - September 7, 1918*. Burt J. Moffett World War I Diaries Collection, Ohio Historical Society (Vol. 1425), Columbus, Ohio.

Moss, James A. *Field Service*. George Banta Publishing Company, Menasha, Wisconsin, 1917.

Neiberg, Michael S. *The Second Battle of the Marne*. University of Indiana Press, Bloomington, Kindle Edition, 2008.

New York Times. New York, New York.

Ney, Virgil. *Evolution of the US Army Infantry Mortar Squad: The Argonne To Pleiku*. Technical Operations, Incorporated, Combat Operations Research Group, Fort Belvoir, Virginia, 1966.

Official Roster of the Soldiers of the State of Ohio In the War with Mexico, 1846 -1848. (Reprint Edition). Mansfield, Ohio Genealogical Society, 1991.

Ottosen, Peter H. *Trench Artillery AEF*. Lothrop, Lee, and Shepard, Boston, Massachusetts, 1931.

Pershing, John J. *My Experiences in the World War, Volume 2*. Frederick Stokes, New York, 1931.

Reilly, Henry J. *Americans All: The Rainbow at War; Official History of the 42nd Rainbow Division in the World War*. F. J. Heer Printing Co., Columbus, Ohio, 1936.

_____. *America's Part*. Cosmopolitan Book Corporation, New York, 1928.

Reppy, Alison. *Rainbow Memories: Character Sketches and History of the First Battalion, 166th Infantry, 42nd Division, American Expeditionary Force*. Executive Committee, First Battalion, 166th Infantry, Columbus, Ohio, 1919.

Richwood Gazette, Richwood, Ohio.

Robb, Winfred E. *The Price of Our Heritage: In Memory of the Heroic Dead of the 168 Infantry*. American Lithographing and Printing Co., Des Moines, Iowa, 1919.

Robinson, Colonel Wirt, ed. *Biographical Register of the Officers and Graduates of the U.S. Military Academy at West Point, N.Y Since its Establishment in 1802*, Supplement Volume VI-A. Seeman & Peters, Printers, Saginaw, Michigan, 1920.

Setzekorn, Eric B. *Joining the Great War, April 1917-April 1918*. Center of Military History, US Army, Washington, DC, 2017.

Sondhaus, Lawrence. *World War I: The Global Revolution*. Cambridge University Press, New York, New York, 2011.

Stackpole, Pierpont J., ed. Robert H. Ferrell. *In the Company of Generals: The World War I Diary of Pierpont L. Stackpole*. University of Missouri Press, Columbia, 2009.

Stewart, Lawrence O. *Rainbow Bright*. Dorrence, Philadelphia, Pennsylvania, 1923.

Taber, John H. *The Story of the 168th Infantry Regiment, Volume I and II*. State Historical Society of Iowa, Iowa City, 1925.

Taber, Stephen H., ed. *A Rainbow Division Lieutenant in France: The World War I Diary of John H. Taber*. McFarland & Co., Jefferson, North Carolina, 2015.

Takle, Patrick. *Nine Divisions in Champagne: The Second Battle of Marne*. Pen & Sword Books, Barnsley, UK, Kindle Edition, 2015.

Taylor, Emerson Gifford. *New England in France, 1917-1919: A History of the Twenty-Sixth Division U.S.A.* Houghton Mifflin Company, Boston, Massachusetts, 1920.

Thomas, Shipley. *The History of the A.E.F.* George B. Doran Company, New York, 1920.

Thompson, David G. "Ohio's Best: The Mobilization of the Fourth Infantry, Ohio National Guard, in 1917," *Ohio History Journal*, Volume 101, Winter-Spring 1992. Ohio Historical Society, Columbus, 1992.

Tompkins, Raymond S. *The Story of the Rainbow Division*. Boni and Liveright, New York, 1919.

Truss, Ruth Smith. "The Alabama National Guard's 167th Infantry Regiment in World War I." *Alabama Review 56* (January 2003), Alabama Historical Society in cooperation with The University of Mobile, Mobile, Alabama, 2003.

United States Army in the World War, 1917-1919, Volume 3: Training and Use of American Units with the British and French. Center of Military History, United States Army, Washington, DC, 1989.

United States Army in the World War, 1917-1919: Military Operations of the American Expeditionary Forces, Volume 5. Center of Military History, United States Army, Washington, DC, 1989.

Williams, Enoch. *Letters Home from Somewhere in France (P.S. Send cigarettes & chocolate)*, Gary Williams, ed. Unpublished. Accessed at https://archive.org/details/EnochWilliamsWwiLettersHome1917-1919.

Wilson, Woodrow. *War Messages, 65th Cong., 1st Sess. Senate Doc. No. 5, Serial No. 7264.* Washington, DC, 1917.

Wolf, Walter B. *A Brief History of the Rainbow Division.* Rand, McNally & Co., New York, 1919.

INDEX